Praise for Inspiring STUDENT EMPOWERMENT

MW00991754

"In her latest work, *Inspiring Student Empowerment,* Patti Drapeau focuses the spotlight on meeting the social, emotional, and instructional needs of students in the classroom. This book brings student voice and empowerment center stage, which is exactly as it should be. The many, varied strategies that she includes to support effective student learning and engagement are both realistic and user-friendly. Kudos to Drapeau for continuing to highlight the importance of the connection between the teacher and the learner as they create an effective learning environment for all students. Well done!"

—Dr. Anita M. Campbell, University of Maine at Farmington

"This powerful, insightful, and thought-provoking book adds a new dimension to teaching and learning. The four main areas of emphasis are differentiation, personalized learning, engagement, and empowerment. How these concepts differ and how they interact with and build on one another is the focus of this book. Throughout her practical book, author Patti Drapeau shows teachers and administrators ways to empower students to be self-directed, responsible, and confident learners. This book contains a plethora of excellent ideas—such as using games and competitions to develop student empowerment and giving students choices in designing their own learning concepts and activities. Finally, Drapeau emphasizes the importance of social and emotional learning within the framework of student empowerment. Because the topics covered are not only timely but also essential for teaching 21st-century students, I highly recommend this book to both experienced and new teachers."

—Carolyn Coil, Ed.D., educational consultant and author

"Patti Drapeau takes on the bold task of clearly defining some of the big ideas currently being discussed and implemented in schools: student engagement, differentiation, student empowerment, and personalized learning. Drapeau is clear that personalized learning is not differentiation, although differentiation is a component of personalized learning, and that student engagement is not the same as student empowerment. She then introduces us to frameworks, expansive strategies, templates, and tools as she guides our understanding of personalized learning and student empowerment. Drapeau presents an exciting vision for classrooms and enables school leaders and educators to confidently put its elements in practice."

—Diane Heacox, Ed.D., educational consultant and author of *Differentiating Instruction in the Regular Classroom* and *Making Differentiation a Habit,* and coauthor of *Differentiation for Gifted Learners*

"How do teachers move beyond their commitment to meeting individual student needs with a basic menu of differentiation strategies to a deeper understanding of personalized learning that motivates students to engage more fully—and to achieve? *Inspiring Student Empowerment* has answers. Each chapter provides detailed descriptions of evidence-based strategies, sample lessons, templates, and reproducible handouts. Whether you are a new teacher looking for practical ways to get started with curriculum differentiation or a veteran program coordinator, you will find powerful support for becoming a more effective educator."

—Dr. Sally Krisel, director, Innovative and Advanced Programs, Hall County Schools, Gainesville, GA, and past president, National Association for Gifted Children

Inspiring
STUDENT
EMPOWERMENT

Moving Beyond Engagement, Refining Differentiation

Patti Drapeau

free spirit
PUBLISHING®

Library of Congress Cataloging-in-Publication Data
Names: Drapeau, Patti, author.
Title: Inspiring student empowerment : moving beyond engagement, refining differentiation / Patti Drapeau.
Description: Minneapolis, MN : Free Spirit Publishing Inc., 2020. | Includes bibliographical references and index
Identifiers: LCCN 2019040575 (print) | LCCN 2019040576 (ebook) | ISBN 9781631984792 (paperback) | ISBN 9781631984808 (pdf) | ISBN 9781631984815 (epub)
Subjects: LCSH: Motivation in education. | Individualized instruction. | Student participation in curriculum planning.
Classification: LCC LB1065 .D716 2020 (print) | LCC LB1065 (ebook) | DDC 370.154—dc23
LC record available at https://lccn.loc.gov/2019040575
LC ebook record available at https://lccn.loc.gov/2019040576

ISBN: 978-1-63198-479-2

Edited by Christine Zuchora-Walske
Cover and interior design by Emily Dyer

10 9 8 7 6 5 4 3 2 1
Printed in the United States of America

Free Spirit Publishing Inc.
6325 Sandburg Road, Suite 100
Minneapolis, MN 55427-3674
(612) 338-2068
help4kids@freespirit.com
freespirit.com

FSC
www.fsc.org
MIX
Paper from
responsible sources
FSC® C005010

Dedication

This book is dedicated to educators who dare to question, try new ideas, and help move the field of education forward. This book is also dedicated to educators who inspire their students and empower them to be all they can be.

Acknowledgments

I'd like to thank all the teachers, administrators, and colleagues who contributed to the ideas presented in this book. They provided me with suggestions, feedback, and classroom examples that helped me transform conceptualized ideas into practical applications. They continue to be my source of inspiration. Special thanks go out to: Dr. Anita Campbell, Jade Anderson, Evelyn Kinney, Tina Kinney, Josh Bosse, Nick Scott, Shelly Pelletier, Kim Oakes, Rachel Hamlin, Tammy Hilton, Kathleen Ball, James Siegal, Gus Goodwin, David Mann, Ed Dettoratius, Erin Lehmann, Jeffrey Blue, James Chiarelli, Sara Bodi, Kasey D'Amato, Candy Anderson, Zachary Brown, Lisa Harvey, Samantha Mills, Larry Peters, Mary Rehak, Lauren Rivera, Ben Segee, Zachary Whitehouse, Lorna Henley, Lori Knight, Jennifer Rosado, and Debra Thibodeau.

I'd like to thank Dr. Heidi Hayes Jacobs for writing the foreword for this book. Heidi is founder and president of Curriculum Designers and is well known for her models on curriculum mapping, curriculum design, and developing twenty-first-century approaches to teaching and learning. I am honored that she was willing to write such words of endorsement.

I'd like to thank Judy Galbraith for believing in this book and for embracing the topics of empowerment and personalized learning. I'd like to thank Meg Bratsch, who helped me formulate and clarify ideas right from the start, and Christine Zuchora-Walske, who painstakingly worked through the rounds of edits with me. I very much appreciate her editing expertise. Thanks to Kyra Ostendorf, Alison Behnke, and Alyssa Lochner for their manuscript reviews and edits. Thanks to Emily Dyer for her cover and design work.

Most importantly, thanks to my family and friends. Their support keeps me going, and they remind me how important it is to find balance in life. They are my constant source of joy.

Contents

Digital Content

See page 196 for instructions for downloading this
content and digital versions of all reproducible forms.

List of Reproducible Pages

Foreword by Heidi Hayes Jacobs, Ph.D.

How do we infuse genuine power into learners' hearts and minds? In *Inspiring Student Empowerment: Moving Beyond Engagement, Refining Differentiation*, Patti Drapeau inspires us to inspire our students. With grounded reasoning and thoughtful conviction, she launches us on a dynamic professional journey to lift our practice to a new and timely level.

Discussions about curriculum engagement, learner engagement, and instructional engagement are ubiquitous in professional learning communities and leadership planning. Even so, Drapeau has opened my eyes. She proposes a striking and powerful shift in the way we hold current practice. She contrasts engagement with empowerment, explaining that empowerment is distinctly more important than engagement to our learners. As a reader, I find her thinking to be both expansive and highly practical.

She begins by detailing various forms of engagement—behavioral, cognitive, and emotional. An arsenal of engagement strategies and tools for classrooms from early childhood through high school are on offer. She also provides easy-to-use rubrics and guides, such as the Engage-O-Meter, to reveal the degree of student involvement in a given undertaking. Any educator will benefit from employing Drapeau's suggested engagement strategies. But she doesn't stop there. Her discussion of engagement lays a pathway to empowerment.

Drapeau develops a clear and practical distinction between big *E* and little *e* empowerment. Rather than judging the level of empowerment a teacher aspires to, she provides a menu of possibilities. For example, a chapter devoted to game-based education and competitions shows how we can support and channel learner focus on a journey to empowerment. Drapeau demonstrates how these strategies can lead to power and confidence in students' school lives.

In her view, empowerment grows from relationships, capabilities, and accomplishments. She deftly makes the case that lurking behind many school-based accomplishments is compliance—following rules and meeting expectations. Empowerment, she argues, is cultivating

independent learners with a keen sense of purpose, competence, and impact. Drapeau demonstrates particular compassion in her detailed discussion of what empowerment might look like in—and why it is so critical for—specific student populations. Her exploration of the needs of girls, boys, nonbinary children, English language learners, and students with special needs is extraordinary. This exploration underscores the need for both big *E* and little *e* empowerment. It also sets the stage for the second half of the book, which clarifies the importance of personalized learning in modern classroom life.

Motivating students by empowering them to personalize their learning is the ultimate goal of this book. Drapeau takes on this challenge by exploring the relationship between differentiated instruction and personalized learning. She asks us to consider eight key elements of differentiation that require high-quality choices by educators: learner academic, social, and emotional characteristics; preassessment and formative assessment; pacing; flexible grouping; open-ended tasks and questioning; simple to complex content; low- to high-level thinking; and product options for summative assessment. She examines each of these elements in detail, with rich examples that make sense to teachers. These elements help us recognize what our students need, how to group them effectively, and how to calibrate curriculum choices to match students' needs in various learning situations. Drapeau's fresh look at differentiation leads us to the heart of the book, personalization.

Personalization is a subject of much debate and discussion among today's educators. Their pedagogy is shifting to more student-facing methods, providing learners with critical competencies to determine their own futures. Yet we are in need of an inspirational and practical definition. Readers will find one here. Drapeau says, "Personalized learning has three objectives: learning content, learning how to learn, and learning about the self." She shows us how we can customize instruction to match our learners' needs and grow their ability to be independent and self-navigating. She provides strategies for engaging learners in investigating meaningful content and, more importantly, for lighting a fire of fascination to propel individual inquiry.

As the culmination of her rich discourse on personalized learning, Drapeau investigates and integrates social and emotional learning (SEL). Educators recognize the importance of addressing SEL skills within meaningful learning experiences in supportive environments. However, it can be challenging to embed SEL into practice. Drapeau answers this challenge by connecting SEL directly to empowerment and personalized learning. She shares a variety of workable models and resources to support the integration of SEL, empowerment, and personalized learning. Her approach is a promising antidote to the complex social, emotional, and intellectual challenges our children face today.

Inspiring Student Empowerment: Moving Beyond Engagement, Refining Differentiation is keenly relevant and exceptionally helpful. Drapeau declares her intention in writing this book to be eminently practical, and indeed, she keeps that pledge. She writes with power and offers critical considerations for our field. Through her personal journey as an educator, she gives us each a compass for our own journey.

Introduction

I always thought engagement was the magic ingredient in learning. After all, when students were engaged, they were on task and focused. Isn't that what we all want? Research indicated that if I used certain strategies, students would be engaged and would learn. This approach was likely to minimize behavior problems and increase academic success. For me, these assumptions proved to be mostly true. My students were learning, and they were generally happy. So why did I have this nagging feeling that my teaching techniques and strategies were still not enough?

Even though students participated in learning and seemed content, they did not appear invested in their learning or particularly excited about it. This level of learning was not changing the way they thought about the content and did not affect the way they might act in the world around them. I realized I was not satisfied when my students were learning at a surface level. I was not satisfied when my students learned content just for a decent grade or to do okay on standardized tests. I was disappointed when some of my students did not seem to really care about their learning—I wanted all my students to be fired up about it.

In Search of the Golden Ticket

In my pursuit of the "golden ticket" to teaching and learning, I read books and attended workshops on differentiation and instructional strategies, and I pursued advanced degrees that focused on students with special needs and English language learners. I devoured strategies that challenged my gifted and talented learners. To learn how to reach my creative thinkers, I took courses in creativity. I differentiated instruction by collecting and using tools that targeted the needs of the outliers in my classroom. My advanced learners received acceleration and content complexity. I organized flexible grouping arrangements for my shy, quiet learners. In math, I provided hands-on options for students who preferred active

learning. I met more of my learners' needs more of the time. And still my students were not particularly fired up. Something was missing.

I examined educational trends to see if I could discover what was still lacking. I decided to research the free school movement, which was an educational reform movement in the 1960s and 1970s (also known as the new schools or alternative schools movement). There was no universal definition for these schools, and each one seemed to march to the beat of its own drummer. Most alternative schools were elementary schools, some continued into middle schools, and a few continued through high school. They were both public and private and often were designed around personalized instruction and student empowerment. During the 1960s and 1970s, about six hundred alternative schools were created, and they varied greatly. Some were formed on philosophies meant to rectify political and social injustices. Some espoused a basic dismissal of standardized curricula. One such school is the School Around Us in Arundel, Maine, which was established in 1970 and is still in existence. The school operates on the premise that all its students, from ages five through fourteen, have an equal voice in the community. Teachers are encouraged to follow the students' interests. Each student's goals include academic, social, and personal goals. Parents describe the experience as having to "unschool themselves" (Jordan 2018).

The free school movement did and still does believe that learning is personal and that students will learn in their own way in their own time. Free schoolers believe in self-directed, hands-on, spontaneous learning. They also believe that learning how to learn is more important for students than what they learn. Free school philosophies gave me the idea to search for a variety of ways to empower students and personalize their learning. Could this be that golden ticket I'd been looking for?

I discovered that many free schools rejected the traditional textbook approaches to teaching. Instead teachers created their own curricula. Textbook sales dipped, and publishing companies started to worry.

The companies responded by creating or acquiring individualized programs, such as the SRA Reading Laboratory. This reading program, still in existence, was designed for students to self-pace through a collection of leveled readers. McGraw-Hill described this reading program as individualized because it helped meet the unique needs of all learners. Some free schools used these individualized programs, but many did not. They relied on their teachers' creativity and empowered teachers to create their own materials.

Regardless of whether free school teachers used published curricula or created their own, they expected that students would learn only when they were ready. This belief is similar to the modern focus on developmentally appropriate practice (DAP) in early childhood education. Unlike in standards-based education, grade-level expectations in these alternative schools were almost nonexistent. Many of them were set up on a continual progress approach. As long as students continued to learn, or show growth, everything was fine.

For many of these schools, the goals were for students to leave with self-confidence and the ability to self-advocate and lead. Academic achievement was a secondary focus, at least in some of the schools. The free school movement was also nicknamed the feel-good movement, because many free schoolers believed it was more important for students to feel good about themselves than to focus on academics. There was an emphasis on praise. Everyone received stickers, happy faces, ribbons, and recognitions for something.

Lessons Learned from the Free School Movement

Along with receiving rewards and praise, free school students did learn empowerment skills while engaging in personalized learning. Students became happier and less stressed. The drawback to the free school movement, however, was that many students fell behind in academic skills. Their writing skills suffered, and their range of general knowledge shrank.

The free school movement dissolved, but some of its tenets remain, and educators have learned some lessons from it. While we still want students to feel good and be less stressed, we also want them to achieve academically.

Empowerment and personalized learning need not sacrifice either of these goals. It is important for students to learn content. Educators should define learning standards and objectives and share them with students. Expectations need to be clear.

Empowerment and personalized learning are still valued in today's classroom. Teachers foster student empowerment by teaching them strategies that help them learn responsibility, collaboration skills, and self-regulation. These skills help students cope with stress and empower them to become changemakers. When teachers give students such tools and when students have opportunities to use them, students find true self-confidence, and they thrive. One such tool used today is Carol Dweck's growth mindset. When students understand that intelligence can be developed and effort does bring results, they become empowered and embrace challenge. They learn that persistence matters and effort is key to mastery. They learn that criticism is a positive thing, because it gives them information they can use to improve. Teaching students about growth mindset supports their desire to learn. A growth mindset empowers students to learn required content in a way that is meaningful to them. It encourages students to become self-directed learners.

A Shift Toward Personalized Learning

How is it that personalized learning is taking center stage in education again? After the passage of the Individuals with Disabilities Education Act (IDEA) in 1997, mainstreaming made it evident that a one-size-fits-all approach to teaching didn't work. General education classrooms adopted differentiation practices. Then the national focus shifted from differentiation to personalized learning for many reasons. Since 2009, the Bill and Melinda Gates Foundation has committed more than three hundred million dollars to developing personalized learning programs in hopes of bringing up student achievement levels, particularly for economically disadvantaged students and students of color. In an attempt to improve student performance, the Investing in Innovation grant program encouraged schools to form public and private partnerships to develop district-wide personalized learning environments. The US Department of Education under the Obama administration gave five hundred million dollars to support personalized learning programs in sixty-eight districts across the United States. The Obama administration also established the Race to the Top program in 2009. This program awarded grants to eleven states and the District of Columbia, providing an opportunity for recipients to incorporate personalized learning into their goals. Many of these grants resulted in improved student performance and motivation (US Department of Education 2015). In 2012, the US Department of Education stated that its top priority for awarding further grants was the creation of personalized learning environments with personalized strategies, tools, and supports aligned to college- and career-ready standards. Under the Trump administration, Secretary of Education Betsy DeVos endorsed personalized learning because she saw it as part of her platform supporting school choice.

At about the same time personalized learning rose in prominence, so did scripted math and English language arts (ELA) programs. Scripted programs are sometimes used in schools where teachers lack training; they tell teachers exactly what to say to all students and when to say it. Scripted programs are also a way to standardize instruction in hope of bringing up test scores. To me, it seemed odd that scripted programs would become popular alongside personalized learning. How could scripted programs work in classrooms consisting of students who come from diverse backgrounds with a variety of needs? Yet as standards and test scores began to take priority over students' needs, low-performing districts sought out scripted instruction to improve test scores. Even high-performing districts bought into the sales pitch. Districts required teachers to use programs that would guarantee their standards were covered, and this, they believed, would result in higher test scores.

In order to preserve the integrity of scripted programs, teachers sacrifice their own creativity and professional expertise. Many teachers who are forced to use such programs become discouraged. They know they need to differentiate instruction so that they can actually support all students' needs. Some of the scripted programs do provide modifications, but teachers often feel these modifications miss the mark. Teachers may end up feeling disempowered—that their hands are tied, and they can no longer trust their own professional judgment. I have seen the joy of teaching subside in the wake of scripted instruction. Unhappy teachers create an unhappy classroom climate.

Teachers may have no voice in decision-making. They comply with what administrators dictate. Whether the initiative is scripted instruction, personalized learning, student empowerment, or something else, I often hear experienced teachers say, "I've seen initiatives come and go. I'm going to wait this one out, and it will go away." To some degree, these teachers are right. The cycle of educational "reform" goes on and on. Some initiatives fizzle out. But student empowerment and personalized learning are not fleeting initiatives or fads. It is not likely that, in the future, we educators will want to disempower students or depersonalize their learning. We cannot go backward.

Our educational system tends to realign itself over the long term. Meaningful, positive change is slow to take place and may be cyclical. Consider how, fifty to sixty years ago, individualized instruction was the focus of educational change. This concept has resurfaced in the twenty-first century with a fresh look.

A NOTE ABOUT LANGUAGE

People are slow to change too. I am aware that pedagogy surrounding personalized learning favors a shift in language from *students* to *learners*. However, I have chosen to continue to use the term *students* in this book. All students are learners, and all learners are students.

We as educators should refine our goals to include personalized learning and student empowerment. Personalized learning is not the same as differentiation, and student empowerment is not the same as engagement. This understanding and these refined goals are reflected in a rising number of published books and information available on personalized learning and student empowerment, separate from differentiation and engagement. Many schools are telling stories of how they not only engage but also empower students, and how they not only differentiate but also personalize their students' learning.

Student empowerment and personalized learning are hot topics in education because teachers want to know how to use them. We know how important it is for students to feel they have control over their learning. They want to know that what they are learning has meaning for them and the world around them. They want to engage in learning that is personal. With the right tools, students can go much further and much deeper in their learning than they—or we—might have thought possible.

About This Book

Inspiring Student Empowerment: Moving Beyond Engagement, Refining Differentiation provides strategies, frameworks, examples, suggestions, templates, and tools to help you shift your teaching practice from engagement to empowerment and from differentiation to personalized learning. This book is for classroom teachers and administrators who are looking for practical ways to empower students and personalize learning. It gives equal attention to both topics. The book describes engagement and differentiation as necessary, but often not enough. It offers you ways to initiate classroom change, school change, and district-wide change.

I wrote this book to provide useful suggestions to help teachers, principals, administrators, and curriculum coordinators move from their current practice—whatever that may be—to the next step on the road to student empowerment and personalized learning. The book takes you from vision to practice by providing examples and posing questions. You can reflect on your own answers to hard questions, to draw your own conclusions. **This book is not meant to be a directive. It is meant to guide teachers, schools, and districts to decide for themselves their best approach to the topics.**

My overall goal in writing this book is to address ten essential questions about empowerment and personalized learning:

1. Why is empowerment a philosophy of teaching and learning?

2. How is empowerment distinct from engagement?

3. What does it mean when we say that empowerment is personal?

4. What ignites empowerment, and what are the barriers that inhibit empowerment?

5. How does empowerment work for the everyday teacher in the classroom?

6. Personalized learning often creates self-directed learners. Why would you want your students to be self-directed learners?

7. Do your students want to become self-directed learners in your content area?

8. How is personalized learning distinct from differentiation?

9. Does personalized learning require a major overhaul of structure, schedule, and curriculum?

10. What role do nonacademic skills and behaviors play in personalized learning?

By responding to these essential questions, this book describes **how to shift the focus of instruction from student engagement to student empowerment and from differentiation to personalized learning**. The beauty of this book lies in the tools it offers to support you and your students in these pursuits. The empowerment tools are designed to foster both teacher and student empowerment. The personalized learning tools are designed to help students direct their own learning. The book includes references to technology tools, but most of the tools assume a district is not married to a particular technology program. The book identifies the problems and challenges facing educators and students today, such as lack of support, lack of resources and materials, lack of time, lack of freedom to create, lack of confidence, and pressure for all students to achieve on-grade-level standards. These barriers are holding teachers back from developing their teaching practices. This book proposes ways forward, demonstrated through vignettes, case studies, sample classroom practices, checklists, and templates.

Figure 1 illustrates the approach to learning presented in this book. It also illustrates the relationship among the ideas discussed. The base of the diagram represents the classroom environment, which must be conducive to engagement, differentiation, empowerment, and personalized learning. The arrows show the relationships between and among the ideas. Engagement and differentiation are related because the same engagement strategies won't work for all students, necessitating differentiation. Engagement and empowerment are related because students must be engaged to be empowered. Likewise, students are engaged when their learning is personalized. Differentiation affects empowerment because students are empowered in diverse ways. Differentiation is part of personalized learning but is not synonymous with it. Personalized learning provides conditions for empowerment to occur, and empowerment does the same for personalized learning.

I have divided this book into two parts, the first focusing on the shift from engagement to empowerment and the second focusing on the shift from differentiation to personalized learning. I demonstrate how empowerment is a vehicle for personalized learning, and personalized learning is a vehicle for student empowerment.

The first half of this book, **Part 1: From Engagement to Empowerment**, describes ways to engage and empower students and reviews the effects of this type of learning on students and their achievement. Chapters 1 through 4 look at the relationship between engagement and empowerment, showing how engagement is one of many igniters that spark empowerment. These chapters also address student behaviors that can warn teachers of false engagement or empowerment. The chapters caution that engagement and empowerment should be assessed in terms of degree. All four chapters contain how-to information, lists of strategies, and practical ways to make engagement and empowerment work in the classroom.

Chapter 1 discusses the **benefits of engaged learning** and describes **ways to encourage engagement**. Everyone likes engagement strategies and tools, but this chapter addresses broader issues beyond just adding things to your teaching tool belt. It discusses student behaviors and degrees of engagement. It explains that one of the reasons why an engagement strategy is effective is because the student's brain responds to and likes particular types of strategies. The chapter ends with a sample lesson that demonstrates an engagement strategy in action. This chapter lays the foundation for the empowerment chapters that follow.

Chapter 2 discusses **types of empowerment** and **ways to empower students**. It explores self-empowerment and group empowerment, the possible impact of gender on empowerment, cultural differences in empowerment, teacher empowerment, and how all these factors play out in an educational context. The chapter proposes action research and offers examples to help you compare student comments on what empowers them to teacher comments on what they think empowers their students. Empowerment is discussed in terms of relationships, sense of accomplishment, power, freedom, control, independence, motivation, grit, and the importance of feedback. The teacher's role shifts from facilitating to coaching. Mentoring and technology both support student empowerment.

Chapter 3 is all about **research-based best practices, strategies, and programs associated with empowerment.**

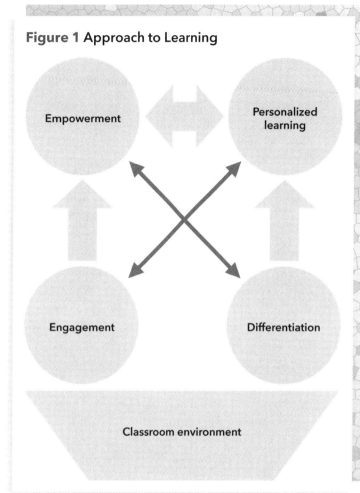

Figure 1 Approach to Learning

The chapter is based on the premise that acts of empowerment may be big or little. Teachers customize their approach to empowerment and determine which type of empowerment they want to encourage and how often. This chapter introduces strategies that empower students, such as the Harkness table strategy. The chapter also identifies starter phrases that ignite empowering discussions. Educators need not think of empowerment as an add-on. Empowerment fits easily within the context of many existing educational curricula and programs. The chapter offers an example of an expeditionary learning middle school to demonstrate how its program empowers both teachers and students. Other program examples, such as global education, inquiry learning, project-based learning, problem-based learning, genius hour, makerspace, and entrepreneurship education highlight a variety of ways to embed empowerment into instruction and curriculum content.

Chapter 4 is titled "In It to Win It" because it examines **the relationship between empowerment and game-based education and competitions.** Games empower students to speak up and collaborate on a team to achieve a common goal. The chapter offers a sample teacher-constructed game to show you how to create a game that engages and empowers students. It discusses large games that continue over time, short games that students play in ten minutes, electronic games and badges, and international competitions such as Odyssey of the Mind and Future Problem Solving Program (FPSP) as ways to empower students. In a personalized learning context, students can use tools provided in the chapter to help them create games that are designed around rigorous learning and challenge their classmates.

The second half of the book, **Part 2: Personalized Learning Plus Student Empowerment**, looks at how student empowerment can thrive in an environment of differentiation and personalized learning. When teachers share their differentiation strategies with their students, the students acquire the tools necessary to personalize their own learning. When students apply these tools and learn to use their voices, they gain control over their learning and their actions. In chapters 5 through 8, instructional tools along with a social and emotional model empower students to personalize their learning and to see themselves as self-directed learners.

Chapter 5 reviews and revisits differentiation (assuming that all teachers differentiate to some degree). **This chapter emphasizes *intentional* differentiation and common sense.** Intentional differentiation means that a teacher is differentiating and using specific strategies to meet the specific needs of a student or group of students. It does not mean an instructional approach in which teachers use a random variety of strategies simply for variety's sake. Chapter 5 discusses eight elements of differentiation:

1. The characteristics of the learner drive the need for differentiated instruction.

2. Teachers use preassessment and formative assessment to inform their differentiated instruction.

3. Each student requires unique pacing of instruction.

4. Purposeful grouping is an effective differentiated instruction strategy.

5. Differentiation supports the use of open-ended tasks and open-ended questioning.

6. A key to differentiation is differentiating the content from simple to complex.

7. Differentiation means that students think along a continuum from low (basic) to high (abstract). High-level thinking can interact with simple or complex content.

8. Differentiation in product options allows students to show what they know in a simple product, a sophisticated product, or new product form.

Chapter 6 examines the **relationship between differentiation and personalized learning** and **demonstrates how and why student empowerment works in tandem with personalization** to foster students' investment in their own learning. It also addresses student voice and choice. Since voice can be a change agent, this chapter offers information about voice as a tool for student leadership. Voice also plays a role in communication and assessment. Student choice occurs when teachers hand over control to students. Teachers identify the standards students need to cover and leave it up to students how they want to learn the content and how they want to show what they know. The more teachers hand over control to students, the more students experience empowerment, but choice can sometimes feel scary or overwhelming for students. This chapter offers several strategies to minimize such fears, help in moving from teacher-driven choice to student-driven choice, and guidance on helping students make good choices.

Chapter 7 discusses and provides examples of competency-based, mastery-based, and proficiency-based education. **These types of education can align with personalized learning and student empowerment.** Districts deal with hard questions when they initiate this type of learning approach. Many districts have a hard time describing what goes beyond the level targeted in a grade-level standard. Districts also need to decide what constitutes competency, mastery, or proficiency. Is it 90 percent or 85 percent mastery? Are competency, mastery, or proficiency levels the same in all content areas? What if a student gets stuck on a standard? How long do students stay on a standard before they can move on? Districts must map their curriculum vertically to align with their state, provincial, or district standards. Everyone needs to know what to teach when, so there are no overlaps. Once curriculum is mapped, teachers can use the instructional design planner described in chapter 7. Teachers can organize instruction using pathways (paths to learning outcomes) and playlists (specific activities that happen along a pathway). The tools in this chapter are designed both for teachers who are starting to personalize instruction and for those who are refining their personalized instruction. Once teachers are comfortable using the tools, they can show students how to use them. These tools empower students to direct their own learning.

Chapter 8 talks about the **social and emotional aspects of personalized learning and student empowerment**. It addresses classroom climate as well as the classroom community. We know how important it is to create a sense of belonging in a physically and emotionally safe place. The climate also depends upon the students' use of their social and emotional skills. The chapter refers to programs such as Open Circle, Superflex, Habits of Mind, Restorative Practices, and Responsive Classroom to foster social and emotional development. It includes information on executive function and self-regulation, along with tips for how to deal with the lack of these skills and students' negative reactive behaviors. This chapter also introduces the Affective Perspectives model. The model consists of five strands: understanding of self and others, leadership, risk-taking, insight, and goal setting.

Each of the eight chapters culminates with discussion questions that you can use to:

- reflect upon the chapter
- guide professional learning community (PLC) discussions
- spark further research on questions and topics of interest
- connect on social media with educators who have similar interests

At the end of the discussion questions, you'll find a web address where you can watch a video in which I share my thoughts about the chapter. For a video review of this introduction, visit freespirit.com/empower-videos.

The **Final Thoughts on Empowerment and Personalized Learning** remind you why we, as educators, want to foster student empowerment and embrace personalized learning. It offers you a list of questions to consider before embarking on any changes in instruction or programming and cautions you to think about not only what the research says, but also what would actually work for you. The conclusion reiterates that there is no one right way to foster student empowerment and personalized learning.

How to Use This Book

Some people always read a book from cover to cover. My hope is that you will find this book so interesting that you read it this way not out of habit, but because you want to. If that's not your preference, I hope you **read the parts of the book that are most interesting and useful to you**.

If you currently engage your students and are always looking for more engagement strategies, chapter 1 may give you some new insights. If you are looking to shift your instruction to include more emphasis on empowerment, I suggest you read both chapters 1 and 2, because many educators confuse engagement and empowerment. These chapters should make the pedagogy clear so that you understand what type of learning you are targeting and why. You should read all three empowerment chapters (chapters 2, 3, and 4) to learn about the various aspects of empowerment and broaden your understanding of the many ways you can empower students.

I know most teachers already differentiate. However, I encourage you to read chapter 5 on differentiation anyway. In it, I may define differentiation in a way that's unfamiliar to you. There are also many tools in chapter 5 that you might find useful and want to add to your differentiation repertoire. It is also important to read chapter 5 so you understand the way I articulate the distinction between *differentiation* and *personalized learning* in this book. If you want to expand your personalized education approach, I encourage you to read all the chapters (5 through 8) in part 2. If social and emotional learning is of particular interest to you, you might want to read chapter 8 first. Since social and emotional learning affects engagement, empowerment, differentiation, and personalized learning, consider reading this chapter regardless of how many other chapters you read.

If you are a specialist, curriculum coordinator, gifted and talented teacher or coordinator, or a school administrator, this book can be a resource for you because it provides practical ideas, strategies, and templates as well as suggestions for big-picture planning. It answers many questions surrounding the shift from engagement to empowerment and from differentiation to personalized learning. If you are a classroom teacher who just wants to know where to begin, the answer is to start small. Use this book to find one idea to use in your classroom. Be willing to try new things. If you are not satisfied with your results, think about how you might use the strategy differently next time. Mistakes are okay; we learn from them.

You can use this book in a PLC, as a required or supplemental text in a university course, or for your own individual needs. You could use it for professional development in a school district that is focusing on engagement, empowerment, differentiation, and/or personalized learning. One advantage of using the book for professional development in a PLC, a webinar, or a face-to-face workshop is that teachers can work together and discuss ideas. A second advantage is that many teachers in one district will receive the same information. A third advantage is that all teachers will be using shared language to communicate their ideas. Many districts prefer to have a consultant explain the ideas from the book in a professional development workshop setting. The information and tools in the book can be shared this way, or the book can stand alone and be used for a small group or individual reading.

Not every idea presented in the book will work for you. Do not worry about that. This book is not meant to provide a step-by-step recipe. You should read its ideas and personalize them. As you read, think about how an idea might work for you. Feel free to alter any idea to suit your situation.

The Journey of Teaching and Learning

Education is a journey without a precise destination. There is no one golden ticket that leads you down a perfect path. There are actually many golden tickets and many paths to empowerment and learning, so choose the ones that are right for you. I hope you collect enough golden tickets from this book to gain courage to move your own student empowerment and personalized learning practices forward.

The journey of teaching and learning is one you take with your students. Enjoy the journey and your travel companions. When you allow your students voice and choice, you also allow yourself voice and choice. When you embrace your own empowerment, you see the value of ownership and freedom. When you embrace student empowerment, you allow your students' young minds to soar. Once you see that look in your students' eyes, the expressions on their faces, and the excitement in their voices, you will understand why infusing your practice with student empowerment and personalized learning is a journey worth taking.

Part 1

FROM ENGAGEMENT TO EMPOWERMENT

Part 1 provides information about how to refocus teachers' efforts and shift instruction from student engagement to student empowerment. Student engagement is important and should not be minimized, but engagement does not ensure that students will experience empowerment. The purpose of this shift in instruction is to promote the development of autonomous, self-directed learners (as opposed to engaged students who may be compliant, dependent leaners). A variety of tools and strategies can be used to help teachers make this shift a reality. Chapters 1 through 4 provide tips and strategies to help students become empowered learners.

Engagement: It Matters

Engagement provides the launchpad for empowering students. I'm sure there are engagement strategies that you and your students like to use. Have you ever considered whether those strategies are effective enough? For example, most students like to work in a group, but is grouping the best strategy to use in every situation? Of course not. Not all engagement strategies work in all situations. Chapter 1 takes a hard look at what engagement really means and the many ways in which strategies can engage the brain. Some commonly used research-based strategies can become more engaging just by making small adjustments. However, it is not only making a strategy more engaging or choosing to use an appealing research-based strategy that matters. What matters is choosing the right strategy for the right purpose and then reflecting upon the results and being willing to adjust if the results are not what you want. Most of us do not take the time to truly analyze the effectiveness of a lesson. We tend to generalize and think a lesson went well or did not. It can be helpful to carefully plan or review how engaging a lesson really is. To make engagement matter, we should make our efforts mindful and intentional.

Engagement Defined

Are your students active, enthusiastic learners in your classroom? Do they willingly participate in learning activities? While it is critical to identify *what* to teach—that is, to know your program's objectives—it is equally essential to know *how* to accomplish these goals. Student engagement is critical to making progress toward learning goals.

According to educational researchers Robert Marzano and Debra Pickering (2011), engagement is based on students' answers to these four questions: *How do I feel? Am I interested? Is this important? Can I do this?* To determine how engaged you are in reading this chapter, you might consider your own answers. How do you feel about the information provided here? How interesting do you find it? How important is it to you? Can you transform the information into practice?

Another definition for student engagement is simply the students' willingness to participate actively. Once they begin to participate, students often demonstrate curiosity, interest, commitment, and achievement. This definition of engagement aligns with Helen Marks's definition of conceptualized engagement as "a psychological process, specifically, the attention, interest, and investment and effort students expend in the work of learning" (Marks 2000, 154).

So, why should you care about engagement? Is it because engagement makes learning more fun and motivates students? Or because engagement makes learning more meaningful? Or because you want to avoid boredom at all costs? These are all good reasons to care about engagement. Another important reason is that research has shown that engagement is a critical component of achievement. According to learning strategists Barbara Bray and Kathleen McClaskey, "Engagement has been found to be a robust predictor of learner performance and behavior in the classroom" (Bray and McClaskey 2017, 42). Literacy researcher John Guthrie points out, "Higher achievers read more and the more engaged these students become, the higher they achieve. Likewise, lower achievers read less, and the less engaged decline in achievement" (Guthrie 2008, 3). In a research report on student engagement, Krystina Finlay writes, "Students who were considered below average in engagement were 30 percent more likely to do poorly on student outcomes" (Finlay 2008, 3).

Since engagement is critical to achievement, try to enhance engagement whenever possible. Engagement increases when students attend to:

- purpose—know why they are being asked to engage in the lesson
- meaning—know and understand what they are being asked to do
- effort—are willing to put in the energy and time to do the work
- commitment—are willing to commit to the content, activity, and/or assignment

- interest—are interested in the content, activity, and/or assignment
- curiosity—are curious about the content
- attention—maintain focus throughout the activity or assignment
- participation—are willing to participate in the lesson
- sense of belonging—feel a sense of community in a safe environment

When these factors are ignored, disengagement can occur. According to the 2016 Gallup Student Poll, 74 percent of fifth graders from three thousand schools said they were engaged in school, while only 34 percent of twelfth graders claimed to be engaged (Calderon and Yu 2017). Engagement figures are similar to these in many countries. How and why does engagement drop over time? One reason may be that a mismatch exists between what teachers think are engaging ideas and what students think are engaging ideas. Teachers may think it is important to engage students with specific vocabulary tied to content; to limit lecture; to provide for high-level thinking; and to target rigorous, relevant, and real-world application of learning. Yet, when asked what engages them, students say things like loving what they do, being understood, having choices, getting out of their seats, and working with peers (Wolpert-Gawron 2015). To rectify this mismatch, we educators need to dig deeper to understand the types and degrees of effective engagement.

Types of Engagement

Let's explore the three types of engagement: behavioral, cognitive, and emotional (Fredricks, Blumenfeld, and Paris 2004). These three types of engagement will help us understand in what ways a student may or may not be engaged.

Behavioral Engagement

Behavioral engagement has to do with following rules. It also includes doing schoolwork, demonstrating effort, asking questions, participating in discussions, and completing homework. It is demonstrated in the student's attendance, participation in classwork, and involvement in extracurricular activities. Behavioral engagement is what we observe while we watch a student who is involved in the learning process (Suárez-Orozco,

Pimentel, and Martin 2009). Research indicates behavioral engagement is linked to academic performance (Archambault et al. 2009). However, according to a 2009 high school survey of student engagement, behavioral engagement is not what students think of when they consider what engages them (Yazzie-Mintz 2010). According to Ethan Yazzie-Mintz, director of this survey, many students said they "would be more engaged in school if they were intellectually challenged by their work" (Indiana University 2010). In other words, they wanted more cognitive engagement.

Cognitive Engagement

Cognitive engagement involves motivation, mental effort, and strategies that students use to exceed proficiency and embrace challenge. It is a preference for hard work and a willingness to go beyond behavioral engagement. Students who are cognitively engaged are doing higher-level thinking. Cognitively engaging lessons have a clear purpose and involve multiple skills. They may ask students to apply learning to a new situation, make inferences, and take their learning to a new level. The teacher has high expectations of students, demonstrates perseverance by sharing personal examples or examples from students, and provides an accepting classroom environment that welcomes mistakes and encourages risk-taking.

Students who are cognitively engaged are often students with high self-confidence and self-esteem. They are conscientious and timely workers. Gifted and talented students are often cognitively engaged. However, some of these students may limit their academic growth because they are unwilling to take an academic risk. They tie their self-worth to their academic achievement, and they will not risk failure. They value effort only if it helps them reach their end goal of doing well in school. When placed in an unsure situation, some gifted and talented students avoid taking academic risks and may be unwilling to take on a true academic challenge. They believe that if they do not exert effort, they can always use that as an excuse that they could have been successful if they had really tried. Students who exhibit this behavior fall back on a fixed mindset, which affects their willingness to cognitively engage.

In order to be cognitively engaged, students need a good working memory. They must rehearse, or use, information to move it from working memory into short-term and long-term memory. Students rehearse information to assign personal meaning and to make connections with prior knowledge. Once information makes it into short-term memory, with more rehearsal, the hippocampus can move it to long-term memory. Short-term memory has limited capacity. For adolescents and adults, the short-term memory can store four items, and for preadolescents, the short-term memory probably stores fewer than four items (Sousa and Tomlinson 2018, 52). It is difficult to remember something that makes no sense or has no meaning. Meaning influences which information gets stored in short-term and long-term memory. Therefore, the most effective engagement strategies target meaning and sense-making.

Emotional Engagement

Emotional engagement involves students' interests, values, and feelings. According to Sousa and Tomlinson, neurons fire when we experience a task or an emotion. The more neurons fire, the more engaged we are. You see emotional engagement demonstrated in students' affective reactions, their appreciation of school success, and their sense of community and belonging. Emotionally engaged students interact with peers and choose friends. They use collaborative learning to solve problems and use inquiry to learn new things.

Students want to be part of a community, but in a 2009 survey of three hundred thousand students, only 55 percent felt part of their high school community (Yazzie-Mintz 2010). If we educators do not provide classroom communities in which students feel comfortable engaging, they will find their own communities outside our classrooms. It's up to us to create classroom communities that are welcoming, safe, and respectful, and that make students feel capable.

Emotional engagement means getting students excited about the content as well as catching and holding their attention. Neuroscientist Jaak Panskepp proposed that the brain contains neural networks that generate emotions (cited in Gregory and Kaufeldt 2015). These emotional networks keep humans motivated, interested, and energized in what they are learning or doing. Emotions help people make connections, and they spark eagerness to learn.

Emotions such as happiness, confidence, enthusiasm, and fascination set the tone for engagement. It is easy to see how an expression of a positive emotion such as laughter alleviates stress, anxiety, and loneliness. Laughter can also increase attention and memory. These are all good reasons to strive for laugher and include it as an

effective engagement strategy. The average four-year-old laughs three hundred times a day (Gerloff 2011). The average forty-year-old, by contrast, laughs four times a day. I wonder how much less a student laughs from age five to age eighteen. Do we lose some of our sense of humor during the school years? When promoting laughter, instead of coming up with adaptations that are humorous yourself, ask your students to alter information in order to make others laugh. (Not all students have the same sense of humor and not all students will think the same thing is funny. Before doing so, have a discussion with your students about the differences between silly and humorous and appropriate versus inappropriate.)

Humans sense and watch facial expressions and nuanced behaviors to determine other people's intentions and feelings. Your attitude, expressed emotions, and behavior affects your students' perception of how capable you think they are as learners. Developmental psychology researchers David Yeager and Gregory Walton have found that "brief exercises that target students' thoughts, feelings, and beliefs in and about school can lead to large gains in student achievement and sharply reduce achievement gaps even months and years later" (Yeager and Walton 2011).

Behavioral, cognitive, and emotional engagement are not isolated processes. These categories simply help us build a conceptual understanding of engagement. Students tend to identify engagement more with emotions and behaviors, because for most students, school is a social experience. On the other hand, many teachers focus primarily on cognitive engagement. Consider whether you are barking up the wrong tree with your engagement efforts. You might be bending over backward to engage students, but what type of engagement are they, not you, seeking?

Student Behaviors

What do student behaviors tell us? Can we use this information to engage students more effectively in learning? Let's look at some data and examples.

When students say they are bored, can they tell you in what ways they are bored? In a survey, Ethan Yazzie-Mintz reported that when students were asked why they were bored, 81 percent said the material was not interesting, and 40 percent said that because the material was not relevant to them, they became bored

(Yazzie-Mintz 2010). Other reporting from this survey found 33 percent of students were bored because the work wasn't challenging, 26 percent said they were bored because the work was too hard, and 35 percent were bored because they had no interaction with the teacher. In another survey, the students said they wanted a learning situation that included control, choice, challenge, complexity, and caring (Kanevsky and Keighley 2003).

In one high school where I was brought in to consult with teachers on differentiation, I observed a science classroom where the teacher was having trouble controlling the class. I was there to observe the differentiation lesson. Her differentiation was skilled and thorough. She differentiated her students' lab work, students moved at their own pace, and she helped struggling students. All students should have been engaged. So what went wrong? I met with a student who was acting out and asked him why he was behaving that way. He replied, "The teacher does not respect me, so I don't respect her." This statement reminded me that we can adapt curriculum for our students, and we can use many varied engagement strategies, but if students don't think we care about them or respect them, all our efforts will be in vain. The statement was a wake-up call for his teacher to be honest with herself and assess her own behaviors, not just student behavior.

Both positive and negative student behaviors can affect degrees of student engagement. These behaviors are based on learner characteristics. If we look closely at these behaviors and characteristics, we can figure out how to tweak our instruction to better attend to the needs of our students. Let's consider the following students and examine how their characteristics and actions relate to their behavioral, cognitive, and emotional engagement:

- **Emilio** is enthusiastically engaged. He can get so involved in a project that it is hard for him to stop. He wants to do his very best all the time. If the teacher is using a rubric for a learning activity, he is not satisfied with proficient performance. He wants to take on a challenge and do advanced work. His effort and commitment sometimes cause him stress, but he seems to thrive on stress. He has a hard time with moderation.

- **Dalia** does her work, gets it in on time, never causes problems in the classroom, and engages moderately in classroom activities. She is not enthusiastic, nor does she demonstrate boredom. She will do whatever the teacher asks of her. She is a rule follower and works for the top grade.

- **Zahra** asks questions because she likes to appear engaged; however, she rarely answers questions. She often leads discussions off track and talks just to hear herself talk. She does not worry about doing her best work, because okay work is fine with her. Just getting by is the standard she sets for herself. She is friendly and likable. Her engagement is dependent upon her comfort level with the activity.

- **Marcos** does not like attention. He rarely contributes in class discussions because he is afraid of what others might think of him. He dislikes working in small groups for this reason and because it is hard to hide in a small group. His level of engagement is limited by his fear of participation, of being wrong, and of what others think of him.

- **Luciana** is highly engaged, but in a negative way. She constantly questions why she must do something or learn something and often says something is boring. She can be disruptive and argumentative and often leads other students toward joining in her negative behavior. When she is absent, teachers notice fewer interruptions, and class goes more smoothly.

- **Jadyn** does not perform in classroom activities or assignments. He is not engaged in schoolwork. He may wander alone or daydream. He works slowly, if at all. He may be engaged in other types of learning at home on his own. However, Jadyn may be at risk for more serious problems beyond engagement issues. When students become loners and set themselves apart from day-to-day activities, it may be that there are problems at home or possibly some social and emotional problems that should be addressed. The teacher needs to keep a close eye on Jadyn so he does not slip through the cracks.

Figure 1-1 shows possible ways to increase engagement for this group of hypothetical students, who have a variety of positive and negative behaviors. As you read about the engagement strategies described in the rest of this chapter, think about which strategy would be the most effective with which hypothetical student—and with your own students. Choose your engagement strategies intentionally.

Figure 1-1 Student Behaviors and Engagement Strategies

Student	Positive Behaviors	Negative Behaviors	Strategies to Improve Engagement
Emilio	Is engaged Is enthusiastic Likes challenge Works hard Performs at a high level	Doesn't like to stop Often expects high-level performance from others Is often stressed	Set clear expectations Agree to time constraints Provide leadership opportunities
Dalia	Does what is expected Meets deadlines Is academically capable	Needs teacher to tell her what to do Lacks independence Lacks self-confidence	Use emotional engagement strategies Reduce teacher dependency
Zahra	Asks questions Is friendly Is likable	Doesn't answer questions Does just-okay work Daydreams	Connect to student's interests Help student make meaning
Marcos	Is quiet Completes work	Doesn't share ideas Won't participate in groups Dislikes being called on in class	Assign a partner who will not overpower him Use emotional engagement strategies Call on student when you know the student knows the answer
Luciana	Is academically capable	Forms identity by opposition Dominates group activities in negative ways Gets attention through anger	Connect with student Foster respect for one another Help student see real value in the work
Jadyn	Attends school May have friends	Feels loss of control Sees no way to accomplish goals Has blank affect	Seek help from guidance counselor for student

Engagement Strategies

In this section, there are a variety of instructional strategies and tools that engage students. I've identified seven types of strategies the brain prefers, based upon neuroscience findings. When we use strategies the brain prefers, it is easier to engage students. I also examine eight common and perhaps not-so-common engagement strategies, and ways to make them just a little more engaging. When using a specific strategy, teachers or students may also use the Engage-O-Meter to identify or predict in what way and to what degree the student is or may be engaged.

What the Human Brain Likes

The brain is wired to like certain things. When the brain likes something, it learns better. Our brains like the following things because they bring us joy. When these elements are present, they enhance engagement.

NOVELTY

The brain likes to be surprised. This can mean anything that diverges from the routine. For example:

- Have your students create plans to rearrange the classroom. Their plans can involve scale drawings or cut paper laid out on a larger sheet of paper. Your students agree on the best layout and proceed to rearrange the room. This engages them in the design process and empowers them to create a novel space for themselves.

- You dress up as a character from a story or a famous person from history. When your students walk into the classroom, they are surprised to see that you look different. To make this novelty even more engaging, let students create costumes for themselves or for each other.

- When your students walk into the room, you immediately engage them in an activity. Don't let them sit down! Don't talk! Let them read written directions from the board and immediately engage in the interactive lesson.

LAUGHTER

Here is a quick reminder to lighten up and laugh. If you are too serious, your students will model your behavior—which is fine some of the time, but being serious all the time will put a damper on engagement. If you are serious by nature, and humor does not come easily to you, here are some activities to try:

- Give students the responsibility of providing a cartoon or joke that teaches a lesson for the day.

- Challenge your students to find cartoons or jokes that relate to the content of a specific lesson. The more students laugh, the more things they will find that are funny.

- Humor is personal, and not everyone will find the same things funny. Discuss the nature of humor. Ask, "What makes things funny? Why is something funny to one person and not so funny to another person?"

- Challenge your students to create a product with something that is funny about the content they are learning. Have other students locate the funny part that the student added to the assignment and explain why they think it is funny.

SENSES

Use sensory experiences, such as images or videos, startling sounds, things to taste, or aromas to draw students' attention. It takes three to five seconds for the brain to process sensory input, and then the input moves immediately to short-term memory. The short-term memory makes connections between the sensory input and content knowledge. Here are some sensory examples that target seeing and hearing:

- Ask your students to find multiple cartoons, images, and quotes that relate to the topic of globalization. Students work in groups to determine which cartoon, picture, and quote they like best. They share their final choices with the rest of the class and explain their choices. By looking at a variety of resources, students build a deep conceptual understanding of the topic, concept, or problem you've posed. Since most students enjoy visuals and cartoons, their degree of engagement, attention, and interest is generally high.

- A video holds students' attention if the music grabs them, if the format grabs them, if the content grabs them, if they understand and relate to the message, if the video is not too long, if the pacing is just right, if the video evokes emotion, or if the video is simply enjoyable to watch. A video notes sheet (see **Video Notes** reproducible, page 25) helps students pay attention to the video and attend to the information in it.

- Videos can be more engaging—even empowering—if students make the videos themselves. If you provide instructions on how to create a video, the products are often more successful. Students are more engaged when they have focus questions to answer before they begin making the video. For example, in planning the video, the students decide whether it will have a narrator or host, and who it will be. Will this narrator or host be a person, a computer-animated character, a cartoon, or just a voice? Will the voice be a real person's voice or an electronically modified voice? Will the video be a demonstration, a game, or a slide presentation? What will the format be? Will the students need to make a list of key words and phrases, vocabulary words, or symbols that should be included in the video? Will there be music or sound effects? Have students view a video with and without music or sound effects to determine which they like better. Do students know how to make a storyboard that delineates scenes?

- Music is a very effective tool that's often underused in the classroom. Most students enjoy music. It has a way of lifting the mind and taking it places. Don't get stuck with only one kind of music, such as classical. Play music that is uplifting and inspiring in addition to relaxing. Use music to key in to content, attention, and mood. You may want to use quiet, calming music if you are about to go over some important information and you need your students focused. If you want to energize your students, play music with a strong beat and with a strong message. For example, songs like "We Are Brave" by Shawn McDonald, "Try Everything" by Shakira, "Torches" by Daughtry, and "Live Like a Warrior" by Matisyahu are fun to play as students are entering the room. Use music to spark discussion. What happens if you play something like "Destiny Awaits" by Audiomachine as students enter the room? Ask them why they think you chose this song to play and what they think will happen next. If you want to change your classroom tone to a light, happy atmosphere, play "Lucky Day" by Tomás Doncker. You can also use music to tie into content. For example, if you are studying globalization, you could play "Conscience of the World" by Tomás Doncker.

INTEREST

When students are interested in the content of an activity or an assignment, they are willing to engage in it. To engage a disengaged student, try to connect the student's interest with the required content. For example, the student's interest is knitting, and you are a math teacher. Although there is no time available in school for knitting, some knitting skills are transferable to math content. A knitter needs to understand how to read and apply number patterns in order to create specific designs and shapes. You could help your student knitter see that patterns serve similar basic purposes in knitting and in math. Patterns repeat, patterns have order, patterns allow for prediction, and patterns help us understand.

QUESTIONS

The brain likes questions. "Questions can generate mild pressure that helps stimulate attention" (Marzano and Pickering 2011, 12). When a student's attention is activated, the student's working memory is keyed into the learning activity. If *you* create questions about a topic, the questions may not interest your students. But if students generate the questions themselves, they are more likely to be interested in the content. Students need tools to generate engaging questions. If you teach your students about the Revised Bloom's Taxonomy, Depth of Knowledge (DOK) framework, or Marzano's strategies, students will be better equipped to create meaningful questions at challenging levels.

The Revised Bloom's Taxonomy connects the level of thinking (or thinking dimension) with the type of knowledge (or knowledge dimension). The dimensions of thinking are remembering, understanding, applying, analyzing, evaluating, and creating. The dimensions of knowledge are the types of content covered in a unit. These dimensions are factual, conceptual, procedural, and metacognitive (Anderson et al. 2000).

DOK is a framework for cognitive rigor in the classroom. The DOK model focuses on the setting, the situation, and the scenario in which students produce learning. The levels are not designed as a taxonomy, which means students do not have to master one level before going to the next level. DOK analyzes the specifics of assignments in four levels: recall (level one), concept and skills (level two), strategic thinking (level three), and extended thinking (level four).

Marzano identifies four thinking processes that include specific verbs. For example, level one is the retrieval level and is associated with verbs such as *recognize*, *recall*, and *execute*. Level two is the comprehension level; the verbs associated with it are *integrate* and *symbolize*. Level 3 is focused on analyzing and consists of *comparing*, *classifying*, *analyzing errors*, *generalizing*, and *specifying*. Fourth is the knowledge utilization level. These mental processes include *decision-making*, *problem-solving*, *experimenting*, and *investigating*.

There are other strategies besides sharing lists of verbs that can help students create engaging questions. One such strategy is question cubes, which you can make or buy. Students are actively engaged when they toss the cube and create questions tied to their content based on the verb on the top face of the cube.

CURIOSITY

Sparking students' curiosity grabs their attention and promotes engagement. You can try to spark curiosity by providing a hook to a lesson, as in the following examples:

- Introduce a topic by showing a quick video. Although this may hook your students' interest, be aware that this strategy targets passive engagement. There is nothing wrong with some passive engagement, but try to avoid too much of it. You can increase the engagement level a little by requiring students to fill out the **Video Notes** reproducible on page 25.

- Another way to spark curiosity is to show your students an object and ask them what they think the object is. Once the students guess what the object is, ask them what they think it has to do with what they will be learning.

- Engage students in a game. Many teachers like to create games using kahoot.com. The teacher generates a list of questions, and the teacher uses these questions to create a multiple-choice game using the Kahoot platform. Students try to answer each question in ten to twenty seconds. The scores are displayed in a bar graph for the whole class to see. If you use this strategy as a hook to spark curiosity, it is unlikely that your students will know the answers to the questions, because you have not yet taught them the content. After each answer is displayed, you can teach the information particular to the question right on the spot. In this way, the Kahoot game can be used both as a preassessment and as a way to engage students and get them excited about an upcoming unit of study.

RELATIONSHIPS

Are you building bridges with your students? "It is not what a teacher thinks and feels about a particular student that forges a positive relationship with the student. Rather, it is how the teacher speaks to and behaves with the student that communicates respect and acceptance" (Marzano and Pickering 2011, 36). Students want to connect with you. Research supports the importance of relationships between students and adults in school. Strong relationships with both adults and peers are predictors of student engagement (Tucker et al. 2002; Perdue, Manzeske, and Estell 2009; Yazzie-Mintz 2010).

In a graduation speech, one high school senior chose not to talk about the accomplishments of the students in his class. Rather, he chose to speak about diversity and relationships. He said that relationships are the strength of our schools. He asked all the students to simultaneously stand up and shout the name of their favorite teacher. The students shouted many names. The student pointed out that school is a web of relationships. The strand that connects each student with each teacher is a unique bond. Each bond, created from interpersonal similarities and differences, creates a relationship that matters. When relationships matter, students engage.

Instructional Practices for Engagement

Instructional practices for engagement are techniques that you can use to engage your students in the learning process. You can tweak these practices to make them more engaging or more personalized for the learner. Even though you can increase levels of engagement in a variety of ways using these instructional practices, it's important to realize that they don't necessarily empower students. That's because you make all the decisions: choosing the technique, grouping the students, identifying the content, and planning the lesson. You are the planner and organizer.

WEBBING

How can we take a simple strategy such as webbing and make it more engaging? In webbing, the concept or problem at hand is placed in a center circle. Students free-associate related words and place those words in circles arranged around the center circle, then connect them with lines to the center circle. This simple strategy is more engaging when teachers encourage students to connect more than two words. The more ideas generated on the concept web with multiple connections made, the deeper the level of understanding. When creating webs, students work alone, with a partner, or in a small group. Generally, a group web is more engaging than one generated by a single student, because the group web represents multiple perspectives and viewpoints.

THINK-PAIR-SHARE

How can we make a Think-Pair-Share simple review strategy in which students work with partners more engaging? To begin this strategy, you ask a question. First, the students **think** individually and write down their answers. Then the students **pair** up, and one partner explains their answer to the question to the other partner, who then agrees, disagrees, modifies, or expands the answer. Together the partners synthesize their response to the question. Finally, the partners **share** their response with the whole class. In order to increase engagement, you can vary this strategy. Instead of pairs sharing with the whole class, one member of each pair travels to share with a different student. The traveling partners then return to their home partners with ideas gained from the other students. The home pairs decide whether to maintain or change their original responses.

VERBAL BRAINSTORMING

Most teachers use verbal brainstorming to get students to generate ideas. This engaging strategy can be more effective when teachers share the following rules of brainstorming with their students: quantity is encouraged, criticism is not allowed, piggybacking is permitted, and wild and zany ideas are welcome. Students who do not like to share ideas orally may prefer written brainstorming, in which students write ideas on a piece of paper and then pass it around for others to add ideas. Written brainstorming can increase engagement for quiet students, who do not have to compete with talkative ones, and allows anonymity and more time for reflection.

VOCABULARY STRIPS AND VOCABULARY CARD GAMES

In this strategy, students cut out small pieces of paper about the size of small index cards or use actual index cards or sticky notes. For each vocabulary term, students use six cards, writing one of the following on each:

1. the vocabulary term

2. the definition of the term in their own words

3. a synonym for the term

4. an antonym for the term

5. a symbol that represents the term

6. a sentence that contains the term

Then students connect the cards to make a vertical strip using a long piece of masking tape. Alternatively, these same cards can be turned into a matching game. Instead of creating vocabulary strips, the student arranges all the cards facedown and finds a partner to play the game with. Each player turns over two cards and tries to find a match. For example, the partner chooses a synonym card that has the word *happy* on it, then turns over a vocabulary card that has the word *elated* on it. The two words are a match, so they are removed from play. Then the card-creating student turns over two cards. If the cards match, they are removed; if not, they are turned back over. The game continues until all cards have been matched, and the winner is the student who located the most matches. Both the vocabulary strip activity and the vocabulary card game strategies are engaging. Both include a hands-on element. But the student works alone with the vocabulary strip activity, while the card game is more social.

GRAPHIC ORGANIZERS

Graphic organizers are useful visual tools for all learners. They are particularly effective with English language learners (ELL students) and students who are unable to or do not like to write a lot. Engagement will vary according to the type of organizer. Story-based graphic organizers, which focus on story elements or character development, are simple and familiar. But graphic organizers can also be more sophisticated. In my book *Differentiating with Graphic Organizers: Tools to Foster Critical and Creative Thinking,* I provide and explain cognitive graphic organizers that target higher-level thinking skills. For example, one critical-thinking graphic

organizer targets prioritizing, one focuses on judging, and one targets inferring. One creative-thinking graphic organizer focuses on making unlikely connections, and another targets elaboration. In order to increase engagement, instead of using templates, students can write their ideas on sticky notes and move them around to organize their thoughts and give verbal justifications for their prioritization, judgements, or conclusions.

SIMULATIONS

Simulations can be based on real or imaginary situations or problems. Begin by posing a situation or problem. For example, in a simulation that focuses on a real situation, the teacher gives her students the following scenario: "We know how important it is to eat healthy foods. Your team noticed that cafeteria food is being wasted because students are throwing a lot of it away. In our study of nutrition, what have you learned in our unit that may be information you could use to defend a new menu that you propose to our food services director? Your team is to come up with a menu for a month that includes healthy eating choices and present it to the director. Make sure you can defend your suggestions both nutritionally and financially."

In an imaginary simulation, the teacher sets up a situation where students must use newly acquired content knowledge to solve an imaginary problem. For example, "The town water commissioner has discovered a high level of iron in the town water. Even though the iron level is high, it is still considered borderline normal. But citizens are complaining that the water turns their white clothes a reddish orange color and they cannot get the clothes white again and that their bathtubs have a reddish orange stain that they can't get rid of. People feel uncomfortable drinking the water, so they feel forced to buy bottled water, which is an added expense and is bad for the environment. The town's water commissioner has asked your team for help to solve this problem."

This imaginary simulation tries to mimic authenticity. You might provide background information packets or links on water quality for students to use. The students will need to make many decisions and work together in teams to come up with a solution. Students must decide whether to organize a town hall meeting. Will they need to interview parents or survey opinions? How might the team find out if this water problem is affecting everyone in town or only some people? Students usually take on roles, such as the water commissioner, the person who laid the town water lines, the town manager, the town budget person, the water chemical engineer, and so on, when they work on simulations. Student teams then present their solutions to the class. In a simulation, students learn specific content skills tied to standards as well as extended skills such as communication, teamwork, and consensus-building. To make this practice more engaging—even empowering—have your students set up their own simulation and create their own scenario for another team of students to solve.

TIERED QUESTIONS

You can use the Revised Bloom's Taxonomy to help you created tiered questions. The Revised Bloom's Taxonomy, as noted previously, refers to levels of thinking and types of knowledge. Using this taxonomy, create sets of easy, medium, and hard tiered questions. For example, an easy question about a story for a first grader is to retell the story. *Retell* focuses on a low level of thinking. A medium question is to compare and contrast the characters in the story. *Compare* and *contrast* are more challenging than *retell* and direct student thinking to a higher level. A hard question is to find examples in the story that illustrate a specific principle. This question is harder because the content, a specific principle, is a difficult concept. Students work in pairs to answer the questions.

VISUALIZATION

Let's look at a solitary visualization activity with an engaging application. In a fourth-grade unit on water, the teacher asks the students to close their eyes and imagine they are in a giant city square. Old buildings surround them. People are busily coming and going. Some people are shopping, and some people are tourists wandering around looking at the unfamiliar environment. You notice some people are strolling on walkways over the water, which is shin-high in the city square. The people realize they are very close to the ocean. In fact, all this water *is* the ocean, flooding the low parts of the city. Where in the world is this? When students open their eyes, the teacher asks them to brainstorm locations and listens to hear if anyone comes up with the correct answer: Venice, Italy. Then the teacher asks the students to watch a video (youtube.com/watch?v=Zj2aTj1bXrs) and see whether what they visualized resembles the real thing. The students and teacher talk about the effects of flooding on daily life, costs to the city, erosion, and the future of Venice.

Some engagement practices are more engaging than others. Do some informal action research to assess your instructional practices and determine whether you need to make any changes to increase engagement. Try to predict the effectiveness of your strategies. Be intentional about the strategies you use and the results you expect. The interaction among the strategy, the content, the learners, and how you set up a lesson determines the degree of engagement.

Degree of Engagement

In the old school paradigm, the teacher gave the students goals and objectives and activities to help students learn the required content. It did not really matter if students were interested in learning the material, because they just did what they were told. They needed to know what they were learning and how to learn it, but educators did not question whether the learning was relevant to students' lives or had personal meaning for them.

At some point in time, the paradigm shifted. Students started to question what they were doing and why they were doing it. Educators became concerned as to whether their students were interested and if students saw relevance in the material. As more and more research showed how students learn best, educators started paying attention to the various ways in which they could reach and teach students.

When John Hattie's work on effect size was released in his 2009 book *Visible Learning*, and research-based strategies became more widely known and consulted, districts started paying attention to degrees of effectiveness. Hattie's work describes the synthesis of fifteen years of research that he spent analyzing eight hundred meta-analysis studies on what influences student achievement. I heard Hattie speak at the 2009 ASCD National conference, where he explained that if we want to know what strategies work—they all do. It's just a matter of how much they work.

For example, Hattie says that providing students with timely, specific feedback yields a greater effect than enrichment does. This does not indicate that enrichment is a waste of time. On the contrary, enrichment is an effective strategy. However, if teachers decide to place more emphasis on providing students with feedback and less time on planning enrichment activities, Hattie's analysis indicates that students will make greater academic gains.

Hattie makes the point that teachers should use their time wisely. Since we all have limited time, where do you want to concentrate your efforts? What type of engagement strategies will give you the most bang for your buck?

Teacher Engage-O-Meter

Hattie's work provides base knowledge and context, but teachers can use their own professional judgments to make decisions about strategies and their effectiveness. I designed the Teacher Engage-O-Meter (see **figure 1-2** and the reproducible on page 26) to help you reflect on the degree to which you think students are engaged and whether that level of engagement affects achievement. The Teacher Engage-O-Meter allows you to identify the type of engagement and refers to whether you intentionally engage students through the content of the lesson, the process of the lesson (the activities and/or assignments), or the product that the students produce. In looking at which instructional strategies engage students the most, are we asking how much the students enjoy using the strategy? Or are we asking how effective the strategy is in helping students learn? If students enjoy the strategy but do not actually learn most of the required content, is it worth using the strategy?

Figure 1-2 demonstrates how one teacher used the Teacher Engage-O-Meter. When the teacher observed the whole class during this activity, she noticed that the visualization strategy sparked lots of student engagement. However, the lesson fell short when she asked students to respond in their science journals. The notes at the bottom of **figure 1-2** explain how the lesson went.

How might the Teacher Engage-O-Meter be useful to you? If you keep track of various activities over a month or so, you may find a pattern. Perhaps it is your content that's less engaging. If so, you could help students make more connections between the content and their interests. If the activities seem to be lacking, you may want to reconsider how you used the instructional strategy or differentiate the strategy for students who did not seem to like it. If the products seem unengaging, perhaps you

Figure 1-2 Sample Teacher Engage-O-Meter

Write the activity prompt in the space below. For each row on the chart, name the lesson element, then place an X in the column that indicates your students' engagement in that element.

Prompt: Imagine you are a plant on a warm, sunny summer day. Visualize what you look like, what you see, and how you feel. What do you need? Respond in writing in your science journal.

	Name It	Not Very Engaging	Somewhat Engaging	Wow! Very Engaging
Simple Content	Parts of the plant What plants need to grow		X	
Complex Content	None			
Process: Activity	Visualization			X
Process: Assignment	None			
Product	Response in science journal	X		

Notes:

The content was accessible to all students because it was fairly simple; it was somewhat engaging for most students, but certainly not a "Wow!" The process in this activity was visualization. This was very engaging, and students really used their imaginations to visualize being the plant. However, when students wrote their responses in their journal, it sort of brought the enthusiasm down to a more ho-hum, matter-of-fact level. Maybe if the students wrote how they felt and what they needed and made an abstract drawing of what they looked like, the product engagement might have been higher. Next time, I will try changing the product form.

can offer more choice. You know a strategy can fall short with one group yet be effective with another. You know if you use a strategy with one type of content, you may get a different result than when you use it with another type of content. The Teacher Engage-O-Meter can help you keep track of the effectiveness of your engagement strategies and provide you with information that will help you make intentional changes. Of course, you will not use the Teacher Engage-O-Meter all the time. It is for those times when you really want to observe your classroom and reflect upon your practice. It can also be used when an administrator or peer is conducting a formal or informal teacher observation.

Student Engage-O-Meter

In addition to the Teacher Engage-O-Meter, I've created a Student Engage-O-Meter. (See **figure 1-3** and the reproducible on page 27.) This student tool is similar to the teacher tool. If we want our students to be engaged, we must pay attention to their needs. The Student Engage-O-Meter lets students self-assess their degree of engagement and discover the most effective way for them to study and to learn. This knowledge empowers

them to choose their own way to learn, process information, rehearse information so they can remember it, and create products.

Look at the individual student's response in **figure 1-3**. This student clearly does not like this lesson. If this student continues to respond to lessons in this way, how long do you think it will take for her to become a disengaged learner?

An Engagement Lesson Plan in Action

Let's take a look at a lesson plan that includes engagement as part of the plan itself (**figure 1-4**). For an eighth-grade ELA lesson, Jade Anderson uses the book *The Giver* by Lois Lowry to target the following Common Core Standards: "Determine a theme or central idea of a text and analyze its development over the course of the text, including its relationship to the characters, setting, and plot; provide an objective summary of the text" and "Write arguments to support claims with clear reasons and relevant evidence" (Common Core

Figure 1-3 Sample Student Engage-O-Meter

Write the activity prompt in the space below. For each row of the chart, name the lesson element, then place an X in the column that indicates your engagement in that element.

Prompt: Imagine you are a plant on a warm, sunny summer day. Visualize what you look like, what you see, and how you feel. What do you need? Respond in writing in your science journal.

	Name It	Not Very Engaging	Somewhat Engaging	Wow! Very Engaging
Simple Content	Parts of the plant What plants need to grow	X		
Complex Content	None			
Process: Activity	Visualization	X		
Process: Assignment	None			
Product	Response in science journal	X		

Notes: I do not find learning about parts of the plants exciting in any way. I thought the visualization activity was lame. Why would I imagine myself as a plant? I do not like writing. If I could have acted this out or at least make a game out of it, maybe I would have been more engaged.

Figure 1-4 Sample Engagement Lesson Plan

Designing a Lesson That Targets Student Engagement

Grade level: 8

Discipline: ELA

Content: *The Giver* by Lois Lowry

The Giver	Standards:		Topics:	Subtopics:	Skills:
	CCSS:		Character	Personality	Analysis
	RL 8.2		Plot	Ability	Synthesis
	W 8.1		Setting	Appearance	Creating
			Writing with evidence	Problem	Justification
				Issues	Writing technique
				Resolution	
Essential question	Why is resolution important?				
Assessment	Rubric: The teacher assesses and provides students with written feedback to supplement the rubric.				
Student learning objective	Elaborate on the ending of The Giver by creating a news broadcast announcing what really happened to Jonas and Gabriel.				
	Target level of engagement:				
Content: Plot	Not Very Engaging		Somewhat Engaging X		Wow! Very Engaging
Thinking process: Elaborate Create	Not Very Engaging		Somewhat Engaging		Wow! Very Engaging X
Product: News broadcast	Not Very Engaging		Somewhat Engaging		Wow! Very Engaging X
Instructional strategy: Think-Pair-Share	Not Very Engaging		Somewhat Engaging		Wow! Very Engaging X

The student will:

1. Review the ending of the story by completing a Review and Complete plot diagram for the story.

2. Engage in a discussion with the class to determine if there is a true resolution in the story.

3. List ideas about what happened to Jonas and Gabriel at the end of the book.

4. Meet with a partner to participate in a Think-Pair-Share activity. Partners will share ideas about what they believe happened to Jonas and Gabriel at the end of the book.

5. Travel to other groups to find out their ideas and take notes if necessary.

6. Return to original partner and share the ideas from the other groups.

7. Along with partner, choose the best idea(s) to create an elaboration on the end of the story.

8. Along with partner, use the rubric to create a mock news broadcast.

9. Along with partner, present their broadcast to the class.

Adapted from Jade Anderson, Sanford Public Schools, 2017. Used with permission.

State Standards Initiative 2019). Jade lists these standards on the plan as well as the topics, subtopics, and skills addressed in the lesson. Next, she identifies the essential question *Why is resolution important?* The essential question provides a key way for Jade to encourage students' cognitive engagement. She hopes to spark the students' curiosity by thinking about the broad concept of resolution. The *why* in the essential question helps students understand the purpose of learning about the content.

The lesson plan also indicates that Jade will be using a rubric to assess the lesson. Once Jade has made her overall content decisions, she is ready to state the student learning objective. Below the student learning objective, Jade breaks down the content, thinking process, product, and strategy she plans to use in the lesson. What is unique to this lesson plan is that it has a place for the teacher to indicate how engaging she expects each part of the lesson to be. This makes her intentions clear. Jade knows it is unlikely that every part of the lesson will be highly engaging. She tries to be realistic about how she thinks her students will respond.

Jade is happy to see that she designed a lesson in which she anticipates three of the four elements to be very engaging. She plans out the body of the lesson by listing the steps the student will follow. After she lists the steps in the lesson, she goes back to reassess whether the levels of engagement match up with the description in the body of the lesson. Now she is ready to give the lesson a whirl.

It is unlikely you will use an engagement lesson plan like the one in **figure 1-4** for every lesson. However, I do recommend using something like this until the types and degrees of engagement become automatic in your mind. If you are already required to use a particular lesson plan format, perhaps you can modify it to include language specific to engagement. If your school or district does not allow you to modify your lesson plan format, you can use sticky notes and just remove them when necessary. The point is to identify when you anticipate student engagement to occur in a lesson and to what degree you think your students will be engaged.

Chapter Summary

There are many ways to engage students. If you give students interesting content and challenge them to think deeply about it; if you provide novelty, humor, and questioning techniques; and if you spark curiosity and integrate the senses into their strategies, students will be more likely to engage. You can engage students through numerous types of products and projects. Where to start? It is all about relationships first. As middle school teacher Beth Morrow says, it's a myth that "adding or changing classroom elements, doing a new project, or exposing a student to a new technology or method of instruction will magically transform apathy into a white-hot fire of curiosity. . . . Caring about students beyond the boundaries of the classroom is the first step of sparking engagement" (Morrow 2014).

Discussion Questions

Are the following statements true or false? Why?

1. When a student is attentive, this is at least one clear indicator that the student is engaged.

2. If a student is on task, the student is engaged.

3. This student is polite and waits for a turn to speak. It is obvious at a glance that the student is engaged and paying attention.

4. This student finishes work on time. The work is complete. Surely this student is engaged.

5. This student jumps up with excitement about the content. There is no question that this student is engaged. Maybe too engaged!

After you've thought about your answers to these questions, visit this website for a video chapter review with the author: freespirit.com/empower-videos.

Video Notes

My name:

Video name:

Now that's worth quoting:	At least three things I want to remember:
I learned something new:	**This really made me think or wonder:**

I rate this video:

☐ Not worth watching

☐ Just okay

☐ Don't miss it

Optional comments:

Teacher Engage-O-Meter

Write the activity prompt in the space below. For each row of the chart, name the lesson element, then place an X in the column that indicates your students' engagement in that element.

Prompt:

	Name It	Not Very Engaging	Somewhat Engaging	Wow! Very Engaging
Simple Content				
Complex Content				
Process: Activity				
Process: Assignment				
Product				

Notes:

Student Engage-O-Meter

Write the activity prompt in the space below. For each row of the chart, name the lesson element, then place an X in the column that indicates your engagement in that element.

Prompt:

	Name It	Not Very Engaging	Somewhat Engaging	Wow! Very Engaging
Simple Content				
Complex Content				
Process: Activity				
Process: Assignment				
Product				

Notes:

CHAPTER 2

Introducing Empowerment

Engagement places students on the road to empowerment. As engagement and autonomy increase, students become more and more empowered. Empowering students and creating a culture that supports empowerment helps students succeed academically.

Empowerment Defined

When students are empowered, they learn more, they learn more deeply, they use thick thinking, and they experience joy in learning. Thick thinking takes place when students think intensely and passionately about something. It is likely that this type of deep thinking occurs when students are empowered and not when they are just engaged in what they are doing. They have a strong commitment; they feel that they can accomplish the goal at hand. They are enthusiastic, excited, and energized because they believe that what they do matters. Empowered students gain a sense of self-worth and self-confidence, and their self-esteem soars.

Empowerment is not just another tool for your teaching tool belt. Empowerment is so much more than that. It is a philosophy of teaching and an approach to learning. It can be as simple as the feeling you get when your opinion is validated, or it can be as complex as taking action to reduce ocean pollution. Empowerment is personal, unique to each individual. Think of a time when you experienced empowerment. Was it in school or at home? Did it involve another person? Was it related to an achievement? How did you feel? Did someone empower you to do something, or did you empower yourself without encouragement from anyone else? You can help students understand empowerment—and the importance of experiencing empowerment—by sharing examples of experiences that previous students say empowered them (see Sample Student Responses at right). You can also ask your students to share their own experiences (see reproducible **Share Your Empowerment Experiences** on page 42). Create a bulletin board with your students' experiences or compile and share them

SAMPLE STUDENT RESPONSES

- A fifth grader felt empowered when he was chosen by his peers to participate on an Odyssey of the Mind team. Usually, nobody chose to work with him on academic projects, but this time his classmates recognized his strength, which was to build and create. They needed someone with his skills on their team. Through this team, he made friends, and his self-esteem soared.

- A fourth grader felt empowered when his teacher asked him to interview some other teachers in the school. This was special because the teacher asked only him.

- A kindergartener felt empowered when her teacher asked her to read aloud to the class. She was an excellent reader and enjoyed reading aloud.

- A seventh grader was asked to lead a discussion about a homework assignment. The student felt empowered because the teacher had confidence in his abilities.

- A ninth grader felt empowered when her artwork was displayed in the town hall. This encouraged her to continue to work on her art.

- The high school football team felt empowered when they came in first in their division. They felt their effort paid off.

- A tenth grader felt empowered when she made the honor roll. This gave her a can-do attitude from then on.

electronically to demonstrate to students the many ways we experience empowerment.

Figure 2-1 offers a synthesis of responses from high school teachers and students who filled out empowerment questionnaires. The students were asked what empowers them in school. The teachers were asked how they empower their students. Compare the two perspectives. Do the students and the teachers view student

Figure 2-1 Student and Teacher Views on Student Empowerment

What Students Say Empowers Them in School	What Teachers Think Empowers Students in School
communication	accountability
independence	mutual respect
when teachers listen beyond the students' words	providing students with opportunities to lead
ability to choose	teaching to inspire
when students are okay with messing up	being flexible
when schools value willingness and desire to learn	teaching based on what is happening in the world
when teachers are willing to change	mutual trust
when teachers understand that students have lives outside school	willingness to go off syllabus and take advantage of the moment
when teachers inspire students	trying to be purposeful change makers
when teachers are passionate about what students are doing	
when teachers are good role models	
when teachers are willing to change their teaching style	
when teachers are patient and wait for kids to get it	
when teachers spend time explaining rather than covering content	
when teachers focus on the real world	
when teachers focus on growth	
when teachers are real and honest	

empowerment in the same way? If you'd like to survey students and teachers at your school, see the reproducible **Student Empowerment Questionnaire** and **Teacher Empowerment Questionnaire** on pages 43 and 45.

Empowerment focuses on capabilities. It is both a process and an outcome (O'Byrne 2018). Empowerment involves participation in activities that result in positive or negative outcomes. A student who tries repeatedly to accomplish a task and fails may become disempowered and discouraged. Instead of focusing on deficits, empowerment theory encourages scaffolding or finding an alternate strategy to help the student experience success. Students experience empowerment when they learn these strategies and know when and how to use them.

Empowerment, like engagement, is about relationships. It is essential for the teacher and student to have a positive working relationship; they create a team. The teacher's role is to cultivate relationships with students. Teachers and students acknowledge that "we are in this together" rather than the teacher imposing instruction on the student. Teachers acknowledge the right to make changes, while students acknowledge that the classroom is theirs and not just the teacher's. Teachers empower

students to make decisions about what they want to study, how they want to study, how they will show what they learned, and how long they want to spend on a topic. Teachers and students make goals and action plans, which students are expected to carry out responsibly. Think about which decisions you currently let your students make and consider when and in what context you feel comfortable increasing your students' opportunities for decision-making.

In your classroom, which of these elements are teacher-driven? Which of these elements are a combination of teacher-driven and student-driven, where the teacher starts out by giving options and the students may add to the options? Which are purely student-driven? Which of these options are student-driven only some of the time?

- what to study

- how to study it

- how students will show what they know

- how long students will spend on the topic

Empowerment goes beyond accomplishment. Students feel a sense of accomplishment when they are compliant. Compliant students follow rules and meet expectations; they may be submissive when completing tasks. Teachers tend to like compliant students, who cause little trouble and do what they are told. They often receive good grades. Nobody needs to remind them to do their homework or to stay on task. They are experts at "doing school." What is wrong with that? Lifelong learning—not compliance—is the goal of education. "If our students are truly compliant when they walk out of schools, they will always need someone else's rules to follow" (Spencer and Juliani 2017, vii).

> At the end of my sophomore year in college, my advisor told me I had to declare a major. I attended a liberal arts university and had no idea what I wanted to do with my life after college. I wanted my advisor to tell me what I should choose. After all, for years teachers had told me what to study, what books to read, and what courses to take. I had been compliant all those years. I had little experience in directing my own learning.
>
> Luckily for me, my university advisor had no idea how to advise me. I had many interests, but no overriding interest that would point toward one major. Then it dawned on me that I had the freedom and the power to make my own decision. I asked my advisor what area of study I had the most credits in, so I would have the least required courses left to take. I did not ask this because I wanted to take the easy way out. I asked because it made sense to me. This would give me the most freedom to choose from the many courses I was actually interested in taking. The freedom to choose, to carve my own path, became an element of empowerment that has continued to be important throughout my teaching career and my personal life.

In the past, schools placed great value on compliance. In fact, many teachers continue to encourage compliance. This is not always a bad thing. Students do need to learn to respect deadlines. They do need to follow rules that ensure safety and care of self and others. There is a place for compliance in schools and in our world. However, compliance isn't enough. It can no longer be the goal in education. Compliant students want good grades and they may be easy to teach, but we must encourage them to be autonomous learners. Compliant students may be immobilized by choice and may sacrifice their freedom to choose. They may not know how to make informed, logical decisions. They may be paralyzed by the prospect of making the wrong decision. Some are frozen by perfectionism. These students run the risk of losing their ability to become academic risk-takers.

When you move students from compliance to engagement to empowerment, you give up some of your power over students. When your students are compliant, you control their learning. When your students become engaged, they relate to the learning, and the learning is more likely to move into long-term memory, making it easier to retrieve later. When students take ownership of their learning, they experience a sense of freedom that is empowering. When students are engaged, they perform; when students are empowered, they learn more (see **figure 2-2** on page 32).

As students transition from compliant learners to engaged learners to empowered learners, they grow in independence. They figure out how to connect what they are required to learn to what they want to learn. They begin setting their own goals and creating action plans.

Independence is an essential component of empowerment. To empower students, teachers need to create a classroom environment that enables students to experience independence. For example, if you are a kindergarten teacher, you might foster your students' independence by setting up routines. You might have your students place their completed work in baskets. After you review the work, you hand it back to your students and tell them to place it in a file that houses all their individual work. The students take responsibility for placing their work in the correct places. You might ask your students if anyone can think of a better system for keeping track of their work. If not, you could encourage them to think about how you came up with your system. Discuss the importance of organization and responsibility and ask them to share examples of ways they organize things at home. If you are a teacher in middle school or high school, you might hand reviewed work back to students and ask them to take it home. You expect the students to figure out how to get the work from their desks to their homes. This simple example demonstrates the shift from teachers organizing everything to learners taking on the responsibility for organizing themselves. When students create their own systems for organizing their time, their

Figure 2-2 From Compliance to Empowerment

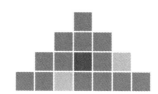

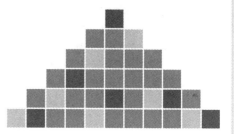

Compliant: The teacher has the power, freedom, and control of the lesson. The student says, "I am doing this because the teacher asked me to."

Engaged: The student may have some power, freedom, and control in least some of the aspects of a lesson. The student feels a sense of involvement. The student says, "I am interested in this because . . ." or "This is fun because . . . "

Empowered: The student has the power, freedom, and control to make most, if not all, decisions about the learning. The student says, "I want to learn this in this way because . . ." or "This makes a difference to me because . . ."

space, their classroom community, their work, and their belongings, they feel empowered. Remember that some students may need help figuring out how to create systems that work for them; other students will be ready to take this on at an early age.

Control

According to student engagement researcher Adam Fletcher, student empowerment happens when adults share any amount of power with students (Fletcher 2018). To empower your students, you need to let go of some or all the control over their learning. This cannot happen overnight. First, you must do much up-front teaching of skills and strategies before your students will be ready to apply those skills and strategies on their own.

The engagement strategies you use are tools your students can use themselves to become empowered. For example, if you use the Revised Bloom's Taxonomy to create questions, your students may be engaged but not empowered. When students use the taxonomy to create their own questions, they feel empowered. They are in control of their own learning. This type of shift in control is a helpful way to start. It feels safe to teachers when students use the same tools that the teachers would have used.

How can you let go of control if you work in a system that uses scripted programs or a textbook series that expects all students to be on the same page on the same day? Such a school usually wants its teachers to use the program with fidelity so administrators can see if it is actually working. They expect the students to be compliant and (hopefully) engaged, but not empowered. If you are trying to transition from this type of program to one with more student autonomy, you might request to do some action research to answer the question, *Will the students who engage in empowerment lessons achieve more than the students who use only scripted or textbook lessons?* If your action research determines that empowerment works better for your students (a likely outcome), this data may convince administrators to allow you to make program changes and gain control over your individual classroom.

Another way to build in empowerment in the context of a scripted curriculum is to identify the content and skills from the program or textbook and let your students know what they are. You can call it nonnegotiable content—material that students are required to learn. Then, let students create their own practice lessons and move at their own rate. This strategy can help you move from a scripted program or a textbook-driven curriculum to one in which students control their assignments, assessments, and pacing. This gradual release of responsibility allows students to learn the same content while empowering them to drive their own learning.

Motivation

Motivation is an essential element of engagement and empowerment. Empowerment is "the process of creating intrinsic task motivation by providing an environment and tasks which increase one's sense of self-efficacy and energy" (Frymier, Shulman, and Houser 1996). Teachers increase student motivation and empowerment when they provide voice and choice, when they allow students to set their own learning goals, when they allow students to determine ways to demonstrate competency, and when they provide a safe and accepting classroom environment.

Motivation matters because it contributes to achievement. The Programme for International Student Assessment (PISA) test is designed to assess fifteen-year-olds' achievement in math, science, and reading. This assessment compares participating countries' achievement results. The results of the 2012 PISA test indicated that on average, students who are motivated to learn math earn eighteen points higher than students who have lower levels of motivation in math. Eighteen points translates to about half a year of math instruction (Achiron 2014). When students lack motivation, their achievement suffers.

The concepts of trait motivation and state motivation offer one way of understanding motivation. Students who enjoy learning have *trait motivation*; it's part of their personality. *State motivation* refers to students' desire to learn in a contextual situation—in a class, for an assignment, or in a content area. State motivation is a predictor of learning. It is influenced by relevance. Students who find academic meaning become motivated. Most students are not lazy. They just have difficulty making meaning of what teachers think is important.

Motivation can be tricky to figure out, because not all learners are motivated in the same way. Some students are motivated primarily by interest and purpose, some by grades. Some students are motivated by working with peers, while others are motivated when working alone. Challenge motivates some but discourages others. Motivation is often dependent upon the student's self-confidence, self-esteem, and self-efficacy. Students must feel they have the ability and the tools to succeed at a task; they won't be motivated to sustain effort if they have no hope of success. The more frustration they experience, the more likely they will be to disengage. The Yerkes-Dodson law of arousal is a theory that says when stress and pressure rise, performance usually improves. However, there is a maximum performance level. At a certain point, stress and pressure no longer improve performance (Gregory and Kaufeldt 2015). In other words: if challenge is too high or too low, it is hard for students to maintain their motivation. Students develop self-confidence through the just right level of challenge.

MEANINGFULNESS, COMPETENCE, AND IMPACT

Researchers have found that empowerment is positively correlated with meaningfulness, competence, and impact (Frymier, Shulman, and Houser 1996):

- **Meaningfulness:** If students do not see any meaning or importance in their work, they have little cause for motivation. They slip into compliance and do the work without much personal investment.

- **Competence:** If students do not feel confident and capable of accomplishing a task, they might attempt the task with teacher support, but they will probably perform only at a compliant level. As long as they know exactly what to do and receive the help they need, they feel okay about doing the work. These students need additional support as they move from engagement to empowerment.

- **Impact:** If students do work for the sake of doing the assignment but the work does not make an impact on anyone else, then they risk becoming compliant learners. When students feel that the work really matters, then they will be motivated to work hard.

Other ways to understand motivation are through the lenses of task commitment and ego. With task commitment, students are motivated by paying attention to the task and the skills needed to master it. Students determine their ability to acquire and process content information, their willingness to make personal connections, and their need for teacher support. They are motivated by feeling a sense of control over and responsibility for their learning. With ego-based motivation, students focus attention on the self. They are motivated to look either smart or dumb in front of their peers. They might be motivated by grades, creating original projects, and presenting projects to an audience. The attention feeds their ego. Conversely, many students are afraid to get up in front of their peers because they fear how they will be perceived. This lack of confidence and self-esteem diminishes motivation and empowerment. In order to motivate fearful students, you must redirect their emotions. Acknowledge the student's needs and feelings, help the student set not just practical but also philosophical goals, and help the student recall feelings of self-worth.

Curiosity is an important motivator. Albert Einstein told his biographer in 1952, "I have no special talents. I am only passionately curious" (Calaprice 2000). Curiosity drives the need to explore. Along with effort, curiosity has as much influence on student success as intelligence does (von Stumm, Hell, and Chamorro-Premuzic 2011; Goodwin 2014). In a 2014 study, researchers wanted to know why people remember some things and forget others. They wondered if it had anything to do with curiosity. They asked volunteers to review trivia questions and asked them to rate each question in terms of how curious they were to find out the answer. While monitored with MRI, participants' brains "lit up" when they were curious about something. The hippocampus (responsible for memory making) and the part of the brain responsible for pleasure both lit up. One of the researchers, Charan Ranganath, explained, "There's this basic circuit in the brain that energizes people to go out and get things that are intrinsically rewarding." This circuit lights up, for example, when we get candy, when we get money, and when we are curious. When participants were tested on what they learned, they best remembered what they were curious about (Singh 2014). This study has clear implications for education: teachers can motivate students by connecting their curiosity to the nonnegotiable content, even if that content appears unrelated to the students' curiosity.

For example, students are studying the Oregon Trail. It is clear some students are anything but curious about it. The teacher's challenge is to spark their curiosity about this nonnegotiable content through an activity. The teacher tells her students that she has three things that are related to their study of the Oregon Trail. She asks for a volunteer to come to the front of the room and choose one of the three things. The first choice is a list of the messed-up things that really happened on the Oregon Trail. The second choice is a free pass to play the Oregon Trail card game. The third choice is something in a paper bag. The teacher says that the volunteer will be able to keep whatever is chosen. Most often the student chooses the paper bag because the student is more curious about the unknown option than the known ones. (Wondering what's in the bag? It's a miniature model of a wooden Conestoga wagon.) The students' brains will remember this activity and the discussion about the content because the students' curiosity served to motivate them.

Motivation drives passion and effort, which are key elements of grit. Grit is the determination required to engage in multiple rehearsals until students get it right. It is the ability to react positively to failure and demonstrate resilience to try again. Grit can lead to a strong feeling of accomplishment, which in turn leads to student empowerment. Does grit correlate with talent? According to University of Pennsylvania psychology professor Angela Duckworth (2016), the answer is no. Many talented students are not motivated to work hard, because they receive easy A's. They are denied an appropriate level of challenge and so they do only what they need to do to get the A. They do not have to work hard. These students don't know academic failure, they don't know what it means to struggle to learn, and they haven't developed resilience or determination. Students who want to learn for learning's sake are the exception to this rule. Duckworth calls these students "ambitious" and says they demonstrate both talent and grit.

Research indicates that punishments and rewards adversely affect grit. Constructive and specific feedback is a better choice; it motivates students because it tells them why they did or did not succeed and gives them suggestions for improvement. Allowing students to revise work is also motivating. You might worry that if you allow revisions, your students will not do their best the first time. Actually, the opposite may be true. When you give an assignment, note when the draft is due and when the final assignment is due. You and your students can generate a rubric together. Tell the students that if they receive "advanced" or "proficient" on the draft, they do not have to resubmit the assignment. A revision becomes a choice, not a necessity. This information empowers students to do their best right away so they do not have to do the revision.

Gender and Empowerment
Girls

Social scientists often discuss empowerment as a way to counter powerlessness. Girls are a group of students who often feel disempowered. According to the International Conference on Population and Development, "Education is one of the most important means of empowering women with the knowledge, skills and self-confidence necessary to participate fully in the development process" (Hunt 2013). However, many educational programs focus on formal skill-based training and do not include opportunities that foster empowerment.

Girls need to become self-aware and have opportunities to raise their self-esteem. This need is even more vital for girls who live in poverty. Poverty is a factor that has the potential to disempower. It is difficult for economically disadvantaged girls to overcome familial and societal obstacles to education. Economically disadvantaged families may have less access to educational opportunities—and less time, money, and mental bandwidth for education because they are expending so much on survival. It is often left to the girls to take care of younger children at home because the family is not able to pay for child care. The girls end up with less time to focus on schoolwork. They attend school unfocused because they are tired from carrying out household responsibilities and they are unprepared because they do not have time to do their schoolwork. These girls sometimes come from families who do not value education. The parents, parent, or guardian may have had negative experiences in school that resulted in their negative attitudes regarding education. These attitudes transfer to their children.

Girl empowerment thrives in an environment where girls feel safe, have self-confidence to express themselves, and have equal opportunities. Girls are empowered when they make their own decisions, have access to information, have options, and believe they can make changes, influence others' perceptions, and improve their own self-image. Girls define happy environments as ones where they are respected, communication is open, and their feelings and opinions are solicited, heard, and respected. In light of this definition, consider the following facts compiled by Girl Talk, a nonprofit organization that helps girls become confident leaders through peer-to-peer mentoring networks:

- A girl's self-esteem peaks at age nine (Girl Talk 2018).

- Only 21 percent of all girls believe they have the qualities to be a good leader (Girl Talk 2018).

- Only 5 percent of Fortune 500 companies are led by women (Girl Talk 2018).

- According to studies conducted at New York University and Princeton University, starting at age six, girls are already growing less likely to believe that girls can be "really, really smart" (Strauss 2017).

- A 2017 study revealed that one in four girls is depressed at age fourteen (University College London 2017).

If we want to raise empowered women, then we need to start no later than middle school and encourage girls to be academic risk-takers. Some girls strive to perform perfectly. We need to remind them they do not have to be perfect. If they focus on getting all things right all the time, these girls will not risk trying. Girls tend to blame performance on a lack of ability rather than lack of effort. Carol S. Dweck's work on effort can help girls understand the relationship between performance and effort (Dweck 2016). Girls become empowered when they take ownership of their successes. They need to understand that owning their successes and sharing their achievements with others is not bragging. We should teach girls how to advocate for their needs as well as owning their accomplishments. You can encourage girls to learn effective communication skills by asking them to contribute to or lead class discussions, encouraging them to join a debate or speech team, or supporting them as they stand up for a community cause.

Girls can also learn skills and build self-confidence by working with mentors. Mentors are people who work *with* students rather than directing, judging, or critiquing them. Women are ideal mentors for girls, but male mentors work well too. One useful resource is the website Girl Talk (mygirltalk.org). This website is devoted to inspiring girls to become leaders through a mentoring program that sets up high school girls to mentor middle school girls. The mentorship program includes leadership literacy for girls ten to eighteen years old.

Boys

British educator David Brockway of the Great Men Project says it's important to teach boys to be empowered—not ashamed—to show emotion. Even in modern society, boys say it is still difficult for them to express emotion, demonstrate emotional vulnerability, or admit to any weakness (Brockway 2015). Parenting coach Marie Roker-Jones outlines ten ways to empower teen boys (Roker-Jones 2015):

1. When he needs to vent, I need to listen and not rush in to fix the problem

2. When he makes a mistake, address the behavior but don't judge his character.

3. Be patient with myself and with him.

4. If I'm unsure, ask instead of making an assumption.

5. Stop thinking that I have the power to protect him from life.

6. Focus on the solution, not the problem.

7. I can lead him in the right direction but I can't control the outcome.

8. He is responsible for his actions. I can't blame myself for his poor choices.

9. If I want to hear the truth, be prepared to handle the truth.

10. Stop trying so hard to raise a great man.

Boys may end up making poor decisions due to their inability to control their impulsivity. Their impulsivity is magnified by their need to fit in. Boys will impulsively follow their peers in order to be part of the gang. They often will not use good decision-making skills that teachers have worked so hard to teach them. Some boys who do make logical rather than emotional decisions feel they must hide it. Middle school boys often think it is cooler not to try than to expend any effort in school. They think they should not have to try because they think it is important to be good at something immediately. Like boy athletes who perform great in a game but don't take practice seriously, academically gifted boys who perform well on assessments may not want to do homework because they find the practice exercises unnecessary. They think practice is important only when they are striving to improve or when they're presented with a challenging goal. To counteract these attitudes, middle schools can emphasize effort and grit along with a growth mindset. You can create a culture of empowerment so boys will develop the courage to overcome peer pressure and practice risk-taking.

The GLOW program for boys (glowprogram.com /boys-program) advocates empowering boys by building in them a strong sense of self. It encourages boys to discuss healthy relationships and the roles they play in those relationships. This program (based in Canada), like the Great Men Project (in the United Kingdom) and The Boys and Girls Club of America (in the United States) encourages community building and connection rather than competition.

Trans and Nonbinary Students

Transgender (often shortened to *trans*) is a term associated with gender identities where the person does not identify with or totally identify with their sex designated at birth. *Nonbinary* students do not identify as male or female but identify with more fluid aspects of gender. There are

federal laws that protect transgender students from discrimination and bullying. Title IX is a federal civil rights law that bans discrimination on the basis of sex in schools.

In addition to the federal laws, there are several advocacy groups that provide guidance and information for the public. The National Center for Transgender Equality provides information about laws that protect transgender students at school (transequality.org /know-your-rights/schools). The Trans Student Educational Resource (TSER) organization is led by young people who are committed to transforming the educational culture through advocacy and empowerment. GLSEN was formed by a group of teachers in Massachusetts in 1990 who originally came together to address challenges faced by the LGBTQ community. The National Center for Transgender Equality (NCTE) and GLSEN created the 2018 Model School District Policy on Transgender and Gender Nonconforming Students. This resource provides guidance and policy language to support safe school learning environments. The policy includes information on many controversial topics such as bullying, sports, dress, student privacy, and equal access to school facilities (GLSEN 2018).

Despite the existence of protective laws and the work of supportive advocacy groups, young people who are transgender, nonbinary, and gender nonconforming still face problems at school. The GLSEN national survey found 75 percent of transgender young people feel unsafe at school (National Center for Transgender Equality 2019a). The survey also indicated that these kids had significantly lower GPAs, missed school because they did not feel safe, and were less likely to continue their education. In some schools, students have been denied access to the restroom consistent with their identity. In a high school in Massachusetts, the teachers met to discuss this problem. After much deliberation, they decided to allocate a restroom for trans and nonbinary students. When teachers discussed their restroom decision with students in their advisory groups, the students wondered why this was even an issue. In this instance, the students thought the teachers were making a big deal over something that was obviously already acceptable to the students. Of course it made sense to provide a restroom that is comfortable for any student to use. The trans and nonbinary students in this school are totally accepted by their peers. Unfortunately, not all schools are like that. Many students come to school and are made fun of because of the way they look or the clothes they wear.

In some schools, these students are sometimes denied opportunities to participate in sport teams or even attend field trips. It is the responsibility of educators to foster school environments that affirm, support, and empower trans and nonbinary students.

Transgender and nonbinary students feel empowered when teachers and students:

- ask them what name they go by
- ask them what their pronouns are
- allow them to use the restroom that corresponds with their identity
- listen to their stories if they choose to share what it is like to be trans or nonbinary
- ensure that LBGTQ characters are represented in literature in English classes
- ensure that LBGTQ history is part of American history and world culture discussions
- allow them to form or join Genders and Sexualities Alliance (GSA) clubs
- invite PFLAG speakers to come to the school
- place rainbow and safe place stickers on guidance office and classroom doors
- respect them

Empowering English Language Learners

It is critical to empower English language learners (ELL students) because they already feel at a disadvantage due to the language barrier. Without the proper academic and social and emotional support, the students run the risk of becoming discouraged. It is important for ELL students to feel welcome. In one school that I visited, flags of sixteen countries from which the school's students hailed hung in the school foyer. Upon entering that school, I was moved by this visual message that the students from all the countries that attended school there were recognized and welcome. ELL students should feel welcome, recognized, and experience academic success—but the evidence leads us to believe this is not happening fast enough. In 2013, ELL fourth graders scored 39 points lower than their peers on a reading scale. The gap widens to a 45-point difference among eighth graders (Murphy, Redding, and Twyman 2016). In math, the

gap is 25 points lower and 41 points lower respectively (Kena et al. 2014). The dropout rate for ELL students is almost double that of their native-English-speaking peers (Callahan 2013).

To empower linguistically diverse students, the school culture must accept and respect differences so that students feel empowered enough to risk getting involved and confident enough to try. Some negative teacher attitudes must shift in order to eliminate bias that may exist toward the students. Instead of becoming frustrated due to lack of ability to communicate with ELL students, teachers can use pictures, hand motions, or facial expressions to aid communication. Instead of feeling that the students are taking away time from the other students, teachers should think about how much the students have to offer to the school community.

Teachers who feel their ELL students cannot do content work can differentiate for these students—for example, by reducing the amount of work rather than making the work easier. The assignments can be the same, but the language component should be minimized or changed to fit the needs of the students. The language targets could be differentiated. Along with differentiation, teachers can also:

- display signs in multiple languages
- provide opportunities for students who speak the same language to gather regularly
- provide resources in various languages
- display visual representations of student cultures throughout the school
- provide opportunities for students to use their first language whenever possible
- encourage all students to express and share their experiences through genuine dialogue between teachers and students and among students

Respecting Preferences and Strengths

Find out what your students' preferences and strengths are and find opportunities for students to showcase them. All students have preferences and strengths, and students perform best when they're working in these areas. Some students prefer to study facts, details, and rules while others like to jump right in and tackle issues, problems, and themes. Students might prefer to think about information and apply it, or to think critically or creatively. The students who are practical thinkers may prefer to think about how things would really work. Students also have style preferences regarding the modalities in which they learn and show what they know. Although research does not support the notion that students will achieve better when they process or produce information in their preferred modality, students still like to produce certain products. Many students like to create posters whether they are good at it or not. Products commonly fall into the oral, visual, written, or kinesthetic categories. Students may also identify with one or more areas of strength according to developmental psychologist Howard Gardner's multiple intelligences: verbal-linguistic, logical-mathematical, musical-rhythmic, visual-spatial, bodily-kinesthetic, naturalistic, interpersonal, intrapersonal, and existential. Some students like to work alone, while other students prefer to work with their classmates. Other student preferences include whether students like to work in a quiet classroom, whether they like to work uninterrupted, and whether they prefer to direct their own learning. To help students in middle school and high school identify their strengths and preferences along with corresponding products, you can use the **Student Strengths and Preferences** reproducible form on page 47. (Feel free to modify the form for younger students.) This type of information empowers students to make effective decisions about their learning.

When your students need to accomplish tasks in groups, put students who have complementary strengths together. For example, you might consider grouping students who are good critical thinkers with creative thinkers. This way, the group will consist of students who like to generate many ideas with students who prefer to use criteria to evaluate ideas. You might also place in this group a student who stays on task and completes work on time. This student can help keep the group focused and productive.

Be aware that when you define a task and choose who will be in what group, you are engaging students—not necessarily empowering them. If you want to empower students, you'll want to first teach students what makes an effective group and why. Talk about the various strengths and ask students to identify their strengths using the reproducible on page 47. Then ask students to share

their strengths with one another. In this way, students learn who among their classmates are idea people, music people, graphs and data people, and so on—and they know who to go to when they need those strengths. When you empower students to form their own groups, they learn to organize themselves in the most effective ways they can (and that choosing to work with their friends sometimes isn't effective). They feel empowered to choose and empowered to share their products.

For students to feel empowered, the students' voice and choice must be heard and considered. (For more information on voice and choice, see chapter 6.) You need to remove messages that promote powerlessness in your students and replace these with messages that foster student responsibility, self-efficacy, and motivation to learn. Some "power messages" include these starter phrases:

- *I am interested in . . .*
- *The purpose of learning this is . . .*
- *I like this challenge because . . .*
- *I know I can . . .*
- *I can break down this task into these parts and complete this by . . .*
- *I am curious about . . .*
- *I am responsible for . . .*
- *I have control over my own learning because . . .*

Teachers as Coaches

Teachers empower students when they do good coaching. A good coach does not just engage students; a good coach empowers students. Coaches help students develop competency by encouraging them, questioning them, and challenging them. Coaches provide the tools students need to tackle content, think about it, and take action; they explain these tools to the students and show how and when to use them. Empowerment is action-oriented and action-driven; teachers who are good coaches offer support for student action at the right time and at the right level of challenge. Coaches create accurate action descriptions and make tasks clear. Coaches then teach their students how to create clear actions and tasks so that next time, students can do it themselves. Students figure out steps to explain what action needs to be taken and identify materials and resources that they need to complete a task. The coach supports the students' efforts by providing any additional resources, and together they acknowledge the students' successes.

When does a student need a coach? When the student:

- lacks knowledge
- lacks skills
- lacks self-confidence
- needs help to understand the problem or content
- is disruptive
- does not produce
- needs clarification
- lacks organizational skills
- pursues extensions of required work
- desires to do in-depth study

What makes a good coach? When the teacher:

- uses common sense language or student language to help students create meaning
- demonstrates how something has worked before
- provides nonjudgmental feedback

- provides students with graphic organizers and tools to build comprehension
- teaches students how to be a productive team member
- shows how effort pays off
- provides examples and exemplars

There are many types of teacher coaching. For example, act as a coach when behavior issues arise. Instead of using a traditional behavioral contract, you can use the reproducible problem-solving template **Oops—I Messed Up** (page 48) with your students as a way for them to identify and control their behavior problems. (See **figure 2-3** for a sample filled-in version of this reproducible.)

Another way teachers can coach students is to have students create their own classroom organization. Have students come up with a room design, figure out where to place homework assignments, where to store classroom materials, and the like. Coach students to think about noise factors, movement between classes, space allowances for projects, and so on. This may take a few class sessions,

Figure 2-3 Oops—I Messed Up Sample

1. In your own words, what seems to be the problem?
   Singing in the hallway

2. What else is the problem?
   I was supposed to go directly to the boys' bathroom. I wasn't supposed to do barrel rolls in the hall. I sometimes just do what I feel like doing.

3. What do you think is the real problem?
   I didn't really think about what I was doing. I just felt like singing.

4. Why is this a problem?
   It bothers other classes and if everyone sang on their way to the bathroom, our school would be really noisy.

5. Describe as many ways as possible to fix this problem.
   Don't sing in the hall. Think about what I'm doing before I do it. Don't do barrel rolls in the hallway, just do them in PE. Ask the teacher if I can go somewhere to sing. Ask the teacher if I can take a break.

6. Which way do you think will actually work?
   Don't sing or do barrel rolls in the hall.

7. Come up with a plan to solve the problem. Let's see it.
   Who: Me
   Does what: Walk directly to the boy's bathroom and back to the classroom.
   When: Every time

8. Try out your solution. Did you fix the problem? Why or why not?
   Yes, I fixed the problem, because I didn't sing in the hallway the next time I went to the restroom.

9. Is this a long-term solution for you? If not, what else can we do?
   Yes, I think this is a long-term solution for me. I think I described some other good ideas that will work for me too. I know I can talk with the teacher if I need more ideas.

but the buy-in is worth the time. Students will feel invested in *their* classroom, and they will feel empowered.

You might also think about coaching your students' social skills. Social skills come into play whenever students communicate or interact with other people. Social skills include accepting and respecting personal differences, disagreeing politely, encouraging others, listening actively, participating, sharing, risk-taking, and following directions. You can coach these skills as the needs arise, such as on the playground or in the parking lot, hallway, classroom, or cafeteria. You can also coach students on these skills through planned meetings or observations.

You can also show students how to coach each other. Set the stage for the peer coaching process by meeting with students and going over the responsibilities of a peer coach. Then students act as mediators when conflicts arise. They learn how to build consensus, organize implementation, and review effectiveness. Students practice withholding judgment, analyzing assumptions, and becoming open to varying points of view. If necessary, you can provide students with a coaching process form. (See **Student Coaching Process** on page 49.) If the student coaches are unable to help, then the teacher steps in. As students learn coaching skills, they begin to feel empowered when they are able to help others.

Often when teachers think of coaching, they think of a deficit model. That is, coaching is needed because something is wrong or needs to be fixed. Coaching can also be an asset model. That is, coaching is needed because something is great, and the student wants to become even better. For example, think of the players on a professional sports team. They are all excellent players. This does not mean they no longer need coaches. Their coaches help them improve their performance. In schools, this example could translate to the highly capable students who are already getting A's in the classroom and are mastering content. Just as with professional athletes, this does not mean these students should be left alone because they can improve on their own. Just imagine how far these students can go with a coach. All students deserve access to a teacher coach, and all students deserve access to a student coach. In your school, who is the academic coach of the gifted and talented students? When it comes to academics, these students look toward the teacher, their academic peers (regardless of their age), or a mentor.

Mentors

A mentor has knowledge in an area of interest shared by the mentor and mentee. They act as role models and instructors. They help students dive into a topic. They often serve as a friend and an ongoing support. Academic mentors can be older students or community members.

If you are establishing a mentorship program, you should recruit, screen, and train mentors. It is critical to make the right match between mentor and mentee. Look for mentors who have patience and like kids. Think about where students will work with their mentor and how often they will meet. For students who want to develop life skills, you may want to set up internships or job shadowing. If you like the idea of using mentors in the classroom, meet with them before they meet the students to be sure they know how you want them to work with students. It is important for mentors to understand that your classroom focuses on student empowerment, and because of that, mentors should not fall into the trap of didactic teaching. The National Mentoring Partnership recommends writing up a volunteer's code of conduct to outline appropriate activities. You can find free materials to help you start a mentoring program on the National Mentoring Partnership website (mentoring.org).

Not all students want or need mentors. Ask students about it and empower them to make their decision and have control over who they spend time with. Questions you might ask your students are:

- Do you know what a mentor is?
- Do you know what the benefits of working with a mentor are?
- Do you want to work with a mentor?
- What type of mentor would you like to work with?
- What do you hope to get from this relationship?
- Are you hoping the mentor has any particular skills?
- What type of work are you looking to do with your mentor?
- Do you want to work with a mentor on only one specific project or would you like to work with a mentor throughout the year?

Supply mentors with some information about student mentees to make sure the mentor wants to work with the student, but confidentiality is an important consideration. See the **Student Mentee Information** reproducible on page 50.

One of the fastest growing mentoring programs is the telementoring program at mentoredpathways.org. This program connects business leaders with students to help them acquire skills and develop their interests. The website contains a professional network of leaders, industry work plans, and career and academic plans. This organization offers a way for students to connect with professionals in the field and provides an empowerment forum for students to pursue their interests and passions beyond the classroom. It can help you recruit mentors when they are not available in your local community.

Chapter Summary

This chapter helps you move students from compliance to empowerment. A transitional student is beginning to feel empowered and experiences empowerment in some but perhaps not all areas of learning. As students assume more and more ownership of their learning and demonstrate self-confidence, they begin to realize what it's like to be a self-directed learner. There is no one formula that you can use with all students. Empowerment is personal and unique to each learner, teacher, and classroom.

Empowered students are successful students. They believe in themselves, and they know the teachers are there to support them in their learning. Empowered students know that learning is not just something they do in school; it is not just something they do because someone tells them to do it. Empowered students find out about what they want to know and what they need to know. They learn how to learn and embrace the joy of learning.

Discussion Questions

1. Compare and contrast engagement and empowerment.

2. Why do we want to move students beyond compliant learning?

3. How can you foster student empowerment if your district uses scripted programs and required textbooks?

4. How might we empower students while taking gender into consideration?

5. Summarize the shifts explained in this chapter.

After you've thought about your answers to these questions, visit this website for a video chapter review with the author: freespirit.com/empower-videos.

Share Your Empowerment Experiences

Describe a real experience that helped you feel empowered. Explain why you felt this way. Next, imagine a situation that might empower you.

Real Experience	Imagined Experience

Student Empowerment Questionnaire

Name:

Grade:

Subject area:

1. Would you rather let teachers assign your work or would you prefer to decide for yourself what you need to do? Give an example.

2. Do you feel your teachers listen to your ideas?

3. Do you feel other students listen to your ideas?

4. Do you like to work with others or do you prefer to work alone?

5. Do you feel inspired at school? If so, when?

≫⟶

6. What do you do when you feel uncertain about what to do?

7. Do you feel self-confident and comfortable speaking and presenting your ideas in front of the class, to community members, or to online classmates?

8. Do your teachers offer you choice? If so, do you like that? Why or why not?

9. Are you comfortable asking your teacher or classmates for help?

10. What does empowerment mean to you?

11. Do you ever feel empowered in school? If so, when?

Teacher Empowerment Questionnaire

Name:

Grade:

Content area:

1. How would you define student empowerment? Please provide examples.

2. If someone asked you to brag shamelessly about your students or your school, what would you say?

3. How would you define teacher empowerment? Please provide examples.

4. Would you rather use a scripted program, follow a published program, or create your own materials? Why?

5. Do you feel your administrators and other teachers listen to your ideas?

➢➢➢ ⟶

6. Do you like to work with other teachers or do you prefer to do your own thing with your students?

7. Do you feel inspired at school? If so, when?

8. Do you feel inspired at home? If so, when?

9. Do you feel self-confident and comfortable speaking and presenting your ideas in front of other teachers, to administrators, to parents, to community members, or to online colleagues? If so, in what contexts?

10. Would you like to add any other comments?

Student Strengths and Preferences

Check your strength areas below.

I prefer to think about content in terms of:
☐ facts, details, rules   ☐ issues, problems, patterns, themes

In my thinking process, I prefer:
☐ knowing and applying information   ☐ synthesizing or adapting information
☐ analyzing and evaluating information   ☐ creating new ideas
☐ thinking of many different and unusual ideas   ☐ thinking in practical terms

I like to show what I know:
☐ orally—in a song, poem, broadcast, podcast, debate, presentation, limerick, travelogue, dialogue, interview, recording
☐ in writing—a report, bibliography, autobiography, short story, five-paragraph essay, script, TV show, multimedia presentation, letter, diary, storyboard, web page
☐ kinesthetically—in a skit, performance, board game, bulletin board, campaign, costume, dance, puppet show, magic show, role play, scavenger hunt, virtual reality hunt, field trip
☐ visually—in a cartoon, bumper sticker, poster, infographic, comic strip, collage, flowchart, diagram, outline, graphic organizer, sign, pamphlet, brochure, Venn diagram

I like to work in the following area(s), or I'm smart in the following ways:
☐ verbal-linguistic (word smart)   ☐ naturalistic (nature smart)
☐ logical-mathematical (numbers/reasoning smart)   ☐ interpersonal (people smart)
☐ musical-rhythmic (sound smart)   ☐ intrapersonal (self smart)
☐ visual-spatial (image smart)   ☐ existential (life smart)
☐ bodily-kinesthetic (movement smart)

I prefer to work:
☐ alone   ☐ with a partner   ☐ in a small group   ☐ with the whole class

I prefer to work:
☐ with no noise   ☐ with some noise   ☐ with music

I prefer to work:
☐ uninterrupted for long periods of time   ☐ taking small, frequent breaks

I prefer to:
☐ be told what work I should do and how to practice it
☐ choose what work I do between choices offered by my teacher
☐ come up with my own work and the way to do my work

My strengths include:

Oops—I Messed Up

1. In your own words, what seems to be the problem?

2. What else is the problem?

3. What do you think is the real problem?

4. Why is this a problem?

5. Describe as many ways as possible to fix this problem.

6. Which way do you think will actually work?

7. Come up with a plan to solve the problem. Let's see it.
   Who:
   Does what:
   When:

8. Try out your solution. Did you fix the problem? Why or why not?

9. Is this a long-term solution for you? If not, what else can we do?

Student Coaching Process

1. Isolate the problem.
   What is the problem?

2. Collect information.
   What do I know?

3. Generate solutions.
   What are some solutions? Name your criteria. Prioritize your solutions.

4. Prioritize solutions according to criteria.
   What are your criteria? Which solutions will work best?

5. Choose a solution. Implement it. Evaluate process and progress.
   Which solution did you choose to implement? How did it go?

6. Follow up on the situation.
   What's next?

Student Mentee Information

Place an X in the appropriate box for each student characteristic. Add comments if you like.

Student Characteristics	Not So Much	Sometimes	Regularly
This student is often bored by traditional classroom work.			
This student's skills are on grade level or above grade level.			
This student is curious.			
This student is very interested and/or involved in the topic.			
This student is willing to learn.			
This student is willing to take feedback into account.			
This student interacts well with adults.			
This student is easy to work with.			

Additional comments:

CHAPTER 3

Empowerment: Best Practices, Strategies, and Programs

In this chapter, we'll explore the concept of empowerment in terms of "little *e*" experiences (small, personal ways students are empowered) and "big *E*" experiences (empowerment that occurs on a large scale and affects more than the self). Some empowerment experiences occur spontaneously, but you can plan them too, using a variety of educational models and strategies. This chapter takes a brief look at empowerment through the Harkness method, global education, inquiry learning, expeditionary learning, project-based learning, problem-based learning, genius hour, makerspace and design thinking, and entrepreneurship.

Big *E* and Little e Empowerment Experiences

Big *E* and little *e* empowerment experiences are equally important. Neither is better than the other. Both should be encouraged as much as possible. One type may be easier to plan for (such as a save-the-rainforest project in an environment unit in a science class), and one type may be more conducive to spontaneity (such as empowering a student to join a group discussion). One type may impact more people and have a broader effect, but both types will impact the self.

When you think of student empowerment, you might tend to associate the idea with students conducting huge, long-term projects that affect many people. These are big *E* empowerment experiences. You can find many examples on the internet of students who engage in this type of undertaking. A quick search leads to a group of students who came up with a new way to provide clean drinking water in developing countries. Some

teachers have opportunities to engage their students in such big *E* projects. However, many teachers do not, for a variety of reasons.

If you're one of the latter, you needn't forsake the goal of empowering your students. You can look for ways to empower your students through little *e* experiences. Mr. Scott, an eighth-grade social studies teacher in Maine, came up with an unusual way to use music to empower his students. Since his students were bored when they had to learn about their state's counties, Mr. Scott decided to take advantage of his students' enthusiasm about the television show *American Idol* (in which talented singers compete each week for a big win at the end of the season) and have his students create songs about the counties in a competition he set up called *Maine Idol*. Students came into his class and talked about the show all the time, so he thought this idea was worth trying.

Mr. Scott set up auditions. Students auditioned by adding a new twist to an old song. He required the students to change the original lyrics of a popular song so at least 25 percent of the song included information about Maine's counties. Then they recorded their revised songs using software provided at school. Students submitted their songs to Mr. Scott for approval before they performed them in front of an audience. They could choose to sing alone, with a partner, or in a trio. Before students performed, Mr. Scott encouraged everyone to participate. He pointed out that the competition was not about singing ability. It was about applying content to a popular tune. News of the competition traveled quickly throughout the school. Participants auditioned in front of the whole school.

For students who were uncomfortable singing and didn't want to get up in front of an audience, Mr. Scott offered the option to create a slideshow. The students who chose this option had to create a script that went along with their slides and present the slideshow to the class. These students did not feel the same pressure to perform that the singers felt. After the first year or so, fewer and fewer students chose the slideshow option. Even students who thought they could not sing found people to partner with so they could participate in Maine Idol. The event grew so popular that students couldn't wait to be in Mr. Scott's eighth-grade class.

Was this experience empowering for students, or engaging? All participants were certainly engaged. Many of them felt little *e* empowerment. Some felt big *E* empowerment, because when they took a risk and got up in front of their peers to sing, it was a really big deal. Mr. Scott thought of an unusual way to empower his students. Teachers can be very creative in finding ways to tweak programs and strategies so they empower students.

Let's look at the difference between little *e* and big *E*. A small way for students to experience empowerment might be to participate on an existing student council. This could be particularly empowering for a student who does not usually get involved with school groups. A bigger—but related—example of empowerment would be to create a student council where one doesn't yet exist. To create a student council, students would formulate rules, present the rules to the staff for approval, create student council positions, and so on. The difference between little *e*, participating on the school council, and big *E*, creating a school council, translates to the degree to which students experience involvement and feel empowered.

In **figure 3-1**, a high school applied geometry teacher identifies strategies that she used in a unit as little *e* experiences. The teacher includes many engaging strategies in the unit, but these are the ones she feels target empowerment. Upon reflection after the unit ends, she lists possible future ideas for the unit, which she hopes will target at least some big *E* opportunities for her students.

If you really want to increase student empowerment, be proactive in your planning and tie your examples to strategies that you use with your content. You'll find a blank reproducible version of the **Categorizing Student Empowerment Experiences** chart on page 68. If you teach at the high school level, you can tie your examples to your content areas or to your advisor-advisee group discussions. If you are an elementary teacher, you can tie your examples to academic content or social skills content such as sharing or taking turns.

You can use the **Quick Engagement and Empowerment Planner** (see reproducible on page 69) to identify places in a unit where strategies, activities, and assignments target engagement and empowerment. When you use the quick planner, you can see how often you are empowering students and whether you are providing empowerment experiences regularly. It is unrealistic to think that all or even most of your lessons will offer big *E* experiences. I recommend that if you can, target big *E* empowerment in one content area at least once a quarter or trimester, and target engagement or little *e* empowerment regularly.

Figure 3-1 Sample Categorizing Student Empowerment Experiences

Unit	Big *E* or Little *e* Experience	How Did Students Feel?	Future Ideas for This Unit
Class geometry	Little *e*: We used the school track and field to learn about geometry terms.	Engaged Happy Positive	Use the school track and field to learn about geometry terms and then create your own problem and solution using the geometry terms. Use the ShowMe app to describe how you solved the problem.
Khan Academy	Little *e*: This was a good option for students who were more advanced.	Proud Challenged Engaged	Connect with a math mentor from the community.
Computer use and technology	Little *e*: We used the Desmos app to model terms and provide lessons.	Interested Happy	Use virtual reality to identify the math terms you see applied around the school. Record your findings and share them with the class.
Creating models	Little *e*: Groups worked together to create models of collinear and noncollinear points.	Frustrated Respected Challenged	Transform your models of collinear and noncollinear points into a three-dimensional superhero with superpowers. List your points so someone else can recreate your superhero.

Classroom Empowerment Strategies

Just as you can use classroom strategies to engage students, you can also use them to empower students. Many strategies lend themselves to big *E* and little *e* empowerment. In the rest of this chapter, we'll discuss how these strategies empower students within the Harkness method, global education, inquiry learning, expeditionary learning, project-based learning, problem-based learning, genius hour, makerspace and design thinking, and entrepreneurship.

The Harkness Method

The Harkness method is an engagement strategy that also provides little *e* empowerment. Named after Edward Harkness, the American philanthropist who introduced it, the Harkness method encourages students to use good reasoning skills. Students must also demonstrate their ability to communicate with others. The method was created in the 1930s at Phillips Exeter Academy in New Hampshire and is used—there and elsewhere—to this day.

The Harkness method is empowering because it minimizes the teacher's role in leading discussion and maximizes the students' role. Rather than using a question-and-answer format, the method encourages deep discussion among students. Every student is encouraged to participate. The teacher or the students pose a question. The questions and the student responses must be tied to a subject area and/or the standards.

A high-quality Harkness discussion is one in which the responses bounce around from student to student. The Harkness method encourages the use of a Harkness table, around which all students sit so they can see one another. Students need not raise their hands to speak. Your job as teacher is to observe who is speaking and keep track of student responses. You might choose to give each student a speaking stone. Whenever students speak, they place their stone in the center of the table. This provides a cue for when to speak and a visual reminder not to dominate the conversation. The result of a Harkness discussion is it "challenges students to sit at the center of education, making meaning of new information together, talking, listening, and ultimately *thinking*" (Mullgardt 2008).

The Harkness method incorporates a shared assessment that gives students feedback. The teacher looks for student participation and sees how the students' thinking reflects the designated topic and standards. At the same time, a student recorder keeps track of the flow of the conversation too. Halfway through the discussion, the teacher and the student recorder compare data. The class receives a formative grade for speaking and listening. This formative assessment provides an opportunity for the group to self-correct. At the end of the discussion, the class receives a summative grade.

Is it fair to give a group grade? We know some students will participate while others remain reticent. The nonparticipators could drag down the group grade. Students learn in a Harkness discussion that the goal is group participation because the variety of viewpoints is valued. The many, varied comments drive the discussion deeper. The culture that the Harkness strategy inspires is one of acceptance and obligation to be an equal contributor. In the end, of course, it is your decision whether to give a group grade or any grade at all. Students are also encouraged to self-assess.

> The Harkness method is often used in high school English classes, but this method can work well in most content areas and most grade levels. In 2014, 139 independent schools, 70 public schools, and 16 countries sent teachers to Phillips Exeter Academy to learn more about the Harkness method (Robinson 2015).

You can use the fishbowl strategy with the Harkness method. The fishbowl strategy places a group of four or more students in an inner circle. They respond to a question by carrying on a discussion with one another. The rest of the students form an outer circle and take notes on the discussion. The fishbowl strategy works well with controversial issues and discussions that may become heated. It concludes with a whole-group discussion of the points posed by the inner circle.

The gallery walk is another strategy that works with the Harkness method. Start the class by posting four to six questions around the room (or assign a team of students to come up with the questions and post them). Groups of four students visit each station and record their responses. After five minutes, groups rotate to the next station and write down their comments. After all groups have visited all stations, they come together and use the Harkness method to discuss their responses.

The following prompts are designed to help you and your students create questions that could be used with the Harkness method to promote deep discussions about topics, issues, and problems. After reading this list, see if you can add a few prompts of your own:

- What would happen if . . . ?
- What are some possible consequences of . . . ?
- In what ways might we improve upon . . . ?
- What are different ways to think about . . . ?
- What are different situations related to . . . ?
- In what ways might . . . ?
- How might we add to . . . ?
- How could we extend upon . . . ?
- Let's consider . . . from many viewpoints.
- What do you think about . . . ?

Here are some video links that show the Harkness method in action:

- youtube.com/watch?v=QCORvIYKMMQ
- youtube.com/watch?v=189Miz-C6sU
- youtube.com/watch?v=PMuQnXsji4M
- youtube.com/watch?v=m3TOtTzTR50
- youtube.com/watch?v=SiAbrjbybfA

Global Education

While the Harkness model is generally considered little *e*, global education lends itself to big *E* opportunities. Global education aims to empower students to better themselves, their community, and their world by shifting education from a curriculum-focused approach (math, language arts, social studies, and science) to one that emphasizes the universal skills of thinking, acting, relating, and accomplishing. The nonprofit organization Global Future Education Foundation and Institute promotes real-world projects and empowerment education. It identifies more than twenty skills in each of these three areas: effective thinking, effective action, and effective relationships.

The US Department of Education, along with other US government agencies (2012–2016), set goals of strengthening education and advancing international emphasis (US Department of Education 2012). The goals target a world-class education for all students that

includes four global competencies (Mansilla and Jackson 2011):

- Investigate the world: Students' ability to investigate the world includes their own environment and beyond. Students are encouraged to identify issues and discuss significance.
- Recognize perspectives: When students recognize their own and others' perspectives within various content areas, they also identify who and what influence perspectives.
- Communicate ideas: Students' ability to communicate effectively with many audiences also affects how audiences perceive meaning.
- Take action: Students take action to improve conditions.

These four global competencies can be integrated into specific content areas. The Asia Center for Global Education offers grade-level rubrics for each competency and a K–12 Global Competence Framework that describes how globally competent students progress through attitudes, skills and knowledge (asiasociety.org /education/leadership-global-competence). These competency indicators are used to specify and communicate growth and are used in both formative and summative assessments.

AFS-USA and the National Society of High School Scholars (NSHSS) have identified qualities that top global learning schools share. They found that these schools have a commitment to diversity, welcome exchange students and international students, change focus to emphasize twenty-first-century challenges, prioritize global standards through a global perspective, and foster a belief that the world is a classroom (AFS-USA 2017). Global education at the classroom level depends upon what teachers and students are most concerned with. It fosters the ideal that students become deeply engaged, make local and global connections, see the significance of their actions, realize what they are learning, and know they are making progress.

Global education provides students with both big *E* and little *e* opportunities. Students learn about global issues and have an opportunity to take action. Here are several examples:

- Second graders might learn about and do a project on the effects of a hurricane after they learn about Hurricane Matthew in Haiti in 2016.

- Fourth graders might learn about and do a project on refugees arriving in Europe from the Middle East and Africa.
- A high school class might do a project on the Zika virus.
- Fifth graders at one US elementary school partnered with a school in Colombia on a 3-D printing project.
- A third-grade teacher from the United Kingdom partnered with teachers from Qatar and Abu Dhabi. Their students wrote multiplication and division word problems focusing on aspects of their town or country. They sent one another videos and photos of themselves solving one another's problems.
- At Fortuna Union High School in Fortuna, California, students take two years of global studies for English and social studies credit, culminating in their senior project, known as a Change the World project.

Many global education resources are available. For example:

- The Center for Global Education (CGE) provides encounters in which students can explore global issues through partnerships with international peers and graduate student mentors (globaled.us).
- Classrooms that use ePals connect through Skype to collaborate with other classes on a special project (commonsense.org/education/website/epals or epals.com/#/connections).
- Skype in the Classroom is a free community that allows students to take virtual field trips, collaborate, and hear guest speakers (education. microsoft.com/skype-in-the-classroom/overview).
- Students can use the WorldVuze platform to conduct global discussions on current events, the environment, and space exploration (blog.worldvuze.com/about-us/).
- Empatico allows students ages seven to eleven to explore the world through activities designed to spark empathy, kindness, and curiosity (empatico.org).
- The Partnership for 21st Century Learning (P21) is a great resource for teachers that provides many examples of school projects (battelleforkids.org /networks/p21/frameworks-resources).

- EdgeMakers is a middle and high school program that provides educators with tools to empower students to change the world. It focuses on cutting-edge solutions to extreme worldwide problems (edgemakers.com).

Educators must help students understand how various cultures interpret information differently so students can develop the skills necessary to thrive in the world. To deal with shared global issues, students should know how to effectively communicate, value differences, benefit from diversity, and coexist with people of many cultures.

Language and communication are especially important when it comes to global education. As teachers, we must help students learn language that empowers. Education researcher Ron Ritchhart talks about the subtle yet profound power of language in his book *Creating Cultures of Thinking*. He identifies seven key kinds of language (Ritchhart 2015):

1. The **language of thinking** refers to the verbs we use in our questions or statements. Empower students to use words that explicitly state what they mean. Share verb lists with students so that when they communicate with their global partners, each will know what the other means. Make sure students understand that the verb directs the way in which we think about something. For example, *summarize the story* differs from *analyze the story*.

2. The **language of community** means using pronouns in their plural form. Instead of saying, "I do this," we can say, "We do this." If we talk with our global partners using plural pronouns, they will feel part of the conversation and part of the project. This reminds *us* that global partners are part of the project as well. The plural pronoun makes the conversation inclusive.

3. The **language of initiative** helps students feel empowered by saying, "This is what we plan to do next." The word *initiative* implies future action.

4. The **language of praise and feedback** draws attention to students' efforts and actions. It gives not just praise, but *praise with feedback* that is specific and timely. The feedback may suggest future action.

5. The **language of listening** is critical in communicating with students from other countries. Cultural characteristics may lead people to interpret ideas in unique ways. After listening, it is useful for students to paraphrase and repeat back what they hear.

6. The **language of identity** is when students see themselves in the role of the professional in the field. For example, global students working together on an ocean cleanup project should try to think like scientists.

7. The **language of mindfulness** is not trying to quiet one's mind but to think in terms of possibilities.

Inquiry Learning

Inquiry learning emphasizes a thirst for knowledge and the development of skills to acquire that knowledge. It involves both critical and creative thinking and promotes an investigation of the world around us in pursuit of answers to students' own unanswered questions. Students pose questions, explore answers, evaluate possibilities, generate conclusions, defend their conclusions, and present their explanations to an audience. The teacher is both a facilitator and an information provider. Inquiry learning empowers students to construct understanding through authentic, hands-on experiences. It is student centered and values *how* we know something, not just *what* we know.

Inquiry learning is based on an issue, a problem, or something that a student is wondering about. To get your class started using the inquiry process, you may need to model questions. However, the goal is for your students to initiate the questions to be investigated, which should relate to real-world issues and be linked to standards. As students begin to research, they may modify or refine the question. They tease out what they already know about the issue and identify related unanswered questions they have. You can use the reproducible form **Inquiring Minds Want to Know** (page 70) to help guide your students to create inquiry questions. The research process may involve using primary source documents, note-taking, or conducting interviews or surveys. As a result of direct teaching or because of teacher-generated support structures, students should become proficient in these types of research skills.

If your students cannot think of a topic for an inquiry, they can use a strategy called Chunk and Crunch (**figure 3-2**). With this strategy, students start with a broad idea that's part of a content unit. Then they brainstorm related ideas, assigning them to categories. Students begin by folding a piece of paper to divide it into six columns. At the top of each column, students write a category. For older students, the categories could be cross-disciplinary, such as *political, social, economic,* *environmental, physical,* and *biological*. Younger students might use only four columns with headers such as *people, animals, places,* and *things*. If you want students to conduct an investigation specific to a unit of study, the categories at the top of each column might be vocabulary words or subtopics. Students work in groups to brainstorm as many ideas as they can for each column. Then, they circle, highlight, or underline their favorite idea or ideas in each column. They look for patterns across the categories and consider whether these patterns suggest any trends, issues, problems, conflicts, or dilemmas students might want to investigate. Encourage students to create inquiry investigations that go deep in order to build understanding beyond a basic level.

Feedback is critical to the inquiry process. Give students feedback on their choice of topic for investigation. You can also give your students checklists and rubrics like the **Inquiry Rubric** reproducible on page 71 to help them understand their level of mastery. This rubric delineates the steps of the inquiry process. It includes assessing the student's ability to plan the inquiry investigation, carry it out, analyze the information, synthesize the information, and communicate the results effectively to an audience. You might also include students' time management on the rubric. In addition, a student reflection piece could empower students to think about how they felt about the process, what surprised them, or what they might do differently next time.

Here's a real-life example of inquiry learning. One teacher leads her students through the scientific inquiry process in which they explore the natural world to solve real-world problems. Her students observe birds, plants, and mammals in the Sonoran Desert in Southern Arizona. Students build their own understanding of the desert environment through their explorations. They work in teams to answer their inquiry questions, which focus on several stages of animal disturbances. They look for patterns and trends, formulate conclusions, and defend their reasoning.

An inquiry resource that you might find helpful is the National Geography Geo-Inquiry website: nationalgeographic.org/education/programs/geo-inquiry. The Geo-inquiry process consists of five steps: ask, collect, visualize, create, and act. The website provides several examples of empowered students who have conducted inquiry investigations and includes additional resources.

It is well documented that inquiry learning works; many schools have used it for a long time. It promotes curiosity, social learning, and academic learning. In

Figure 3-2 Chunk and Crunch

Science unit: Water

1. Brainstorm big and small topics related to water and write them under the appropriate categories.

2. Circle, highlight, or underline the ideas that interest you most. You do not have to choose ideas from each column.

Environmental	Economic	Social	Political	Physical	Biological
Landscape changes	Water energy	Effects on daily life	State and federal laws	Forces	Plants
Landslides	Water Disasters			Erosion	Animals
Coastline	Tourism			Abrasion	People
Gullies	Costs to the town/city			Waves	
Levees				Tides	
Flood controls				Reservoir	
Flooding				Water cycle	
Reservoir				Ground water	

3. Using the ideas that interest you most, identify trends, issues, problems, conflicts, or dilemmas. Create an inquiry question based on these.

I am interested in the effects of hurricanes on the coastline because I live by the ocean and I have seen the beach erosion. I know we planted seagrass to try to hold the sand in place, but erosion is still happening. This is affecting our plants, animals, and tourism. Tourism is the main industry in our town. People are not coming to the beach because they don't have much space to sit on the sand. I want to know what state and federal laws exist regarding what we can and cannot do to save our beach. I want to investigate ways to help this problem, because what we are doing now is not enough.

a study conducted in four states, researchers found discussion-based inquiry approaches improved student performance. They also concluded that these effects applied across gender, socioeconomic levels, and ethnicity (Applebee et al. 2003). In 2002, a school district used inquiry-based learning with ELL students. The educators found that students made significant gains in English language, reading, and math (Amaral, Garrison, and Klentschy 2002).

Expeditionary Learning

Expeditionary learning schools use a type of project-based learning. Expeditionary learning is "learning by doing" and is similar in some ways to environmental education or outdoor education. The learning occurs through explorations, referred to as "expeditions." These are not expeditions in the traditional sense: they are expeditions in learning. Through these expeditions, students study topics, develop cumulative products, and make public presentations. Expeditionary learning provides a framework and strategies that are intentionally designed to change the culture of the school. It provides big *E* experiences for students.

Expeditionary learning can be undertaken by students of all ages. In one expedition, called bird cards, kindergarten students made note cards with bird drawings on them and sold the cards to raise funds for bird habitats. In another expedition, middle school students created four books of interviews with unsung local civil rights heroes. In yet another, students studied rewatering parts of the Erie Canal that ran through their city. They met with officials, surveyed residents, and researched other successful water projects. Then the students prepared and presented two reports to the city.

At King Middle School in Portland, Maine, students complete two expeditions a year. The entire school population is split up into groupings called houses. They got the idea of forming houses from the Harry Potter novels, in which students who attend Hogwarts School of Witchcraft and Wizardry are placed into houses. At King Middle School, each house has a regular community meeting, which consists of all the students in the house getting together to share information and make presentations. During one such community meeting, teachers announce a new expedition. Each expedition culminates in the students presenting to a real audience, such as professionals in the field, city councils, community members, and global viewers. By eighth grade, King students are very comfortable taking the lead and standing up in front of groups of people to share what they have discovered. They know how far they have come. They step up proudly, and the audience lifts them up. When students present to audiences beyond their teachers, they feel empowered because the world is listening to them. Because they work as a team, they learn to use their strengths for the betterment of the team. Some students at King Middle School did a Smart Cities expedition focused on increasing green space in the city. The students presented a city plan at their city hall. One student said, "Expeditions feel less like school and more like learning. Expeditions are more unpredictable, so that makes it more fun."

Expeditionary learning can be used at any type of school, but it may work particularly well for turn-around schools (schools performing in the lowest 5 percent) and Title I schools, because it is an instructional model based on student needs and because it provides social and emotional and community-oriented services and supports. At one school, a student who appeared to be disillusioned with and disengaged from school participated in a march calling for action on climate change as part of an expedition. Before the march, the student did not engage in school and had trouble making friends. She was not invested in completing her work or doing it well. This march changed her attitude and helped her feel more connected to the community. It empowered her because she was proud of the purposeful work the group was doing. After the march, the student was happier at school, made friends, and attended to her classwork. The experience helped turn things around for this student.

Since expeditionary learning teams are designed with student strengths in mind, a student who has difficulty writing may voice record research notes or be an interviewer. The student does not have to be the one in the group responsible for any formal writing. The same considerations apply to advanced students. Students who can handle reading passages at higher levels with more abstract concepts may read from more difficult resources. The team pools together its strengths to create sophisticated products.

Teachers at expeditionary schools often say they feel empowered. They teach what they love and connect with their students, their communities, and their environment. They model being learners themselves and show excitement. This excitement is contagious, and it is easy

to sense once one steps through the door of an expeditionary school. For teachers to feel empowered with this type of teaching and learning, administrators must support the expeditionary learning process. Administrators can allow teachers to create their own schedules, capture student interest, and connect with professionals in the community. They can empower teachers by letting them take on leadership roles. Administrators can make sure goals are transparent, with no hidden agendas. They can enable teachers with time, resources, and off-site planning; ask for teacher input; and celebrate successes.

Project-Based Learning

According to John Larmer of the Buck Institute for Education, project-based learning is any combination—with an extended project at the heart of the learning—of designing or creating a tangible product, performance, or event; solving a real-world problem (simulated or authentic); or investigating a topic or issue to develop an answer to an open-ended question (Larmer 2014). Like expeditionary learning, project-based learning offers not only engagement, but also both big *E* and little *e* empowerment. Both expeditionary and project-based learning encourage authentic learning through projects that relate to the real world and to the lives of the students and their communities. Both offer projects or expeditions that focus on problems that exist beyond the classroom and are relevant to the student's life.

The differences between the two learning systems are small. The Buck Institute recommends using seven design elements with project-based learning: challenging problem or question, sustained inquiry, authenticity, student voice and choice, reflection, critique and revision, and public product. The seven teaching practices are aligning to standards, building a culture, managing activities, scaffolding student learning, assessing student learning, engaging and coaching, and designing and planning. Expeditionary learning's performance tasks are based on three dimensions: mastery of student knowledge and skills, high-quality student work, and character. Project-based learning can also start with a fictional scenario that includes an underlying real-world problem, whereas expeditionary learning does not.

How can you shift from engagement to empowerment in project-based learning? This shift might happen naturally, but you can also think it out ahead of time. For example, let's say you are teaching a math class. You ask your students to apply their math skills to design a new school playground. They must decide what equipment they want to buy and how much space it will require. If they include a slide, they must figure in space at the bottom of the slide for students to land. Students then do a scale drawing of the new playground. This is an engaging project, but it is not particularly empowering. You can take it a step further to make it a little more empowering by asking students to work in teams and compete against each other to design a playground within a given budget. Then, they present their design and scale drawing to a panel of teachers and students, who use a rubric to determine the best design. This assignment takes more time than the first one, but it is also more empowering, and students learn additional skills. To create a big *E* experience, challenge your students to carry their playground design plans even further. The students might survey other students to ask them what they want on their playground, consult with a local architect, research neighboring schools' playground designs, come up with a design, price it, pitch it to the school administrators, and pitch it to the school district's board of education. Through this pitch process, students may discover that there are regulations they must follow. They may have to go back to the drawing board to make adjustments. Their design may not actually be used, but students would experience what it's like to work as a professional in the field. The school's or district's administrators can file the students' design for future reference to use when they are ready to redo their playground.

Here's another example of shifting from engagement to empowerment through project-based learning. Let's say your class is studying recycling. Students decide their project is to clean up the school grounds. They start with a plan that states who will do what and when they will do it, and they list tools they will need to do the cleanup. Students brainstorm potential problems and provide solutions to anticipated problems. Then they set up a work schedule. So far, this project is engaging but it is only somewhat empowering. It isn't until students present their plan to the principal, receive permission to carry out their plan, and complete their work that they begin to feel empowered. The students end the project by classifying the kinds of things they cleaned up and analyzing them in terms of how long it would have taken those things to decompose if they had not been picked up. Now, the students realize the larger effects of their efforts, and their feeling of empowerment increases.

For project-based learning ideas for your classrooms, try visiting the following websites:

- 7 Examples of Project-Based Learning Activities: thetechedvocate.org/7-examples-project-based-learning-activities
- Examples of Project-Based Learning: cambridgeport.cpsd.us/academics/examples_of_project_based_learning
- 50 Smart Ideas for Project-Based Learning: teachthought.com/project-based-learning/a-better-list-of-ideas-for-project-based-learning
- 17 Examples of STEM Project Based Learning Activities: projectpals.com/project-based-learning-blog/17-examples-of-stem-project-based-learning-activities

Problem-Based Learning

Problem-based learning and project-based learning are closely related instructional approaches. Both offer opportunities for students to become engaged, empowered learners. Both follow the inquiry process. But the two approaches differ in some key ways too:

- In project-based learning, the students usually have less input in goal setting and outcomes. The teacher generally sets the goals. In problem-based learning, the students are given a scenario and they must figure out how to solve the problem posed in the scenario. The students set the goals.
- Project-based learning may or may not involve a problem. The main emphasis of problem-based learning is to integrate the core content with the problem-solving process.
- Project-based learning sparks curiosity by asking questions and engaging students in critical and creative thinking and problem-solving. It is student centered and promotes active learning. Problem-based learning is often more specific and based on a scenario that is to be solved.
- Project-based learning may involve more authentic tasks with real-world applications than problem-based learning.

Education professor John Savery defines problem-based learning as "an instructional (and curricular) learner-centered approach that empowers learners to conduct research, integrate theory and practice, and apply knowledge and skills to develop a viable solution to a defined problem" (Savery 2006, 9). John Larmer identifies the six prescribed steps of problem-based learning. They are:

1. presenting an ill-structured problem

2. defining or formulating the problem

3. generating a knowledge inventory

4. generating possible solutions

5. formulating learning issues for self-directed and coached learning

6. sharing findings and solutions

To promote problem-based learning, you must provide your students with a "fuzzy" or "messy" ill-structured problem. Students must determine the underlying problem and solve it. The students become engaged through problem-solving—and also empowered, as they become more self-directed learners. The students must figure a way to present information to an audience in an engaging way. Students collaborate as they reflect on the work. They have an opportunity to revise their work based on their reflections. Each unit closes with self-assessment and peer assessment.

To develop your own problem-based learning activity, start with the topic, subtopics, skills, and standards that you want to cover in the lesson. Design a standards-based problem for students to solve. When you develop your own scenario, consider whether the problems or potential problems are authentic. If they are not, student engagement may falter. Also consider relevance. Do students really care about the problem? If they don't care, how engaged will they be? Students generally care more about local problems and problems that directly affect them than broader problems. Create a problem that is open-ended and has more than one solution. Not all solutions must be equally effective, but more than one solution should be effective. The more students have to think through the solutions, the more engaged and empowered they will be. A good problem to be solved is one that is cross-disciplinary, conceptual, and multifaceted. The concept/problem should be something real—a problem that already exists or has the potential to exist in a field of study.

In **figure 3-3**, the teacher identifies the main elements of the lesson, and develops the scenario from these elements. For students to solve the problem, they must

learn about how water affects the earth. They learn about erosion, weathering, sediment, and flood controls. They also learn about the city of Venice, Italy, the causes and effects of flooding in Venice, and what has been tried to date to curb the rising water. The students develop their own products to show what they know.

Many elementary, middle, and high schools have active problem-based learning programs. Edutopia is a great place to begin a search for inspiration. Here are some other examples:

- The Bed Project: Real-World Problem Inspires Social-Justice Response (grade 2): educationworld.com/a_curr/stenhouse/authentic-learning-social-justice-leadership.shtml

- The Toy Unit: Problem-Based Learning Puts Students in Charge (grade 4): educationworld.com/a_curr/stenhouse/project-problem-based-learning.shtml

- Bright Futures, Power of Words, On the Museum Wall, and Curtains Up! (grade 9–10): etd.fcla.edu/CF/CFH0004397/Millard_Michelle_C_2013April_BS.pdf

Problem-based learning positions the student as a stakeholder and the teacher as a coach. The structure of a problem-based learning unit is divergent in nature; that is, there is more than one answer to the problem. Students are evaluated based on their use of logical reasoning to solve the problem. Let's compare three problem-based scenarios:

- **Problem A:** Along with four other students, you are responsible for ordering supplies for the school store. You are the leader of this group. You have two dozen fancy file folders for sale at the store. Jack comes in and buys four. Mike wants to buy four also, but he has only enough money for three. If Mary buys eight for her birthday party, and Latisha buys six for her brothers and sisters, when David comes along looking for those fancy file folders, will you be sold out? Why or why not?

- **Problem B:** Along with four other students, you are responsible for ordering supplies for the school store. You are the leader of this group. The other students at school are complaining because you keep running out of fancy folders. Your budget is tight, and you are required to offer variety at the school store. You and your school store teammates

Figure 3-3 Problem-Based Learning: How Water Changes Earth

Content Areas	Nonnegotiable Learning
Content	Effects of water/flooding
Concept	Changes over time
Disciplines	Science, social studies
Critical/creative thinking	Logical reasoning, problem-based learning

We know that various forces shape the landforms that make up Earth's surface. People try to control the effects of these forces for better or for worse. The year is 2030. Venice's tourism industry is just about eliminated. Nobody wants to go on vacation and have to wear rubber boots the whole time. The city's buildings and bridges are eroding. The city smells musty, and the rat population is growing exponentially. The effects of erosion on daily life have placed a huge economic burden on the city. You and your team are the last hope. What is your best ecological, economical, and scientific solution to save the sinking city and empower its citizens to do the right thing?

must decide what to do so that the complainers turn into school store supporters.

- **Problem C:** You visit your cousin in another state, and she shows you the cool stuff she purchased at her school store. You wish your school had a school store like hers. You ask her about the store and how it works. She tells you the students run it, make the rules, order the materials, and keep track of the money. The students also handle any conflict that arises between the school store sellers and the school store buyers. You are excited and you want to introduce this idea to your teacher and principal. Your task is to create a team of students, develop this idea, pitch it to the teachers and principal and make it happen.

Do you think the students working on problem A feel empowered? Most probably do not. Some might feel personally empowered if they struggle to solve word problems and they figure out the answer; they've experienced success and learned new skills. This would be an example of little *e* empowerment.

Do you think the students working on problem B feel empowered? They probably are engaged, but still may not necessarily be empowered. They might feel little *e* empowered if they feel the work is particularly challenging.

Do you think the students working on problem C feel empowered? They probably do. A student discovered the idea out of state and decided to introduce it at home. The work of creating a team, developing the idea, pitching it to the teachers and principal, and making it happen is entirely student driven. Students who work

on problem C have the opportunity to make a real difference at their school. This problem offers them a big *E* experience because they are creating something new, and their effort will affect many students.

How can we use problem-based learning to foster empowerment? If the problem is based on a real problem in the field, where students can take action, then the students experience empowerment. They become empowered when they take on team responsibilities, such as setting agendas, timelines, and deadlines. Students learn about bias, role interpretation, real-world problem-solving, and ways to solve a problem from team members' various viewpoints.

The ultimate application of student empowerment with problem-based learning is to have the students create their own fuzzy problem. First, designate the nonnegotiable learning that is required of all students or assign nonnegotiable learning that targets specific students' needs (differentiation). Then ask the students to create a problem scenario that requires them to apply the nonnegotiable learning. Review all the student-created scenarios to make sure they will require students to apply the targeted learning. The students become empowered when they create the scenario and ask their classmates to solve the problem. To make it competitive, the students can vote on the scenario they like best and solve the winning scenario. To use a random-selection approach, shuffle up the scenarios, place them facedown, and ask each team of students to choose a scenario. Whether students choose the scenario they want to solve or vote on the one they want to solve, they have control and power. If you tell them which scenario to solve, you have the control and the power.

Genius Hour

When students engage in project-based learning, problem-based learning, and inquiry leaning, they are often empowered to use their own questions and solve problems rather than be spoon-fed knowledge. These types of little *e* and big *E* experiences provide a great foundation for students to participate in productive genius hours. In education, genius hour is sometimes referred to as "passion projects." Genius hour encourages students to follow their own passions and express their creativity. It is a research-based program that allows students to excel through intrinsic motivation.

The idea for genius hour began when Google gave its employees 20 percent of their time to explore their own passions. Google found this resulted in higher productivity. According to career analyst Dan Pink, over half of Google's developments came out of the 20 percent time (Pink 2009). This idea spread to education, and now some schools empower students with genius hour explorations.

You can help your students discover their passions by using such sites as wonderopolis.org, thrively.com, or diy.org. Once students identify their passions, they plan their time, identify materials, and may contact outside experts to help them. Students keep track of their progress in a planner or use a project management app such as Trello (trello.com). Encourage students to share their products with an audience beyond the classroom. In this way, you encourage them to produce products that are good enough to share with the outside world.

Genius hour provides an opportunity for students to learn about social and political issues and injustices. It promotes student autonomy because students learn and use skills, develop probing questions, and spark their own curiosity. Students participating in genius hour often experience intense feelings and reactions through a sense of purpose and mastery.

For genius hour to be successful, students need to know where and when it takes place, what materials are available, and how and if they will be assessed. Ask students, "What would you want to learn about if nobody told you what you had to learn about?" (Matteson 2016). Once students establish a topic, help them find resources, teach them research skills, and respond to their needs (Rush 2015). I recommend following these guidelines and asking yourself these questions:

- Control internet content according to the guidelines set forth by your school.

- Let students do genius hour a few times a year. This does not have to be a year-round commitment.

- Encourage students to take risks and accept failures.

- Genius hour can be genius half-hour and can occur once a week for six weeks. Define the amount of time that makes sense for the students and for you.

- Decide what type of materials will be available to students. Can they use paint? Can they use wood, saws, and drills?

- Will the students be required to stay on topic? How much freedom to explore ideas will they have?

- Do you need permission to conduct a genius hour?

- Do you want to team with another teacher and classroom?

- Provide a controlled classroom, not a free-for-all environment.

- Provide opportunities for students to be both engaged and empowered.

Texas teacher Meshelle Smith gave her fifth graders one genius hour per week. Her students explored topics for four weeks, narrowed down topics for three weeks, then worked on their projects all but the last four weeks of school. Since these projects were long-term, she asked her students to break them into five-week mini-projects submitted along the way. Students kept working journals, and they responded to prompts she posted online. These prompts challenged the students to reflect on their progress, list challenges, and discuss possibilities. Smith also encouraged collaboration. Students took part in partner and group chats. They helped one another with their individual expertise. For example, if students were good at making presentation slides with voice-overs, they showed others how to do it. The students were proud of their accomplishments and felt empowered as they overcame obstacles (Smith 2017).

Although Smith spent a long time on genius hour projects, you should not feel you must give up that kind of time. You can arrange for your students to work for forty minutes rather than one hour, or two times a week for three weeks rather than every Friday for the whole year. Generally, a longer amount of time works best, but some students find it difficult to maintain their interest for long periods of time. If your school year is divided into quarters, you could arrange passion projects by the quarter. Some students in your classroom could work on one project for two quarters, while other students work on one project for one quarter. There are no rules about how to best structure your genius hour. In fact, some teachers don't like using the term *genius hour*. They think this name implies that students are only geniuses for an hour. No matter how you set it up or what you call it, the point is to empower students with the gift of time to pursue what they are passionate about.

Makerspace and Design Thinking

Another popular movement in education is the makerspace movement. It too provides plenty of opportunity for student empowerment. The makerspace movement supports academic learning and encourages experimentation and collaboration. STEM education consultants and authors Sylvia Libow Martinez and Gary Stager credit Seymour Papert as "the father of the maker movement" (Martinez and Stager 2013). A makerspace is a place where people get together to create something. It can contain electronics, woodworking supplies, or just common craft materials or odds and ends. This space is designed to provide social interaction and support the idea that innovative thinking is valuable. "Students who have unique learning needs thrive in a makerspace because it allows them to express themselves without fear of failure" (Fleming and Krakower 2016).

The Makerspace Playbook provides a guide on how to create a makerspace (Maker Education Initiative 2013). A makerspace is a place where students are given an opportunity to focus on broad-based problems. Usually the disciplines are integrated, which allows student to pursue a topic in-depth. The students engage in open-ended tasks independently or in small groups and use critical and creative thinking skills throughout the process. The most obvious goal is for students to produce creative innovations. This means they may use unusual materials, designs, or techniques that are put together in some unique way.

In June 2016, President Obama declared one week in June as the National Week of Making. The US Department of Education was hoping makerspaces would help educators rethink career and technical education. As teachers become more and more frustrated with high-stakes testing, they are embracing the makerspace trend. But tension is growing between a somewhat unstructured movement and a highly regulated system. Questions are arising: Should makerspaces

occur within or outside the classroom? Should maker education be tied to standards or should it let students truly explore? Sometimes districts convert unused space into makerspaces and then find that teachers are not using the space. Even though research says that making gives students agency over their learning, teachers and administrators need to be convinced that making is an effective way to learn. To get teachers on board, structured maker challenges may be the best place to start. In elementary schools, teachers can begin by assigning art projects at the end of a lesson to reinforce learning. For example, after students read a book, they create a three-dimensional representation of their favorite part of the story and explain why it's their favorite. Or at the end of a unit on Egypt, students create pyramids and mummies. The makerspace provides space and materials for students to create these products. When teachers start to back away and let students determine a hands-on project, students begin to feel empowered to make their own choices that reinforce their learning.

In makerspaces, students who use the engineering design process feel empowered because they have a structure and a process to follow yet still experience the freedom to create. Here are the basic steps of the design process (NC State University 2019):

1. Identify problems and limitations.
2. Imagine solutions and determine the best one.
3. Plan out a solution. Draw a diagram or sketch in order to see what materials are needed to create the solution.
4. After gathering materials, create the solution by following a plan and testing out the creation to see if it works.
5. Evaluate how the creation could be better.
6. Use ideas for improvements and begin the design process again in order to improve the original.

Even though the design process appears linear because each step is specifically stated, it is not linear. Students start in one place and may end up in a totally different place. However, all students need to be involved in setting up norms, identifying safety procedures, and articulating some sort of goal (even though the goal may change). Makers use design thinking, which starts with defining what students want to do, moves into ideation, and results in creating a prototype. The prototype is tested, and the maker receives feedback. The maker usually refines the creation and goes through the process again. This contrasts starkly with the linear process that is used in the scientific method. In that method, the researcher states what the problem is and conducts research to find out about the problem. The researcher creates a hypothesis and develops a procedure to test the hypothesis. The researcher analyzes the results and compares the hypothesis to the experiment's conclusion. By contrast, making grows and evolves. Makers use their imaginations and are empowered to become experts. They experience little *e* empowerment as they go through the process of making.

Teachers who are comfortable allowing students to truly embrace the maker mindset let their students take things apart, explore new things, and do things in new ways. Students are often inspired by new ideas that emerge, because making can be a source of innovation. Making is student-centered, not teacher-centered. It is idea-driven, not textbook-driven. Making encourages divergent, open-ended thinking, and creating, not regurgitating. Making fosters integrated skills and content. It is unpredictable, not predetermined (Maslyk and Miller 2014). Making engages and also empowers students.

Teacher educator George Couros explains that seven things happen when students truly embrace the maker movement (Couros 2017):

1. Students demonstrate iterative thinking. This means they try, fail, try again, revise, and continually improve their work until they are satisfied with it. This takes modeling, because often students do not like to revise their work.

2. Students become problem solvers. They embrace challenges because they learn how to use critical and creative thinking to solve problems.

3. Students learn to think divergently when they begin to connect unrelated ideas to create something new.

4. Students learn that they must take risks in order to become a maker. Risk-taking might mean trying something new or presenting their ideas to a real audience.

5. Students are proud of the fact that they are makers. They use a making process and bring their creation to fruition. Students learn a making mindset. It is thinking like a designer, an innovator, and a problem solver.

6. Students learn to create management systems to help them engage in their creative work.

7. Students gain empathy, learning what others think and feel through interviews or needs assessments.

Here are a few examples of what teachers are calling "making" in the classroom. Do you agree that these are true examples of makerspace learning?

- In a third-grade classroom, the teacher asks the students to design a roller coaster. Students work in small groups to create a roller coaster that incorporates several scientific principles.
- A group of fourth graders must design, create, and complete a sewing project.
- A teacher creates a robot. The students will design their own robot.

These are all maker projects that empower students. In all three examples, students create something without following a set of directions. They experiment with ideas, collaborate, and get feedback from others. Teachers usually set up their classrooms in centers where students work together. Students usually keep track of their progress in their journals. Their designs and creations are shared with others outside the classroom.

Here are some websites you can visit for design challenge ideas:

- Make: Community: makezine.com
- Invent to Learn: inventtolearn.com
- Instructables: instructables.com
- Exploratorium: exploratorium.edu
- Makedo: make.do
- Code.org: code.org
- Design Squad: pbskids.org/designsquad
- The LAUNCH Cycle: thelaunchcycle.com

Entrepreneurship

According to a recent report on entrepreneurship education published by the European Union, young people "will need to be innovative, adaptive, resilient, and flexible to navigate an ever-evolving labor market" to be employable in the future (British Council 2017). If it is our responsibility as educators to prepare our students for the future, then this preparation should include introducing our students to entrepreneurship. Many students will not turn out to be entrepreneurs. But many students do not turn out to be historians or scientists either, yet we require that they take history and science classes. We as a society determine what all students should know in order to be college- or career-ready. Shouldn't this include entrepreneurship education?

Entrepreneurship education prepares students for twenty-first-century competencies such as creativity, collaboration, critical thinking, communication, global citizenship, passion, and purpose. It also encourages research, planning, and implementation. Students experience real-world lessons and skills integrated through multiple subject areas. They learn what it means to come up with an idea and carry it through development phases until it reaches implementation. Entrepreneurship education gives students opportunities to dream big and empowers them to take action by building and managing a business. Entrepreneurship projects provide real and relevant experiences.

Entrepreneurship education inspires students and motivates them to achieve. It empowers them to create something from nothing. It provides a forum in which students can engage in rigor, develop skills, and be competitive. Entrepreneurship should be integrated into multiple disciplines so students can see that it is not just about inventing gadgets to sell. Our national economy relies on entrepreneurs to innovate and drive it forward.

Education technology researcher Cheryl Lemke believes there are five skills that are essential to becoming a successful entrepreneur: calculated risk-taking, persistence, tolerance for ambiguity, evidence-based reasoning, and self-direction (Pierce 2016). Lemke's firm has developed an online learning platform to help educators foster these skills in their students. Teachers want students to put together ideas in new and usual ways. They want students to ask questions and dig deeper and not settle for the first answer. As in Socratic questioning, one student responds, and then other students generate questions about that response. Students answer those new questions and then generate more questions. An entrepreneur can use Socratic questioning to explore complex ideas to analyze concepts and discover assumptions. Socratic questioning is a method of argument that is thoughtful and disciplined. It was named after Socrates, the Greek philosopher who believed that questioning enables one to explore ideas logically. There are six types of Socratic questions: clarifying concepts, probing assumptions, probing reasons and evidence, questioning viewpoints, probing implications and consequences, and questioning the question. Teachers can empower students by teaching them these six types of questions and then asking their students to use them when they begin to think about their business ventures.

How would students know whether they want to be entrepreneurs? Many people think that if someone has a passion or is particularly inventive, they might want to go this route, but not everyone is cut out to be an entrepreneur. It is often particular characteristics that determine whether someone is a successful entrepreneur: Entrepreneurs are risk-takers. They invest time and energy in their pursuits, not just to design and invent but to create a business, with no guarantees of success. They have no road map or how-to manual. This means that students need to be confident in their ideas as well as in themselves. They need a can-do attitude. They must stay curious and have the tenacity to solve problems that crop up along the way. Their ability to think flexibly will help them solve both small everyday problems and big problems. Entrepreneurs focus on the big picture and are driven by their desire to build something. Often their competitive spirit translates into restless behavior. If you have students who fit this description, you might recommend they channel their energy into an entrepreneurial pursuit.

It is important for entrepreneurs to have a growth mindset. They must embrace challenge and persist through difficulties. Student entrepreneurs acknowledge that effort is the path to success. They learn from criticism and adapt their ideas rather than ignore negative feedback or give up. They understand what they are not good at and figure out what they need to get good at it, or they find someone with these skills who can help them succeed.

Entrepreneurship is not the domain of only highly able students. Entrepreneurs believe anything is possible regardless of their academic ability. They take big leaps into the unknown. In the entrepreneurial world, success is often a matter of grit rather than intelligence. Grit allows students to push past failure and disappointment and to stay with a question long enough to develop a comprehensive view of the topic. Entrepreneurs are not people who say in just a few minutes, "I've got the answer. I'm done."

Often entrepreneurship is taught in a design-thinking format. Hands-on design challenges foster active problem-solving and should not be limited to STEM classrooms. For a design challenge, students must decide if they want to invent something new or modify an existing invention. You can use the "once upon a napkin" technique as a hook to get your students thinking like designers and entrepreneurs. "Once upon a napkin" is a popular strategy based on the notion that people often create and develop new ideas in a coffee shop or restaurant and write their ideas on a napkin. To use this technique in a STEM or science class, give your students napkins and ask then to write their passions, interests, or hobbies on the napkin. Then, ask them to identify a challenge that exists in one of those areas. To use this technique in an English language arts class, ask students to identify a passion, interest, or hobby they think a character in a story might have. Students can justify their responses with textual evidence. Then ask students to identify a challenge in one of those areas.

Challenge your student entrepreneurs to create something to market. To get started, have students work in teams to identify problems by researching and reviewing information, interviewing stakeholders, and looking for recurring patterns, problems, or themes. Then have each team focus on one issue or problem, brainstorming physical solutions to solve it and determining which solution will work best. Teams should consider elements of practicality, such as whether the solution will really work, whether the needed materials are accessible, and whether they can make their deadline. Students may seek out local experts or their peers for specific feedback. The feedback should include praise as well as suggestions for improvements. Students should anticipate problems and determine solutions up front in order to avoid them. Student teams divide the labor and address each weak element of the design before creating a prototype. Then the team creates a prototype and presents it to a real audience. After making any needed adjustments, the team is then ready to set up its entrepreneurial pursuit.

When students launch their own business, they learn organization skills, marketing skills, math and writing skills, basic bookkeeping skills, and communication skills. Even young children can start a business. Take Evelyn, for example:

I started my bottle business, called Lil Happy Bottles, when I was seven years old. I started selling my bottles at a couple of craft fairs with my mom, and I sold a bunch of bottles. I always loved fairies and magic, so a bottle that held a little bit of happiness and magic seemed like a good idea. I love to read, dance, and make art; that is why I put the bottles, quotes. and charms together.

I have fifteen different bottles, which include Pixie Dust, Imagination Dust, Pearls of Wisdom, Sleep Dust, Time in a Bottle, and more. I plan on adding new bottles to my business. I have just started to think about getting my own website. I hope to market my business on my website and to wholesale the bottles to other stores.

I hope my business will be a success and help me learn more about how to run a business and save money for college and my future. I have so many interests, and I know that the money I'm earning with this business will help me in the future with school, and maybe traveling too.
—Evelyn Kenney, 2012

When Evelyn created her business, she experienced little *e* empowerment. When she launched her business, her experience shifted into the big *E* zone. Evelyn created her own company on her own time, after school. But we cannot expect that all students have this opportunity. To level the playing field and close the empowerment gap, we as teachers should encourage all students to design, market, and publish their entrepreneurial projects during school time. All students deserve the opportunity to find and pursue their interests and passions.

Social entrepreneurs are people with innovative solutions to social problems who offer new ideas on a wide scale. A few examples of such entrepreneurs are Maria Montessori, who introduced a new approach to education; Henry Ford, who made automobiles affordable for the middle class; and Nelson Mandela, who led anti-apartheid efforts in South Africa. Social entrepreneurship in education usually involves class projects in which students develop initiatives to change the world, their community, or their school. Organizations such as Kiva U (kiva.org/kivau/intro) can help students and teachers in the classroom get started creating a business that will make a difference in their community and the world.

When a student-run business is altruistic in nature, students experience a deep sense of purpose. You'll find many such examples on the internet. Share these stories with your students to inspire them. For example, at age nine, Dylan Mahalingam founded a nonprofit to raise funds for developing countries that has grown to a roster of twenty-four thousand regular youth volunteers. Alexandra Scott started a lemonade stand to raise money for childhood cancer research at age four. Alex herself had cancer. By the time of her death at age eight, the Alex's Lemonade Stand Foundation had raised more than one million dollars. At age twelve, Katie Stagliano founded Katie's Krops, a network of youth-based gardens that grows and donates thousands of pounds of fresh vegetables to people in need. Malala Yousafzai, who fights for the rights of girls to get an education in her home country of Pakistan and other countries around the world, was shot in the head by the Taliban when she was fifteen. She started a movement in Pakistan that has led to worldwide support.

If you are interested in teaching students about entrepreneurship, here are several books that model the entrepreneurial spirit:

- *The Amazing Kid Entrepreneur* by Zohra Sarwari
- *Better Than a Lemonade Stand! Small Business Ideas for Kids* by Daryl Bernstein
- *The Making of a Young Entrepreneur: A Kid's Guide to Developing the Mind-Set for Success* by Gabrielle Jordan
- *The Most Magnificent Thing* by Ashley Spires
- *What Do You Do with an Idea?* by Kobi Yamada

Chapter Summary

This chapter looks at empowerment through the lens of strategies and programs categorized as big *E* and little *e* experiences. To direct your empowerment instruction, you should know if you intend to target little *e* or big *E* empowerment. If you plan to incorporate empowerment activities and strategies proactively, you can ensure that your students will feel more empowered over time. This chapter provides a quick planner for keeping track of your empowerment ideas. Strategies such as the Harkness method, global education, inquiry learning, expeditionary learning, project-based learning, problem-based learning, genius hour, makerspace and design thinking, and entrepreneurship lend themselves to little *e* and sometimes big *E* experiences.

Discussion Questions

1. If you really want to make an impact and have your students feel empowered, how many little *e* and big *E* activities should you do?

2. Should you use all the programs and strategies described in this chapter? Is any program or strategy better to use than another?

SOCIAL ENTREPRENEURS IN ACTION

In 2002, David Wish was named a social entrepreneur by the Draper Foundation. He created Little Kids Rock (littlekidsrock.org), a nonprofit organization that provides music education for K–12 students nationwide. Since then, the organization has served more than 850,000 students, providing them with modern band music classes. Its mission is to restore music classes in schools where budget cuts have eliminated music from the curriculum. The program works with economically disadvantaged schools and provides teacher training and musical instruments free of charge. It requires that schools must be willing to offer music classes at least once a week. Little Kids Rock methods are based on the types of music students listen to.

The Maine Department of Education created the Maine Kids Rock initiative, developed with the Little Kids Rock program. Josh Bosse, a music teacher in Fryeburg, Maine, participated in this program. While students in the program practiced their music, he saw them go above and beyond what was required of them, work harder to better themselves, help other students, discuss their songs with other students, get better at playing their instruments, and choose to stay after school to practice. The Maine Kids Rock program provided a forum for Josh to empower his students. He seized this opportunity and successfully ran with it.

3. What idea described in this chapter are you willing to try? When? What will it look like?

4. Should you emphasize a metacognitive approach with your students and see if they can transfer the feeling of empowerment to other situations?

5. What do you like about the ideas in this chapter? What questions do you still have about these ideas?

After you've thought about your answers to these questions, visit this website for a video chapter review with the author: freespirit.com/empower-videos.

Categorizing Student Empowerment Experiences

Choose a unit of study. Describe how you empowered your students during this unit in the past. Were these big *E* or little *e* experiences? How did your students feel after the experience? Add any ideas you now have that might pump up the level of empowerment in the future.

Unit	Big E or Little e Experience	Feelings	Future Ideas for This Unit

Quick Engagement and Empowerment Planner

Name of unit:

Activities, Strategies, and Assignments	Beginning, Middle, or End of Unit	Not Engaging or Empowering	Engaging	Little e	Big E

Inquiring Minds Want to Know

What do you know?

How do you know it?

What questions do you have?

What do you think?

Why do you think it?

Tell me more:

Inquiry Rubric

Inquiry Steps	Just Okay	Pretty Good	Fantastic
Include course content.	Inquiry includes some course content.	Inquiry includes course content essentials.	Inquiry goes above and beyond course content.
Create inquiry question.	Question is fuzzy.	Question is mostly clear.	Question is specific and focused.
Conduct research.	Student uses few resources.	Student uses many but common resources.	Student uses unusual resources resulting from digging deeper.
Analyze information.	Student retells information.	Student analyzes obvious points.	Student does deep, reflective analysis.
Synthesize information.	Student summarizes information.	Student synthesizes information.	Student makes unusual connections in the synthesis.
Create recommendations.	Student gives one simple recommendation.	Student gives an obvious but detailed recommendation.	Recommendation is sophisticated and expressed well.
Present solutions.	Presentation is basic.	Presentation is clear and articulate.	Presentation is multifaceted and detailed.
Do work on time.	Work is completed late.	Work is completed on time.	Work is completed early.

Student reflection:

1. Did you like using the inquiry process? Explain why or why not.

2. Did you encounter any surprises while you were exploring your topic? If so, describe them.

3. What, if anything, would you do differently next time?

CHAPTER 4

In It to Win It: Empowerment Through Game-Based Education and Competitions

Game-based education and competitions are ways to teach content and skills in a competitive or cooperative format. You can use gaming or competition as an instructional approach in an individual lesson or to structure an entire unit of study. With some games, students work together as teams to move through various levels; in others, students play alone. Perhaps you see gaming and competition as engagement strategies. But games and competitions can also be empowering. Some students feel personally empowered when they "conquer" a level or a game or successfully complete a competition. Many students feel empowered when they create their own game or competition.

Traditional Games

There are two main types of instructional games: traditional board or card games and electronic ones. If you give elementary students a choice among product forms, they will often choose to create traditional games. In most cases, students create games similar to the ones they know and play. For example, elementary and middle school students might create a board game that looks like Monopoly but uses vocabulary words from a unit of study. Although this game might be fun and engaging for students, it likely provides little in the way of content review. Students often create games that ask players to regurgitate facts instead of using higher-level thinking. If this sounds familiar, ask yourself if students feel empowered and if creating such games is worth your students' time.

Here's an example of a fourth-grade teacher who helped her students improve a game they'd created so it became more challenging, more instructive, and more empowering. Two boys worked together to create a basic rocks-and-minerals board game. First, they created a deck of cards. On each card they wrote a question about rocks and minerals and a number. Then they created a game board. Players took turns choosing cards, and if they answered the question on the card correctly, they moved their marker forward the designated number of spaces on the board. The boys who created the game seemed engaged and somewhat empowered. The teacher looked at the questions on the cards and found that they were all lower-level, factual questions that could be answered with one word.

The teacher asked the boys to revise their questions using Norman Webb's Depth of Knowledge (DOK) verbs, because she wanted them to create a game that targeted a variety of thinking levels, not just recall questions. The teacher gave the boys a list of verbs and explained that these verbs would pump up their questions and make kids think. Then she noticed that other students had also created games with low-level factual questions. So she gave all the students lists of verbs from Webb's Recall and Skill/Concept levels, from the Strategic Thinking level, and from the Extended Thinking level. She wanted all her students to create challenging questions and she wanted all players to be successful when they played the games. She asked students to create questions at a variety of challenge levels because she assumed not all students who were going to play the games could handle the same degree of content complexity at the same point in time. Some of her students would need more practice with the content before they could use extended thinking, while her gifted students would be underchallenged if they were not engaged at the Extended Thinking level. For a reproducible list of gaming verbs you can use with your students, see **Three Tiers of Gaming Verbs** on page 87.

The students used an organizer to rewrite their questions. (See the **Create Just-Right Questions for Game Playing** reproducible on page 88.) The students felt empowered because they had a tool to help them make their questions better. They created questions they were proud of.

Since the students created questions from different lists of verbs, the teacher asked the students to designate their questions as level one, level two, or level three. Gifted students created questions from the top tier of verbs because they wanted to create a challenging game for their academic peers. Other students created questions from a variety of levels. Students who struggled to come up with any questions at all, even with a verb list, needed more support from the teacher. With the help from the teacher, they were able to create simple questions that focused on basic content. Most of these questions did end up being level one questions, but a few were level two and level three questions.

In this way, students are empowered to create the games and players are empowered to choose their own level of questions. Some students like to conquer all levels of questions. They start at level one, which boosts their confidence even though they experience easy successes, and they move on to higher levels as they acquire more content knowledge.

Electronic Games

Judy Willis, a neurologist before she became a teacher, says that video games exemplify mastery-oriented goals and should be a model for best teaching practices. She writes, "A Department of Education 2008 report determined that students who seek to master an academic topic with mastery-oriented goals show better long-term academic development than do their peers whose main goals are to get good grades or outperform others" (Willis 2011b). What lessons can teachers learn from video games?

An important feature of video games is that the player is rewarded for incremental progress, not just for the final win. Willis says this reward is fueled by dopamine produced by the brain, which makes us feel good. Dopamine is released only when cognitive or physical effort is put forth. There also must be elements of risk with an outcome that's unpredictable. In most video games, players receive feedback instantly and are rewarded through a point system. The brain remembers the feeling of the response and seeks out another surge of dopamine, which is why players return to play over and over again. According to Willis, studies indicate that the brain evaluates the probability of success based on past experiences and determines whether it is worth it to expend the effort to try again. She claims that 80 percent of the time, gamers will make errors, but games often provide hints and clues to keep players engaged. Most players will start on level one when they first try a new video game. If the level is too easy, they will quickly progress until they find the right level of challenge. Students learn to determine their realistic achievable challenge level. This is why it is so important for students, when creating their own questions, to create appropriate levels of challenge.

We can use video gaming research to help us teach better and to empower our students. You can empower your students by sharing Willis' five lessons with your students. When your students create their own traditional or electronic games, ask them to consider the answers to the following questions:

- How will you reward your players when they conquer a level?

- How will you determine appropriate levels of challenge for all students? Is each level significantly harder than the previous one?

- What type of instant feedback will you provide, how often, and when?

- What is your point system? How do players get points and how many do they get? What do points mean?

- Are there risks built into your game?

Video gaming is becoming more and more popular with students, and some teachers are taking advantage of this trend. According to a 2017 Pew Research Center survey, 84 percent of US teens age thirteen to seventeen years old say they have a game console at home or have access to one, and 90 percent say they play video games on a computer, game console, or mobile phone (Perrin 2018). Nearly 50 percent of teachers reported using digital games in their classrooms in 2015, according to Project Tomorrow's Speak Up survey, up 25 percent from 2010. Are teachers using gaming in a purposeful way to teach content and promote best practices so that students learn? Gaming that involves systems thinking is often done collaboratively; yet 52 percent of teachers assign digital games as independent activities (Shapiro et al. 2014). In another survey, teachers said 47 percent of low-performing students benefited from using games, while only 15 percent of high-performing students benefited (Games and Learning 2014). It seems that low-performing students benefited from practice and remedial-type games, but few high-performing students did. It would be best for teachers to apply the five questions noted in the previous paragraph before choosing an appropriate electronic game for their students and to remember that the gaming experience is enhanced through collaboration.

Some electronic games are designed for the teacher or the student to insert their own content. Below are a few examples of popular electronic games and game-building sites that teachers use with their students. Whenever possible, teachers should give up power and control and empower their students to create the questions:

- Kahoot! (kahoot.com)
- Quizizz (quizizz.com)
- Quizlet Live (quizlet.com)
- Quizalize (quizalize.com)

Electronic gamification of content can be as simple or complex as teachers want it to be. Remember to keep asking if the activity is engaging students or empowering them. If it is engaging, how can teachers bump it up a notch to empower them? Sparking student thinking is one way to do so. By creating questions that involve issues and problems, teachers empower students with deep knowledge. If students want to take action on these problems and issues, they can empower themselves even further. Some of the options listed below are games that help students learn content:

- Students create a scavenger hunt game that uses QR codes.
- Students use Kahoot to create games and play with their classmates. Kahoot can also be used as a preassessment or formative assessment.
- Students use Quizlet (quizlet.com) to create flash cards, matching games, and guess-and-check games.

- ClassDojo (classdojo.com) can be used to share game playing with the community or with parents. ClassDojo is also an electronic portfolio platform for students. Students post their work and share it with their parents.
- Breakout EDU (breakoutedu.com) is a site that offers physical games, digital games, and a digital game builder.

Using the Game Model for Instruction

If teachers apply their understandings of the video game model to nongaming classroom instruction, like providing instruction with levels, they should make sure a goal is divided into small tasks that students can reach often. Students should be able to correct any misinformation during the goal-attaining process (formative assessment) rather than making adjustments solely when they reach the goal. Students can keep track of their own small-task progress, while teachers chart group progress on wall charts. (Wall charts can be embarrassing for students who do not do well, so teachers may not want to chart individual student progress this way.)

For all students to be successful with a game model, scaffolding and differentiation may be necessary. Teachers may need to provide additional clues and hints to keep students progressing toward their goal; students should be able to receive the help they need in order to play the game. If tasks are based on reading or research, assignments may need to be modified. Some students may read fewer pages or use fewer resources. Some students may need supports such as audio recordings of the readings or tutorials in math. All students should be able to make incremental progress, and all students should have access to game-based education.

The Follett Challenge Model

One game model that you can adapt for instructional purposes is the Follett Challenge (follettchallenge.com). The Follett Challenge is designed for competition, but you can use it as a game structure upon which to build any curriculum unit. First, like with problem-based learning, create a mission for your students. The mission is usually a mystery, a quest, or problem of some sort to be solved.

The students work on the mission in teams of whatever size you prefer. I like teams of three or four. You can assign students to teams or let students choose their own teammates. Students create a name for their team and a symbol that represents their team. This process helps team members bond and form a team identity. It promotes team spirit and little *e* empowerment.

Next, create regular curriculum assignments and call them "tasks." After teams earn a certain number of points by completing tasks, you give them a clue card. Students move through the game by accomplishing tasks and receiving clues; they are motivated to do their tasks (curriculum assignments) because they are part of the game. When a team completes all the tasks and receives all the clue cards, it tries to solve the mystery or accomplish the mission.

It is important to plan out your game's rules and procedures. Follow these eight steps to create your game:

1. Create a mystery or a problem for your students to solve, or a mission for your students to accomplish. Decide how the game will be won and what happens when a team wins. Will students get an automatic A grade for the unit, a homework pass, or some other reward?

2. Create three levels of task cards with curriculum assignments ranging in difficulty from easy to medium to hard. Assign points to task cards according to difficulty.

3. Decide when students will play the game. The game should not sacrifice instruction time. Rather, instruction time is built into the game, because content learning is embedded in the tasks.

4. Create teams or have students create teams based on the results of a preassessment. Students choose their own team name and create a symbol that represents their team. Students can use Google Docs (or another program of your choice) to communicate with one another and with you as they make their way through the tasks.

5. When students answer questions correctly on a task card, they receive the number of points indicated on the card. The team must reach 85 percent mastery on each task card to earn its points. If students do not reach mastery, the team sees you for reteaching and then tries again to complete the task.

6. When a team earns a certain number of points, you give the team a clue card. The clue cards help students solve the mystery or problem or accomplish the mission. Teams may also receive wild cards with points for such things as the team working well together, helping an opposing team, or going over and above the requirements. Use the wild cards to affirm student acts of empowerment and distribute them at unexpected times during the game to motivate the teams.

7. When a team solves the mystery or problem or accomplishes the mission you've laid out, declare the winner and end the game.

When you use a game to teach content and skills, begin with the standards and identify the nonnegotiable content. As for any other unit design, create essential how or why questions about the content. An essential question is much broader than a factual question; it is one that you want students to answer and remember even if they forget all the other information in the unit. Let's say an essential understanding required by your district is "There is a relationship between and among planets in the solar system." An essential question would not ask students to name the planets in the solar system; rather, it would ask students how the planets in the solar system affect one another.

When you use this game format for instruction, you must pose an additional driving question that defines the game's mission. The mission is the object of the game. The tasks within the game help students learn the nonnegotiable content, but the content doesn't necessarily help students solve the problem or mystery or accomplish the game's mission. It is the clue cards students receive after they complete the tasks that help them accomplish the mission.

If you're having difficulty coming up with a scenario upon which to build your game's mission, think about what your students are interested in. The scenario can connect to the content, but it doesn't have to. Here are some ideas to get you started:

- scavenger hunt for something or someone
- problem-solving search
- conquest to capture or take control of something
- spy search to observe and gather information and report it back
- fairy tale–themed search through an imaginary land

- Harry Potter–themed quest with teams identified by Hogwarts houses Gryffindor, Hufflepuff, Ravenclaw, and Slytherin

- superhero-themed mission to solve environmental, political, or economic problems

- quest in which animals have magical powers

- scenario in which students imagine themselves grossly gigantic or microscopically small

- mission in which someone speaks in a made-up language and can't remember how to speak English

- escape room

Some teachers prefer to set up a game in which the tasks themselves help the players accomplish the mission. For example, one teacher built her game scenario on content but placed the content in a precarious situation. She created a computer game about atomic history with the help of the computer tech person in the school (all students had computers and were able to play during class). The teacher told her students that an important scientist was abducted from history. The students' mission was to find out who was abducted and therefore save that scientist's contribution to modern atomic theory. The teacher had created a digital, interactive map consisting of multiple rooms. When students clicked on a room on the map, they saw a picture of a scientist and read a summary about the scientist. Then they had to answer a question specific to the scientist to gain points and clues to solving the mystery of who among the scientists on the map had gone missing.

The Mystery of the DLES Ghost

Shelly Pelletier, a fourth-grade teacher at Dr. Levesque Elementary School (DLES) in Frenchville, Maine, created a game for her students called "The Mystery of the DLES Ghost" as part of her folklore unit. The students' mission for the game was to determine if DLES was really haunted. She told her students that strange things seemed to be happening throughout the school each evening and asked them to find out if a ghost was causing these things to happen—or if something else was the cause. The students' mission was to check out specific areas throughout the school, collect clues, and complete tasks. Only then would they be able to learn if the school was truly haunted. After telling the students the back-story, Shelly showed them a video trailer that she'd made about the game.

The Mystery of the DLES Ghost game includes the task cards described below. You can see that the tasks are questions to be answered that have nothing to do with finding out whether the school is haunted. The questions are based on the folklore content Shelly wanted her students to learn about. Once they complete their tasks, students receive a clue card that gives them information about the school haunting. Teams choose which task cards they want to complete to get enough points to receive the clue cards.

TASK CARDS
Characteristics of folklore:

- Describe two morals or lessons from children's folktales that could help your team in the game. Your team can choose any method to present the information to the teacher. (five points)

- Identify an example of folklore that no one from your team has read. Using sticky notes, find and mark each characteristic of folklore that you can find in your chosen example. You must find at least five characteristics of folklore in the story. (ten points)

Purposes of story elements:

- Create a story map that could be used to write a piece of folklore. (five points)

- Choose two story elements and create a collage to show why they are important to a story. (five points)

Purposes of plot elements:

- Find two pieces of folklore with similar plots. Discuss with the teacher why they are similar. (five points)

- Create an anchor chart to help your classmates remember the characteristics of each element of plot. (ten points)

Influences of theme:

- Find five quotes that symbolize the theme of love and five quotes that symbolize the theme of existence. (five points)

- Describe three themes found in folklore and give examples of stories in which each is found. (ten points)

Plot structures:

- Find two examples of folklore with a plot structure of "rags to riches." Prove to the teacher through discussion why the stories fit this plot structure. (five points)
- Create a two-minute video trailer for a piece of folklore. The story must have the plot structure of "the quest." (ten points)

Patterns of events:

- Using any digital method, describe the pattern of events that your team feels occurs most often in folklore. (five points)
- Choose two themes in folklore. Why could these themes present a problem to the pattern of events in a story? Present the information to the teacher in any written form. (ten points)

CLUE CARDS

Clue 1: Magnets, vinegar, and beakers galore! Oops! I just made them all hit the floor! No one was here but me until just after 10:23! *(Students will click on the science lab icon on the map.)*

Clue 2: Wobble, bounce, and sit on the floor. Flexible seating will be no more! The squeaking of the ball chairs drives me crazy! *(Students will click on the Grade Four words on the map.)*

Clue 3: I visited the COOLEST place in the school. The view was amazing and the train tracks ruled! It's too bad the kids can no longer use it; after all, I helped to build it bit by bit! *(Students will click on the Loft words on the map.)*

Clue 4: I traveled all around the United States tonight and may have toppled over a few plants in the process. It's a good thing I found a mop and a pail! *(Students will click on the Grade Two words on the map.)*

Clue 5: Two points! My jump shot looks great without the net! Did you know that I played basketball here, way back when?! *(Students will click on the Cafeteria/Gym words on the map.)*

Clue 6: Toilet Paper, paper towels, and water, oh my! I had a blast and made a mess so fast! It's nice to have fun once in a while! *(Students will click on the Girls Bathroom words on the map.)*

Clue 7: You now have six clues that will help you find the answer to this mystery. Can you solve it? The map may help you figure out where to go and if I really am a ghost, but you must use your two feet in order to know! *(Students should use the clues to figure out that the ghost is in the music room, specifically, the music room attic. It would be the only place to find each item. They should also know that the ghost is our school janitor, Dave.)*

WILD CARDS

- Woohoo! You've earned five extra points to add onto your team's score at this stop on your mission.
- Well done! You may choose to change any product that goes with your task card.
- Congratulations! You may steal five points from the next team who advances a level! *(Shelly decided to build in stealing points into her game. Many games do this, but it is certainly not a requirement. You can choose whether to allow point stealing.)*
- Oh no! You heard the ghost's footsteps running through the hall! Your team loses five points at this level!
- Keep this one a secret! Your team found a safe house! You may steal five of another team's points at any time during the game!

THE MAP

Shelly created a digital map that designated four areas of the school where the ghost might have left his mark. The areas included the White Wing, which housed the fourth-grade classroom, science lab, work room, and bathrooms; the Blue Wing with the cafeteria, gym, and music room; the Red Wing, which included the art room, grade two classroom, and French immersion classroom; and the Yellow Wing, with the preK–kindergarten room, occupational therapy room, and a loft. Shelly limited access to the map via Google Docs. Team progress was not shared with the other teams. At various areas on the map, students were required to answer some task cards.

Empowerment in the Game Model

Let's now look at this type of game through the lens of empowerment. Do you think Shelly felt empowered when she created this game? Do you think she felt empowered when she watched her students' level of excitement rise while they were playing the game? The game players themselves experience little *e* empowerment. Students might feel empowered to learn by working in a team. The game may make them feel empowered to be more actively involved in the class. Students who are competitive may rise to the occasion because the game format empowers them to do their best.

Students who create their own games might experience big *E* empowerment. If you teach older students, consider empowering them to create their own games. (You still need to create preassessments to ensure that students learn the nonnegotiable content.) Middle and high school students can take the standards, create tiered questions and activities, and create a game for their classmates to play. A student team creates a mission, backstory, and trailer. You and the students can create the teams, or the students can create their own teams. This decision depends on class dynamics and the degree of control you are willing to give up. You also need to decide whether you will assign the teams to do specific tiered questions targeted at their appropriate level of challenge or students will choose their own levels. Will you assess the formative work?

When using comprehensive games for a unit, you should create a game first and have the students play it so they can see how it works. Afterward, debrief with the students and emphasize the content learning that happens in the game. Then, when you feel your students are ready to create their own games, you can empower them to do so. **Figure 4-1** is a sample organizer showing who might be responsible for what part of designing the game. You can give your students more or less control as you see fit.

Academic Competitions

In this section, we look at why academic competitions are successful, how they relate to empowerment, and how we can replicate certain elements of competition in everyday instruction.

Odyssey of the Mind

Odyssey of the Mind (odysseyofthemind.org) is a creative problem-solving competition that began in 1985 and continues to engage and empower students today. The competitive part of Odyssey of the Mind is for students worldwide from third grade through college. (Younger students in grades K–2 solve a problem specifically geared for their age level and present their solutions noncompetitively.) All teams are limited to seven members and are placed in a division according to the oldest

Figure 4-1 Sample Game Design Organizer

Teacher	Teacher and Students	Students
Lists standards	Form teams	Create the mission and backstory
Lists nonnegotiable content	Teacher assigns tiered questions and students can choose additional ones	Create the trailer
Develops and gives preassessment to all students		Create tiered questions
Develops, gives, and reviews summative assessment		Create activities
Provides scaffolding and assistance where and when needed		Create formative assessment and give teams feedback
		Keep track of who is doing what task when

age (international) or highest grade (United States) of the students on the team. Each year five problems are offered and the team chooses which of the five they want to compete in. The same problems are offered to students in all the competitive divisions, but students compete only against other teams in their own division. The five general types of problems in this competition are: creating cars that perform tasks, building some sort of contraption, designing weight-bearing structures, performing based on a given theme, and performing based on the classics in literature, art, and architecture. Each year these problems are wrapped around literary genres or specific scientific principles. Teams must follow these rules:

- The team must come up with a solution to the problem, create the solution, perform the solution, and answer questions posed by the judges with no outside help. An adult may not come up with ideas or make suggestions about using different materials or methods. The team succeeds or fails on its own merits.

- Students must rely on one another. If team members do not pull their weight, the team suffers. Therefore, it benefits the team members to work together.

BADGES

A badge is an emblem awarded for an accomplishment. It can be a physical emblem or a digital one. Scouting organizations award badges, the military awards badges, and video games award badges. Colleges, universities, and professional development organizations award badges for education and training achievements.

Students could earn badges for doing a variety of specific things. For example, if students complete all three tasks in a game-based learning unit, they receive a badge. Teachers might give a badge to students on one team who help students on another team. Or teachers might award badges for doing really challenging things, such as students contacting their senator and presenting their position on an issue.

Many students want badges and are willing to work hard to get them. Badges can encourage students to put in effort and try things differently. They provide external motivation because they are given to students as evidence of what they have accomplished. Some students are not motivated to learn something just because you tell them they should learn it. For these students, externally motivating them with badges can spark their internal drive. If a badge system is set up well, it can inspire students to know more and result in a motivation shift from external to internal. Unlike a traditional grading system, a badge provides positive specific feedback on student achievements. The badge system does not work when it rewards the wrong behavior or rewards a behavior unnecessarily. If students are already internally motivated, badges may not be necessary, but usually students have fun collecting them anyway.

In a 2013 study, researchers found that badges support students in setting goals and motivate them to reach these goals (Abramovich, Shunn, and Higashi 2013). However, they also found that badge types affect learner motivation and learning performance. If badges are designed in a content area where the learner does not excel, it could result in a negative effect. This study suggests that the various levels of questions or tasks should be delegated to students who can experience success with them. By letting students choose their own level, the teacher may set students up for failure because students may have unrealistic expectations and choose to over- or under-challenge themselves.

Some badges showcase what students have learned. Each badge should be tied to an objective or outcome that students demonstrate. The badge represents evidence of learning that students self-report. If students do not care about badges, they may not report their learning. This is why it is important to have badging procedures in place. For badging to be effective, you must identify the nonnegotiable learning, the specific criteria, skills, and standards that students need to master. Then, you decide on a badging platform to use, such as Open Badges (openbadges.org). You can empower students by giving them voice and choice in their assignments, but you determine the criteria for each badge. Be sure to issue badges in a timely manner when students meet the criteria. Decide whether to display badges on a digital bulletin board, a physical bulletin board, or in an individual student's digital portfolio.

- The team must perform the solution to the problem in eight minutes. The team loses points if it goes over time.

- Each team has a budget. Team members must itemize all their expenses even if they don't actually buy something. For example, if a team uses duct tape, cardboard, and markers supplied by the school, the team must still place a monetary value on them and note them in the budget. In this way, no team has an advantage due to economic disparities.

Odyssey of the Mind scores teams in three categories: solution and presentation, style, and spontaneous problem-solving. First, students are scored on how they present their solution to the problem they have chosen. They can receive up to two hundred points in this category. Students are well aware of what aspects of their solution will earn them more points. The elements to be scored are not all of equal worth. The score for how well an invention works may be worth three times the score for what an invention looks like.

Students are also scored on style. This category is worth fifty points. Parts of a team's solution are scored separately on style. For example, a team could be scored on a costume, a prop that transforms from one use to another use, or background scenery.

Finally, students are scored on their spontaneous responses to a verbal, hands-on, or verbal–hands-on problem. This category is worth one hundred points. In a verbal problem, students usually have three minutes to respond to a prompt they have never heard before. For example, they have three minutes to describe all the uses for a pipe cleaner. Students who give an unusual response will score three or five points, while students who give a common response will score one point. A related verbal–hands-on problem might be to give students a pipe cleaner. They must show what the pipe cleaner could be used for and describe what they are showing. A related hands-on problem would be to give students five minutes to physically create something using a pipe cleaner and other provided materials provided and tell what unusual use this creation would serve. A judge keeps track of the spontaneous responses and scores them. The team does not know what type of spontaneous problem it will receive until the competition. Therefore, the team must practice and come up with strategies to deal with all three types of spontaneous problems.

Odyssey of the Mind teams in the United States compete regionally, then statewide. If the team places first in all of those competitions, it moves directly to world finals. There is no national competition in the United States. Teams outside the United States may compete on a provincial level. Each country decides how it will determine which team moves on to the world finals. The world finals always take place in the United States. Since the competition was created in New Jersey, the organization has chosen to continue to host the international competition in the United States on university campuses.

Like a sports team, when an Odyssey of the Mind team reaches this high level of competition, the students are not just engaged. They are empowered. At the world finals, the first-place US state teams compete against other first-place teams from around the world. In order to attend the world finals, most teams raise their own money.

Let's identify what is valuable about the Odyssey of the Mind competition and translate it to classroom practice.

- **Team size:** Seven students may seem like a lot, but when students are working on something big, they often need to work with several teammates to accomplish the necessary tasks on time.

- **Established dates and times:** Students need enough time to complete their tasks but not so much time as to get bored. If students are competitive, they will want to beat the other teams and will likely exceed the time you designate for them. (My students spent more time than they would have on a sports team. Since this involved after-school time and sometimes even weekend time, if students were on an Odyssey of the Mind team, they could not participate on a sports team at the same time. Some students had to choose.)

- **Five types of problems:** Students can choose problems that suit their personal styles and learning preferences. This choice levels the playing field and allows students to do their best work.

- **No adult help:** Students learn to be self-directed and not depend on adults to solve problems for them. Student autonomy also levels the playing field. One team cannot do better than another team just because the parents of its team members help them at home. Student autonomy does not mean the coach sits back and does nothing. In Odyssey of the Mind, a student can tell you she wants to make a hole in a piece of wood. You can show her how to make a hole, but the student must come up with the idea to make a hole, learn how to make a hole with a power tool, and make the hole in her piece of wood herself. A coach must give control to the students. Even if the coach knows a quicker, better, or more effective way to do something, the coach cannot give suggestions; however, the coach can ask enough questions that guide the students to figure it out on their own.

- **Limited budget:** This also helps level the playing field. When all teams have the same budget, one team cannot get ahead just because it has more money. Students do not use real cash to go out and buy materials. Rather, they must determine the value of the materials they use.

MY EXPERIENCE AS AN ODYSSEY OF THE MIND COACH

I was an Odyssey of the Mind coach for nineteen years. I was also responsible for finding coaches for our school's other teams. There are five long-term problems that students can compete in, which means there are five first-place winners, one for each problem, in each division. One year, five teams from our school district placed first and moved on to the world finals. It costs about seven thousand dollars per team to attend the world finals, including travel, housing, and food expenses for the team members and their volunteer coach. This meant, that year, we had to raise thirty-five thousand dollars, and we had eight weeks to do it. The school is in a town of eight thousand people, and it wasn't rich with resources. I knew brownie sales would not help us reach our goal, which was to raise the entire amount for all students and the volunteer coaches.

We decided each of our five teams was responsible for raising its own money. Fortunately, Odyssey of the Mind does not set forth any rules about fundraising. Adults can help, and parents knew that without their help, traveling to the world finals was not going to happen. We held weekly meetings for adults and families. All five teams were at school every weekend and most afternoons into the evenings either practicing or fundraising. Teams supported their members who did not have home support. We accessed the local news media, created a letter-writing campaign, and came up with a variety of other ideas to meet our goal. Students were involved throughout the process. In the end, the school committee gave us half the money and the rest of the money was raised by all involved. Our little town of eight thousand people sent the thirty-five students and their coaches to the University of Tennessee to compete on a world stage without costing the students' families or the volunteer coaches a single penny.

For many of our students, this was their first time on an airplane, flying to a different state, and staying in a dorm on a university campus where the competition was held. It was also their first experience with pin trading. Each state and country has a lapel pin specific to where they are from and what problem they competed in. In my state, a student designs the lapel pins each year. Students trade these pins at the world finals with students from other states and countries. Students quickly learned that some pins were more desirable than others. The pins of great value either had moving parts or were a set or had some unique feature. Students learned that sometimes they had to trade two or more pins for one really special pin. There was an unspoken rule that no money could ever be exchanged for a pin. The competition even had places specifically designated for pin trading. When teams found themselves with free time on their hands, they often would go to the pin-trading tent. This was a wonderful way for students to meet other students from other states and from all over the world. It was also a great lesson in economics.

- **Authentic audience:** It is important for students to present their creations to a real audience before the actual competition. The real audience could be composed of parents or other students in the building. Students can also record their performance and make it available on the school website.

- **Scoring:** All elements of the competition are scored, but not all elements are of equal value. Students learn to spend more time on what counts more. They develop time-management skills.

- **Rewards:** Students compete against other students from their region, state, or province. If they win these competitions, they compete at the world finals. This means a big trip with teammates, meeting peers from other states and from all over the world, and all sorts of adventures. Educators can establish rewards at the school or district level too, such as a pizza party, a gift certificate at the school store, a gum-chewing day, or some other item or privilege that students value.

If you want to create your own competition modeled after Odyssey of the Mind, you could do so. Let's say a sixth-grade ELA teacher wants to use these ideas to create a competition for her class, which is studying fairy tales as a literary genre. Students would need to know the nonnegotiable content, which is that a fairy tale is a type of short story that includes the following specific elements: once upon a time, talking animals, a land far away, enchanted setting, good versus evil, things happen in threes, and magic. The teacher designs the problem choices and the summative assessment for the fairy-tale unit based on the competition described in **figure** 4-2. In this example, the teacher provides the winning team of students with a choice of rewards.

If you choose to hold this type of academic competition, it is important for your students to perform their solution for a real audience, because students will work harder for an authentic audience than they will for their teacher or classmates. Let students perform in front of a whole-school assembly. Let them perform for another classroom. Invite a reporter from the local cable TV station to record students on video and air their performances. Invite a local newspaper reporter to run a brief news story on your unit. If you really want to see your students soar, invite another teacher at your grade level to teach the same unit at the same time and participate in the competition with your class.

Address style points through an additional rubric that defines what performances should look like. In this rubric, students might lose style points for sloppy or unappealing work. They might gain style points if they present their solution with flair. Other aspects of style may be incorporating a theme, such as costuming that reflects a time period or location, or stylizing diction or accent. Address the spontaneous response aspect of the competition by connecting a prompt to the content learning. If students know the spontaneous prompt will be based on their homework from the unit, it is likely they will do their homework and review it before the competition.

If you would prefer to set up a cooperative unit instead of a competitive unit, assign different components of the problem to different teams. Then the teams will have to work together to complete the solution. The teams present their cooperative solution to a real audience, but the presentations are not competitive, and there are no rewards. Teams receive a completed rubric with feedback just as they would with any other type of summative assessment.

Figure 4-2 Sample Classroom Competition Based on Odyssey of the Mind

Teams	Students select their own teams of four. A productive team consists of members who bring a variety of skills to the team.
Dates	The competition lasts one week from start to finish, Monday to Monday. Mandatory team meetings occur during ELA class every day for sixty minutes. Teams can also meet on their own whenever they like.
Problems	Choose one: 1. Create and perform a skit about a specific fairy tale that substitutes one character for a character from a different fairy tale, includes a prop with a moving part, has an elaborate student-designed set, and has a surprise ending. 2. Create a fairy-tale mall that includes stores representing six different fairy tales. The mall must fit on four desktops. Create a magical prop for one of the stores. Create a script in which a fairy-tale character describes the stores and their merchandise to potential customers. 3. Create a fairy-tale amusement park. The park must include at least two typical rides, such as a Ferris wheel and a roller coaster. These rides must demonstrate simple machine principles, such as the use of inclined planes, levers, and pulleys. Name the rides after fairy-tale characters and explain your naming choices.
Rules	Teams may not receive help. Accepting outside help will cost a team points on its project. At the end of the competition, the teacher will ask each team who came up with the ideas and who constructed the solutions.
Budget	Each team's budget is equivalent to seventy-five dollars. The team will not receive or spend actual money. The team will use recycled materials to create its solution to its chosen problem.
Presentation	Once teams create their solutions, they invite a real audience to view their skits or presentations. The audience should not only enjoy each performance but also learn something about fairy tales.
Scoring and Feedback	The teacher will score teams on how well they solved their chosen problems. Specifically, teams will be scored on creativity, uniqueness, and inclusion of standards and content. They will also be scored on how well they stayed within their budget, if they received any help, and if they completed their project on time.
Rewards	1. Each student on the winning team will receive one homework pass usable anytime during the current quarter. 2. Each team member will receive an A grade for the unit. 3. The team members design their own reward, subject to teacher approval.

COMPETITION VERSUS COOPERATION

In the field of education, there is more and more emphasis on cooperative learning rather than competitive learning. Some students find competition empowering, while others do not. Some students have trouble tolerating losing. These students need to learn the skill of losing. Students will be part of a global competitive world, so we should discuss with them what healthy competition looks like and how it can benefit them. At the same time, constant competition is not a balanced approach to education. Students need to learn and practice cooperative skills as well so they can learn how to get along with others.

Future Problem Solving Program (FPSP)

Future Problem Solving Program (FPSP) is another international academic competition that empowers students. It's engaging because students like to see problems in the extreme and set in the future. It's empowering because it helps students think about their own futures. The FPSP chooses a current problem and blows it out of proportion. The team's task is to come up with a solution that prevents the problem from growing to the point that is described in the futuristic scenario. Each year there are five topics that students can choose to research. These five topics provide the foundation for the Global Issue Problem Solving, Scenario Performance, and Scenario Writing Competitions. These three topics, plus the Community Problem Solving and Action Based Problem Solving, are areas in which students can compete against other students in their state at their grade level span (juniors in grades 4–6, middle in grades 7–9, and seniors in grades 10–12). The Program includes a primary noncompetitive program for grades K–3.

Many schools are already involved in this competition. If you are interested in finding out more about it, visit fpspi.org. This competition is particularly suitable for students who are issue-oriented and who like to research and write. Students are asked to think about and research some of the most complex problems we face today as a global society and use their language skills to develop solutions to problems and persuade others to support their ideas. FPSP is a yearlong program in which teams of four students use a step-by-step process to solve realistic problems of the future. Every few months, teams complete a practice problem and mail in their solution. The solution is reviewed by outside evaluators. The evaluators give students specific feedback so they can improve their problem-solving and writing skills for the final competition. As with Odyssey of the Mind, the state winners go to an international competition.

FPSP challenges students to address real-world issues such as artificial intelligence, media impact, rage and bullying, sensory overload, food distribution, and invasive species. The students are given the topic ahead of time and research it prior to attending competition. When they arrive at the competition site, they go to a classroom where they are given the "fuzzy" scenario set in the future that addresses the topic. The team has two hours from start to finish to identify many challenges in the scenario, to determine the underlying problem, to brainstorm up to sixteen solutions to solve the underlying problem, to identify criteria that can be used to rate their solutions, to rank their solutions in a grid in order to determine their best idea, and to develop an action plan to carry out their chosen solution. Students are scored on how many ideas they come up with and how different and original their ideas are. They are also scored on the clarity of their write-up. Solutions are scored on relevancy and the degree of elaboration used to explain the who, what, when, where, and how elements.

You can also purchase FPSP materials and use them in your classroom noncompetitively. I found this program works well for teaching the writing process. The rubric serves as a guide to help students break down specifics in the process. If you do not want to purchase FPSP materials, you can create your own version of the program with problem-solving scenarios just as you would with any problem-based learning. Find issues or problems in any content area and create scenarios set in the future. The following example shows a future scenario for a fairy-tale unit using the FPSP structure. This scenario addresses societal class in the story of Cinderella.

The class system is a theme threaded throughout the story of Cinderella. For example, Cinderella is seen as poor and is bossed around by her richer stepmother and stepsisters. The prince, by contrast, is nicely dressed and is waited on hand and foot. Let's change the scenario and set this fairy tale in 2030. This new scenario might go something like this.

In the year 2030, the class system has become starkly obvious. Society consists of the very rich and the very poor, with few in between. The very poor have little chance to improve their lives. College education is no longer affordable to working-class people. Poor people cannot get the education they need to rise out of poverty. They can no longer afford medical care. The poor are dying at a younger age and in larger numbers than the rich. Few people marry across socioeconomic classes. News alerts announce that fairy godmothers no longer exist. They have finally died out. The poor are resorting to taking magic potions to feel good. They are joining cults so that they feel a sense of community. It seems that society is breaking down. Your team has been asked to attend a global summit at the White House to determine what can be done.

After you give your students the scenario, give them a blank worksheet with the six steps listed below. Have them identify the challenges, choose the underlying problem, brainstorm solutions, set criteria to evaluate solutions, choose a solution, and create an action plan. Then, have them think about in what ways this scenario is the same or different from the Cinderella story. Here are what student responses might look like:

The challenges:

- Poor people see no way to rise out of poverty.
- Poor people are getting sick and can't afford medical care.
- Poor people can't afford education.
- Fairy godmothers have become extinct.
- Poor people are resorting to magic potions and joining cults.
- Societal norms are breaking down.

Underlying problem:
How might we provide poor people with an education so that they can attend college, get good jobs, and raise their standard of living?

Solutions:

- The government provides free college education for all its citizens.
- The government raises rich people's taxes. The government uses the additional tax money for poor people's college education.
- The colleges will close because not enough people will be attending. Then everyone will have to learn what they need to know from other people or on the internet.
- Society will break down, and money will become useless. We will go back to a bartering system. People who know the trades will become the rich ones. The currently rich people who are not in the trades will end up being the poor people. We will create a new type of economy.

Solution criteria:

- relevancy
- breadth of impact
- immediacy
- staying power

The solution:
The government will provide free college tuition for all its citizens because this will affect the most people and will help them rise in economic status and get good jobs. People will then be able to afford better food and medical care.

Plan of action:
The government will collect taxes from the wealthiest people, who are currently exempt from paying taxes or who pay little in taxes. Anyone who makes more than a certain amount of money will be required to contribute to the education fund. All colleges will receive this money, which means college will be free for everyone. When more people are educated, more people will get good jobs, and more people will be able to contribute to the education fund.

Chapter Summary

Game-based education and competitions are two ways in which teachers can empower their students. Both can provide little *e* empowerment or Big *E* empowerment depending on the level of student self-involvement. Teachers can choose to set up a game cooperatively by emphasizing the team interactions and minimizing the "us versus them" mentality or empower students to choose whether they would like to play a game cooperatively or competitively. Teachers may create the games but can also empower students to create their own games. It is likely most students will not have the skills to create electronic games from scratch, but they can use websites such as kahoot.com to plug in content information to a preprogrammed game format. It is important to remind students of the elements of gaming that Willis talks about (page 74) so the student-generated games are instructional and fun to play. The games should not be about tricking their friends but about creating challenging questions, developing a fair point system, and providing their friends with feedback. Academic competitions such as Odyssey of the Mind and the Future Problem Solving Program also provide little *e* and Big *E* experiences. Students can participate in these programs, or you can identify the elements that make these programs so successful and share the ideas with your students so they can apply the ideas when they create their own mini versions of these games and programs.

Discussion Questions

1. How do you feel about game-based education?

2. In what ways might you gamify your instruction?

3. How might gamification provide a forum for student empowerment?

4. What role do badges play in education now? What role might they play in the future?

5. Evaluate the role of competition as a teaching tool.

After you've thought about your answers to these questions, visit this website for a video chapter review with the author: freespirit.com/empower-videos.

Three Tiers of Gaming Verbs

Level Three: Extended Thinking

Design

Create

Analyze results

Apply concepts

Examine alternative perspectives

Prove

Conduct investigations

Synthesize

Provide alternative solutions

Elaborate with detail

Level Two: Recall, Strategic Thinking

Revise

Develop an argument

Assess

Differentiate

Draw conclusions

Cite evidence

Hypothesize

Prioritize

Formulate

Critique

Make connections

Recognize misconceptions

Develop a model

Judge

Justify

Level One: Recall, Skill/Concept

Define

Identify

Tell

Arrange

List

Graph

Classify

Estimate

Relate

Predict

Summarize

Show

Organize

Categorize

Modify

Use

Measure

Illustrate

Interpret

Compare

Create Just-Right Questions for Gaming

Brainstorm questions for your game. Let your ideas flow. Write these questions in the left column of the chart below. Now think about whether these are just-right questions for your game players. You might want to see if you can make better questions by checking the words in the **Three Tiers of Gaming Verbs** list. Choose words from the appropriate level for your players. Now revise your questions in the right column next to your original brainstormed list of questions. The first row of the chart provides an example for you.

Brainstormed List of Questions for Your Game	Revised Questions Based on the Three Tiers of Gaming Verbs
Do sedimentary rocks flake apart easily?	Justify why sedimentary rocks flake apart easily or why they don't, and design a sketch to demonstrate your point using the ShowMe app.

To create good questions, be aware of your audience. It is not fun for the players of your game if they cannot answer your questions. Nor is it fun if the players have no trouble answering your questions; perhaps your questions are too easy. Your challenge is to come up with just-right questions that make the players think.

FROM DIFFERENTIATION TO PERSONALIZED LEARNING

Part 1 began with an overview of engagement and built to a discussion about student empowerment. Part 2 is organized the same way, but here the overview begins with differentiation and builds to a discussion about personalized learning. It is important to understand the underpinnings of differentiation before we shift into the elements of personalized learning. Because teachers provide options and choices when differentiating, it is likely students will be engaged. With personalizing learning, it is likely the students will be empowered because the students provide their own options and choices. Even though teachers take into account students' interests, abilities, and needs when differentiating, differentiation emphasizes a more teacher-driven rather than student-driven approach to learning. After revisiting differentiation in chapter 5, the focus in the subsequent chapters shifts to student-driven learning with much more emphasis on personalization and empowerment. The final chapter embraces social and emotional learning as essential to the well-being of the student. A social and emotional model that can be integrated into curriculum provides a possible way of addressing the affective component of personalized learning and student empowerment.

CHAPTER 5

Differentiation Revisited

Shifting from differentiated instruction to personalized learning is a natural progression. To make this shift happen, it is important for teachers to reflect on their differentiation practice to see where and when they differentiate and determine whether they want to fine-tune their instruction. But first, we must unpack what the term *differentiation* means and consider how we might refresh our practice. As you read the chapter, think about the difference between differentiation and personalized learning. Think about when you differentiate and try to determine whether personalization may be more effective.

Differentiation Defined

Differentiation does not have one universal definition. It is a multifaceted concept. Sometimes educators confuse differentiation with personalization. That's an easy mistake to make, because personalized learning is a natural extension of differentiation. **Differentiation means meeting more of the students' needs more of the time, while personalized learning means students directing their own learning more of the time.**

Differentiation should be intentional and proactive in order to meet the needs of learners. Differentiated instruction is the process of identifying students' individual learning strengths, needs, and interests and adapting lessons to match those strengths, needs, and interests. According to a US Department of Education report, "Differentiated instruction requires teachers to be flexible in their approach to teaching and adjust the curriculum and presentation of information to learners rather than expecting students to modify themselves for the curriculum. The intent of differentiated instruction is to maximize each student's growth and individual success by meeting each student where he or she is and assisting in the learning process" (Hall, Strangman, and Meyer 2003).

Differentiation is based on informed decision-making. Carol Ann Tomlinson, respected educator and researcher in the field of differentiation, suggests

to teachers that differentiation is not meant to be a round-the-clock approach with all students in all content all the time. She says it is more about attending to content based on meaning, authenticity, and who students are and assessing classroom elements to connect content to learners whenever possible (Sousa and Tomlinson 2018). Tomlinson's model of differentiation consists of modifying content (what students will learn), process (types of activities students engage in), products (how students show what they know, understand, and can do), and affect (social and emotional needs). She encourages teachers to address students' readiness, interests, and learning profiles by differentiating one or more of the elements in her model.

Research on differentiated instruction is limited due to its varying definitions and implementations. However, studies on the practices that compose differentiation have proven them effective. Researchers in Connecticut found evidence that the achievement gap "between rich and poor and among different ethnic groups" narrowed at the elementary school level when enriched curriculum and differentiation were used with all students (Beecher and Sweeny 2008). Another study of middle school students showed that students who received differentiated instruction demonstrated significant achievement compared to the control group (Brighton et al. 2005). In a multiyear study at a high school, the dropout rate fell and student participation in Advanced Placement (AP) courses rose almost by half with exam scores holding or rising despite increased enrollment. The differentiation practice continued for seven years, and the achievement gains continued throughout those years (Tomlinson, Brimijoin, and Narvaez 2008). A three-year study of K–12 mixed-ability classrooms found that students with mild or severe learning disabilities benefited greatly from differentiated instruction delivered in small groups or with targeted instruction (Rock et al. 2008). Educational psychologist Carol Tieso found that differentiated instruction in math was effective for high-ability students. These students were preassessed and placed in groups commensurate with their performance level, and received supplemental textbook instruction. They outperformed the students who received whole-class instruction and used the textbook (Tieso 2005).

Differentiation means teachers use a variety of strategies to meet the variety of students' needs when teaching the same objective. It does not mean using strategies at random in hopes that they will reach some of the students some of the time. This random approach is far less effective than specifically matching strategies to students' needs and interests. To be effective, differentiation must be intentional. Intentional differentiation equals high-quality teaching plus common sense. When teachers use intentional differentiation, they:

* create a positive classroom climate

* know their students

* use data from preassessments and formative assessments

* use flexible grouping

* allow for choice

* make learning real and relevant

* set appropriate student goals

* use strategies to motivate, engage, and empower students

Limiting Beliefs About Differentiation

Sometimes, limiting beliefs inhibit teachers' willingness to differentiate. One such belief is the notion that "I can't differentiate because I can take students only so far. I can't teach students what next year's teacher is supposed to teach them." This belief produces a glass-ceiling effect. Students can't advance because teachers believe the content is someone else's territory. But when students master their grade-level content, they should be able to advance to the next year's content. Grade-bound materials also create a glass ceiling. For example, when a district uses a fifth-grade math textbook and students master all the material in the book, they should be allowed to work in the sixth-grade book or work on the fifth-grade skills at a deeper level. It is easier to differentiate when you're not required use one prescribed program. If you are required to use a specific program, you should be able to use it to anchor your content, but not feel restricted by it. You

should be able to make the content simpler or more complex depending on the needs of your students.

Another limiting belief is that whole-class instruction is usually the best choice. This is not to say that whole-class instruction is never the right choice. But when it's used all the time, the advanced students become bored, and the struggling students are left behind. There are so many instructional strategies and techniques that are far more engaging than whole-group instruction. No matter what strategies you use, keep in mind what students need and what motivates them. In the differentiated classroom, students engage in content that's real and relevant to them. Meanwhile, you define the learning, provide choices, let students know what they need to learn, tell them why they are learning it, and explain how they might use this new knowledge.

A third important limiting belief is that it's enough to simply know how to differentiate instruction. But if you don't have a rapport with your students and don't create a safe and caring classroom environment, your differentiation efforts will fall short. First and foremost, you must build relationships with your students. The relationships between you and your students and among your students must be built upon mutual respect. Students need to understand that their classmates are doing different things and learning at different rates—and that is okay. Explain that all students deserve to be challenged and to learn new things. Teach them that students have many strengths and weaknesses, and that if we were all the same, life would be quite boring. Unique opinions, ideas, and preferences help broaden our perspective. In a differentiated classroom, teachers and students often create classroom rules of behavior that include such things as acceptance, listening to others, honesty, integrity, and willingness to help others. You can come up with your own rules or use preexisting lists, such as Bena Kallick and Arthur Costa's sixteen Habits of Mind (Costa and Kallick 2008). For more information on Habits of Mind, see page 175 in chapter 8. Or you could use the Habits of Work developed by the Great Schools Partnership. The Habits of Work address three major categories: ethical awareness, collaboration, and civic mindfulness (Great Schools Partnership 2019). Remember that rules are not effective if students do not pay attention to them. It is up to you and your students to carry out these rules.

The Eight Key Elements of Differentiation

Once you and your students have established the classroom tone and you have built relationships with them, begin to focus proactively on the eight key elements of differentiation:

1. learner academic, social, and emotional characteristics

2. preassessment and formative assessment

3. pacing

4. flexible grouping

5. open-ended tasks and questioning

6. simple to complex content

7. low- to high-level thinking

8. product options for summative assessment

Element 1: Learner Academic, Social, and Emotional Characteristics

When teachers differentiate, they often first consider the amount of content that needs to be covered in a certain amount of time. Teachers certainly should focus on content, but they must simultaneously consider the characteristics of their learners. The students' characteristics and behaviors influence the ways in which teachers should differentiate.

Differentiation means that when students struggle to learn, teachers make adjustments. For example, you might ask them to make a few points rather than many points. You might limit the text portion rather than have struggling readers read the whole thing. When students have limited language ability, you might offer them a multiple-choice quiz rather than have them write an essay. You might personalize their goals or scaffold supports for them.

Differentiation means that when advanced students know content, you do not want them to simply add more points, read more, or write more. We call this more of the same (MOTS). What advanced learners need is more sophisticated or complex content. They may actually read fewer pages, but the pages deal with more abstract issues and concepts. They may need more time rather than less time to tackle the complexity and depth

of a differentiated assignment. All students deserve to be challenged academically. Research has found that a key to intrinsic motivation is feeling that you are making progress in meaningful work (Amabile and Kramer 2011).

Differentiation is not just for struggling and advanced learners. Differentiation is for all learners. Teachers need to know many ways to boost students' interest, grab their attention, chunk and pause information, use prediction to spark curiosity, and hook them through inquiry—all based on learner characteristics. For example, students who are perfectionists might be more comfortable answering why or how questions. When you ask them to justify their responses with text references and quotes, this justification reassures students that their opinions can be backed up and are defensible. Creative learners would much rather formulate their own questions and use possibility thinking to create what-if questions. After working with students all day every day for a few months, elementary teachers can usually identify students' characteristics and needs. It is much harder for middle and high school teachers, who work with more students for shorter periods of time, to figure out individual strengths and weaknesses.

To find out more about your students' preferences, you can use the reproducible **Learner Survey** on page 113, create your own survey, or use one of the many available online. The Learner Survey consists of tendencies and traits students exhibit in the classroom. Students will likely fit into more than one category and, as with any self-inventory, the information you receive may not be comprehensive. However, the information may be helpful for two reasons. You will gain insight into how the students view themselves and you will gain knowledge about students who demonstrate various observable behaviors. The survey is based on the following six tendencies and traits of students (Drapeau 2004):

1. Academic learners are compliant, high-achieving students. They are successful in school but are often dependent upon teacher recognition and constant reassurance. They may like to work faster than others because they grasp knowledge and skills easily. They thrive on complexity and depth, so long as expectations are clear.

2. Perfectionist learners are similar to academic learners but are more consumed with doing their absolute best. They sometimes do not feel worthy of praise. Their perfectionism can disable them. Extreme

perfectionists may stop doing their assignments to avoid making mistakes, which they see as failure.

3. Creative learners like to come up with unusual ideas and often think of other ways to do things. They like to experiment or play with ideas because they are possibility thinkers.

4. Challenged learners find school difficult and may feel as if they constantly have to keep up with others. They can get discouraged and frustrated and may start to exhibit a defeatist attitude.

5. Hesitant learners like to hide. These students do not want to speak aloud in class even when they know the answers. They usually prefer to work alone or with one close friend. They do not attract either positive or negative attention, and they do not want to stand out in any way.

6. High-energy learners have no problem learning if they are moving around. They may have trouble focusing, especially if they have to sit for too long. Lecture is not a good strategy to use with these learners. Kinesthetic activities work best.

The learner survey is short, so as not to overwhelm students. It is designed for students in grades three through twelve. If you work with younger students, you can simplify the language or give students examples to show what the statements mean. Young students may have unrealistic perceptions of themselves, but the survey could still give you useful information about your students. If you work with middle or high school students, you can add questions that seem appropriate for each category. If students are truthful when they complete the survey, you may gain information that will help you differentiate. This survey is not designed to assess readiness, but to address learner characteristics so you can choose specific strategies that will meet more of your students' needs more of the time.

It is best to give a learner survey to your students at the beginning of the year. Students complete the survey individually. Offer support to students who need help reading or interpreting the questions. Once students have written "yes" or "no" next to all the statements, they identify which group they associate with most by determining which category has the most yes answers.

One eighth-grade teacher did the Learner Survey with her students. She used the survey, along with a multiple intelligences survey, to get a broader picture of her students' preferences. The teacher was sensitive about using labels, especially with middle school students. She talked about how students could use labels to think about their own thinking and recognize their learning preferences. After she gave the survey to her students, she discovered that the class that gave her behavior management problems was made up of 90 percent creative and high-energy learners. Using this information, she changed the instructional strategies she used with this class. She also used the information to group students in all her classes. She commented that she learned more about individual students as well. She talked about a student who described himself as a challenged student and a perfectionist. She had already known about how hard he had to work to learn, but she'd been unaware that he was a perfectionist. Now she could imagine the frustration this combination must have been causing him. She began differentiating for the hesitant learner she discovered, whom she now calls on when she knows they know the answer. She also started pushing the academic and perfectionist learners to monitor their own progress rather than constantly checking with her to make sure their work was good enough.

Element 2: Preassessment and Formative Assessment

Assessment is not only a way to chart student growth, but also a key element of differentiation. Use preassessment and formative assessment to evaluate your students' readiness and interest and to inform your differentiated instruction.

PREASSESSMENT

When you're planning a new unit, you must identify the nonnegotiable content and gauge students' prior knowledge with a preassessment. When you create or choose a preassessment, you must know what you want your students to know and be able to do. There are many types of preassessment you can use. In this section, we'll discuss just a few: KTW charts; concept webs, maps, and lists; and journals, quizzes, and conferences.

Regardless of what type of preassessment you use, it should allow you to see differences among your students. Make sure your students understand that the preassessment is not a test of what you have taught them. It is just a way to gather information to guide you, so you can adjust your teaching to make it appropriate for each learner. Tell students that if they don't know any answers, that's great! That means you're preparing work for them that's right on target, and they will be learning new information or skills. If students already do know some of the information, tell them that you will be adjusting the lessons based upon what they already know.

Preassessment occurs before the start of a unit. Take care not to assume that a student knows nothing in a content area just because it's not that student's area of strength. You should preassess all students before each unit, because you never know when a student might surprise you with prior knowledge.

You do not always have to create your own preassessments. For example, you might be using a math textbook that offers a few quizzes in each chapter. You can use one of the quizzes for a preassessment. You could even use the end-of-chapter quiz, with or without a few numbers changed. Perhaps you feel it's okay if students remember the exact questions when they reach the end of the chapter and it's time for a summative assessment—the point is that students learn how to do the math. Whether you devise your own preassessments, modify textbook assessments, or use summative assessments as preassessments is up to you. No single preassessment tool will work for all teachers in all situations. You should decide for yourself what makes sense for you in your classroom.

KTW Chart

One commonly used preassessment is a KWL chart, in which students first identify what they **know** and what they **want** to know, and later what they **learned**. On page 115, you'll find a reproducible variation of this called the **KTW Chart**. In this chart, students identify what they **know** and their source, what they **think** they know and their source, and what they **wonder** about. In the first column, students list what they are *sure* they know and how they know it. Did they learn it from home, from a previous teacher, or on their own? In the second column, students list information that they are *pretty sure* about but not 100 percent sure. They may remember only pieces of information, or perhaps they can formulate only incomplete thoughts. Here again they must write their source. In the first and second columns, students' responses are affected by their ability to remember information on demand, writing ability, and motivation. In the third column, students list what they *wonder* about. This helps teachers find out about students' interests and level of curiosity.

Concept Webs, Maps, and Lists

Another useful preassessment technique is having students create a concept web, map, or list. A concept web or map is a graphic representation of a student's conceptual understanding. It is handy for preassessing students' understanding of an issue, problem, or principle. **Figure 5-1** shows an example of a student-drawn concept map. In this example, the student free-associates what she knows about the problems with space pollution. The teacher is surprised by the depth of knowledge she

FIGURE 5-1 Sample Concept Map

demonstrated. He asks the student where she learned about space pollution, and the student says she learned about it in her previous school. Now that the teacher realizes the student knows almost all of what he plans to teach in this unit, he knows he shouldn't make her sit through introductory-level material about space objects. Clearly, the teacher needs to differentiate for this student.

Some students do not like concept webs. The information looks confusing to them, and they have difficulty making sense of words in circles on a paper. They might simply prefer to list attributes or characteristics. A list may be an effective preassessment tool, especially if you are assessing less complex or factual knowledge—for example, if you want students to identify parts of a microscope or characteristics of a Shakespearean tragic hero. See **figure 5-2**.

It may be helpful to give your students a choice of preassessments. For example, you might say, "Use a KTW chart, a concept web, or a list to describe the rainforest." Some students like to web ideas because it taps into their ability to free-associate. Other students prefer to use a KTW chart because they like to chunk and categorize information. Still others like to simply list ideas. When students have a choice of preassessment, they may feel more empowered and motivated to take the preassessment seriously.

Journals, Quizzes, and Conferences

When you want students to elaborate on their prior knowledge, one effective preassessment technique is to ask them to respond in their journals. A journal preassessment gives you an opportunity to write back to your students for clarification. This technique is particularly effective for students who like to write more than one- or two-word responses. You can also use short-answer quizzes as preassessments. This type of preassessment, like a journal, allows for multiword responses. For students who prefer to talk rather than write or who enjoy one-on-one teacher attention, a student-teacher conference can be a very effective preassessment technique. The conference gives you an opportunity to ask students to explain their answers, to argue a point of view, or to just have students read to you.

ADJUSTING CURRICULUM

A strategy you can use in conjunction with preassessment is the curriculum compactor. Joseph Renzulli and Linda Smith originally designed the curriculum compactor

FIGURE 5-2 Sample List of Parts of a Microscope

Parts of a Microscope
1. Eyepiece (lens you look through)
2. Tube (connects eyepiece to lenses)
3. Arm (supports the tube and connects to the base)
4. Base (the bottom of the microscope and includes the illuminator)
5. Illuminator (light source)
6. Head (upper part of the microscope)
7. Focus knob
8. Nosepiece
9. Objective lenses (primary optical lenses)
10. Stage clips (used when there is no mechanical stage)
11. Aperture (hole in the stage where light goes through)
12. Condenser (collects and focuses light)
13. Iris diaphragm (controls the amount of light)

to be used with advanced students who have already mastered the content (Renzulli and Smith 1979). The compactor consists of three columns. The first column addresses the curriculum areas to be covered. The second column is where teachers list the procedures they will use to determine whether students know the content (preassessment). The third column is where teachers list acceleration and enrichment replacement activities. The compactor works best when teachers receive training in how to challenge advanced learners. It does not matter what students already know if teachers are not willing to replace classroom activities with appropriate activities that challenge their students.

A curriculum adjuster called SCARMA is an adapted version of the curriculum compactor. SCARMA stands for **standards; concepts** (this includes skills); **assessment** type and areas mastered; **replacement** activities, tasks, or assignments; **materials** and resources needed; and **additional** comments. Use SCARMA after your students take a preassessment and demonstrate their prior knowledge.

In the sample SCARMA in **figure 5-3**, before the student takes the preassessment, the teacher lists writing standards in column one and concepts included in the preassessment in column two. In the third column, the teacher indicates the type of preassessment planned.

After the preassessment, the teacher lists the student's prior knowledge. This student knows 90 percent of the information about erosion and weathering. The teacher decides this is mastery and is willing to replace the surface-level activities that the whole class will be doing with something else for this student. "Something else" means, in this case, that the student will work go deeper into erosion and weathering concepts because the student has expressed interest in those areas. The teacher offers a choice of replacement activities. The student chooses to research the worldwide effects of erosion from a scientist's perspective and make comparisons and share them with the class or create a display that demonstrates small to great impacts of weathering. In the fifth column, the teacher anticipates what the student will need to complete the replacement activity. The more proactive you are at this stage, the more you can set up your students to be fairly independent. It is important to consider what materials and resources are both available and realistic. In this example, the teacher thinks the student needs access to a computer, library resources, display materials, and of course general classroom materials. The sixth column is perhaps the most important, because it is a space for teachers to make specific comments about students. In this column, the teacher notes the type of assessment, the type of behavior observed, and anything else that might have affected the student's performance—in this case, that the information from the preassessment was limited because the preassessment was a definition worksheet and allowed the student only to define words.

You'll find a blank reproducible version of the **SCARMA Curriculum Adjuster** on page 116. Why would you bother to take the time to fill out a SCARMA form? If you work with many students, the SCARMA form can help you remember what replacement activities you plan to do with whom. It is also an accountability tool. When a principal observes a classroom, a SCARMA form makes it clear who is doing what and why. It helps you defend your differentiation practice. When family members email or call you and complain that their child is bored or that their child is not doing the same work as another child in the class, you can pull out the completed SCARMA form and document the prior knowledge demonstrated by the child and the type and degree of differentiation that has taken place for the child.

When you plan replacement activities, make sure they're equally fun and equally challenging compared to the regular activities. If replacement activities are seen as more fun than the regular activities, students might view them as a reward. If the replacement activities are seen as too hard, students may underachieve so they don't have to do the harder work.

FIGURE 5-3 Sample SCARMA Curriculum Adjuster

Subject/Content Area: Science: Earth's Changing Surface   **Grade Level:** 5

Standards to Be Covered (Codes refer to Common Core State Standards.)	Concepts and Skills to Be Preassessed	Assessment Type	Areas Mastered	Replacement Activities, Tasks, or Assignments	Materials and Resources Needed	Additional Comments
W.5.2 W.5.2.D W.5.2.B W.5.2.E	Landforms Erosion Weathering Rivers Glaciers Abrasion Wind Plate movement Volcanoes Earthquakes Landslides	Short-answer definition worksheet	Erosion Weathering	Pretend you are a scientist reporting on comparisons of worldwide effects of erosion. OR Create a display that shows small to great impacts of weathering.	1. Computer 2. Library resources 3. Student-identified display materials 4. Classroom materials	The preassessment was a vocabulary definition worksheet, which allowed the student only to show that she knew the definitions. It is hard to tell if she knows more than that.

FORMATIVE ASSESSMENT

Ongoing assessment, or formative assessment, helps drive differentiation. Use it to determine group or individual needs. If the purpose of the formative assessment is to look at the whole class to determine what most students do not yet understand, rather than to give them individual feedback, then students do not have to put their names on the assessments.

Research shows that testing increases achievement by improving students' ability to retrieve information from memory (Brown, Roediger, and McDaniel 2014). The formal use of testing to monitor student achievement and make instructional adjustments on a month-to-month basis can improve achievement, but the effects are generally small (Wiliam and Leahy 2015). Test scores, when used as formative assessments, allow teachers to see who needs more help and who is ready to move on. Formative assessment is valid when it is directly related to instruction. For example, if the assessment is a version of what is presented in class but is not exactly aligned with the lessons, students are not actually being held accountable for the information taught in the lessons.

Education researcher John Hattie ranks feedback among the top ten strategies that affect achievement (Hattie 2009). Assessment scholars Siobhan Leahy and Dylan Wiliam recommend conducting assessments between two and five times a week (Leahy and Wiliam 2012). This keeps students informed about where they are going, how they will get there, and what they need to do next. Graham Nuthall, a professor in New Zealand who undertook forty years of research on learning and teaching, conducted extensive in-class observations and noted that 80 percent of verbal feedback comes from peers, and most of this feedback is incorrect (Hattie

2012). Teach your students to use the ABC peer feedback technique to give more accurate and helpful feedback to their peers. ABC feedback asks students to **agree** with, **build** upon, or **challenge** the answers of other students (Wiliam and Leahy 2015). It can be helpful for students to use a tool when conducting formal peer assessments. For a reproducible **Peer Feedback Form**, see page 117. This form offers guiding questions, cues, hints, and suggestions to create productive peer reviews.

Students can use similar questions to self-assess, as in the reproducible **Self-Assessment Form** on page 118. They can also use a simple flash card technique as an informal self-assessment. Students make flash cards of vocabulary words, then sort them into piles of the ones they know and the ones they still need to learn. They can then create a matching game with the ones they still need to learn. The kinesthetic activity coupled with the visual technique is an effective memory tool.

Another type of formative assessment is a teacher observation checklist. For an example, see **figure 5-4**. This checklist was designed for a differentiated fourth-grade literacy classroom. As the students worked in their groups, the teacher moved around the room and wrote comments on the checklist. Students who had minimal literacy were working on basic skills such as identifying character, plot, and setting. The students in that group who could handle a little more challenge identified kinds of things that happened in the story and characteristics of the main characters. The teacher listed who was participating, who appeared to lead the group, who appeared disengaged, and who seemed overwhelmed. Students in the intermediate group were able to handle basic story elements and think of them at a high level. They analyzed characters, evaluated their actions, and synthesized the

FIGURE 5-4 Teacher Observation Checklist

Basic	Intermediate	Advanced
Names of students:	Names of students:	Names of students:
Character Plot Setting Kinds of Characteristics of	Analysis Synthesis Evaluation Purposes of Influences of/on	Issues relating to Problems with Themes Generalizations Philosophical

relationships among the characters. The more advanced students in the intermediate group were ready to identify the purpose of actions taken and the influences of a character on another character. The teacher used the checklist to note who seemed successful and who needed support. Students in the third group, the advanced group, could already think critically and creatively about character, plot, and setting. They needed more challenge. These students addressed subtle issues and problems in the story. They looked for global themes and generalizations such as inevitable changes that took place in the story, or patterns of behavior that characters demonstrated throughout the story. They also dealt with philosophical concerns such as what is just and fair and whether that is something that everyone agrees upon. Since the advanced group was working at a deep, abstract level, particularly for fourth graders, the teacher observed and wrote down who could handle this level of challenge and who thrived on it.

SUMMATIVE ASSESSMENT

Formative assessment allows teachers to see differences among students, which helps them make timely instructional adjustments. Summative assessment, by contrast, is not used to differentiate instruction. Summative assessment happens after instruction.

However, you can differentiate the types of summative assessments you offer. Not all students can successfully show what they know in the same way. Give students summative assessment choices when the product is not itself the standard. For example, let's say your students complete a study of ancient Egypt. You could ask them to provide certain information in an essay, a travel brochure, or a blog. As long as students include the required content information in their product, they can choose whichever format they prefer. This freedom to choose a preferred product may increase student engagement.

Element 3: Pacing

Each learner requires unique pacing of instruction. When you analyze the results of your students' preassessments and formative assessments, you'll determine whether all your students require the same pacing and the same amount of repetition to learn the required content. You must consider the amount of time you'll spend teaching the content to all students. Some students learn content more slowly or more quickly than others.

For example, students living in poverty may start school one to three years behind their middle-income peers (Campbell et al. 2001). This means primary teachers must help these students achieve up to two years of adequate yearly progress per year so they can catch up. If they don't catch up, after a few years, they may begin a cycle of failure. Meanwhile, research also shows students from poverty have weaker working memories (Luethi, Meier, and Sandi 2008). This means they will not only need to learn a lot in a short period of time but they will also need more repetitions and practice than other students need. Strategies to build working auditory memory include partner or small-group work, games, add-on stories (one student starts a story and the next one adds to it), repeat-after-me directions, and having the student take notes while others speak (Elliott et al. 2010).

Students who are struggling for a variety of reasons can learn when they practice using effective strategies (Jensen and Snider 2013). Brain scans verify that gray matter increases in density with greater mathematical practice (Aydin et al. 2007). Vocabulary instruction and test scores are also correlated with increases in gray matter. The density and volume of gray matter appears to correlate positively with various abilities and skills. Brains do change and grow due to neuroplasticity.

While struggling students may need many repetitions to learn, gifted students may learn science and math two to three times faster than the normal class pace (Rogers 2007). As a result of her research, gifted education professor Karen Rogers recommends that instructional delivery for students who are gifted be differentiated in pace, amount of review, and practice. Gifted students often complain that class is boring, which might be attributed to too much downtime and too much repetition. When students are bored, they do not pay attention to instruction. And when they do not pay attention, they mislearn information.

When your students are working at varying paces, you might worry about how you will keep on top of who is doing what, so create a system that assures you no student is slipping through the cracks. You could make a simple chart that lists your students' names down the left side and lists the activities or assignments that all students will complete across the top. As your students complete the required activities, write the completion date in the corresponding space on the form. Place an X in any space on the form if you feel a student already knows the information or has the skill and does not need to participate in that activity. The form also specifies reinforcement activities providing extra practice for students who might need it and extension activities for students who finish work before the others. See **figure 5-5** for a sample differentiated pacing chart. You'll find a blank reproducible version of this chart, the **Differentiated Pacing Form**, on page 119.

Pacing differentiation can lead to acceleration in a content area. Decide whether you want to accelerate by content or give students enrichment activities. When you provide enrichment activities, the class stays together by unit or subtopics. This may be convenient for you, but gifted students may feel as if they are stalled and waiting for others to catch up even though they are actually going deeper into the content. You run the risk of boring them. There is no single solution to this problem, but you can ask yourself three questions to help you choose a course of action:

- Does the student really know the content, and is the student ready to move on?

- Is the student being challenged if the student stays at the same pacing as the rest of the class?

- Are all students truly learning new content?

Element 4: Flexible Grouping

Purposeful, flexible grouping is an effective differentiated instruction strategy. In fact, flexible grouping is one of the foundations of differentiated instruction (Pettig 2000). According to best practices, teachers should try to minimize whole-group instruction as much as possible. Students learn best when they are grouped according to their affective and cognitive needs. In a differentiated classroom, the teacher groups students according to instructional demands, degree of rigor, task complexity, and the needs of the students. The groups change when the instructional objectives change.

In most classes, teachers work with groups of about four students each, arranged in similar or mixed readiness groupings. For skill-based learning, students are best placed with others at the same ability level. It would be frustrating for students to work in a group learning skills two grade levels above their ability. However, not all groupings need to be determined by readiness. You can also group students according to interest. Students with similar interests pursue more extensive information on

FIGURE 5-5 Sample Differentiated Pacing Chart

Subject/Content Area: Reading—Identifying Alphabet Letters   Grade Level: Kindergarten

Student Names	Assignments and Activities				Extra Practice			
	ABC chart	Matching	Pair and share	Bingo	Letter toss	Jeopardy	Flash cards	Conference
Sally								
Abby	X	X	X					
George								
Henry								
Marsella	X	X	X					
Morticia								
Leo	X	X						
Curtis								
Montgomery								
Maggie	X	X						

					Extension Activities			
					Next letters	Book find	Copying or tracing letters	Writing and reading words
Abby								
Marsella								
Leo								
Maggie								

their chosen topic. In addition, you can group students who work well together, who contribute a variety of strengths, and who are varying types of thinkers and doers.

Consider when you would like your students to work alone, in pairs, in small groups, or as a whole class. Flexible grouping allows you to intentionally differentiate by placing varying groups of students together. Plan the teaching strategies you will use and consider what type of groupings you want for each strategy by using a simple **Flexible Grouping Tracker**. (See **figure 5-6** and the reproducible version on page 120.) The tracker in **figure 5-6** is based on a seventh-grade social studies unit. It shows which activities are best suited for students to work alone, in pairs, in small groups, or with the whole class, which helps you make sure you have allowed for a variety of grouping arrangements.

Random grouping is usually the least effective way to group students. However, it does work well when there are short-term tasks to complete and all students have the potential to be equal group contributors. To form random groups, ask students to count off by fours, or draw craft sticks with students' names written on them. Another technique is to remove from a deck of cards all the cards with face values higher than four (or whatever value works best with your class size) and have each student draw a card. All the students holding ace cards form a group, all the students holding two cards form a group,

and so on. Alternatively, you could ask students to form sequence-based groups. (For example, each group contains an ace, a two, a three, and a four.) This approach gives students more control over their grouping, because they seek out the students they want to work with.

Group size does matter. With three students in a group, sometimes one student is left out of the action. Sometimes a group of four is too big, and one student may not really have anything to do. To avoid problems like these, break the activity up into smaller tasks. This will help you determine the appropriate group size. For example, if a group of students is working on a slide presentation, all students in the group can research information, one student can create the slides, one student can write the script, and one student can present the information to the class. This sounds like a good activity for a three-person group.

Another type of grouping to consider is cluster grouping. This strategy is especially effective when you have several gifted learners. Cluster grouping is when educators group gifted-identified students together in classrooms based on their abilities, while placing all other students in classrooms according to their achievement levels. Ideally, no classroom includes both gifted students *and* students who perform far below average (Brulles and Winebrenner 2019). Research indicates that with cluster grouping, student achievement improves among all

FIGURE 5-6 Sample Flexible Grouping Tracker

Unit: Social Studies—Southwest Asia **Grade Level:** 7

Classify the activities in the unit according to which grouping arrangement would work best.
Do the groupings serve the learning objective?
Does your teaching plan for the unit offer flexible grouping?

Work alone:	Work with a partner:
Preassessment quiz	Tiered questions
KWL chart	Game
Independent reading	Venn diagram
Model	
Work in a small group:	**Work with the whole class:**
Brainstorm activity	Watch a movie
Research assignment	In-class discussion
Create a video	
Work in grouping of choice:	
Surveys	
Interviews	

students, not just the gifted students (Gentry 2014). This type of grouping is most effective when the classroom teacher receives training in gifted education and has a desire to differentiate specifically for gifted students.

Element 5: Open-Ended Questions and Tasks

Effective differentiation includes the use of open-ended questions and tasks. Open-ended questions have more than one correct response. However, not all responses are correct. Students must apply logical thinking and consider criteria when formulating their responses. Open-ended questions encourage students to build understanding and demonstrate their creative thinking. Following are some examples of these questions.

In math:

- The answer is eighteen. Your equation must include both positive and negative numbers as well as both a fraction and a decimal. What is your equation?
- Create a concrete, pictorial, and abstract example that demonstrates the concept of percentage.

In reading:

- You just learned that the main character in the story has measles. How will this affect her actions in the story?
- Why is imagery an essential literary element?

In science:

- Describe one way to conserve nonrenewable resources.
- Describe why potatoes physically change.

In social studies:

- Find a song that reflects Marco Polo's accomplishments.
- The answer is civil rights. What might the question be?

In any discipline:

- Develop a way to . . .
- How is . . . like . . . ?
- How would it be different if . . . ?
- When might . . . do . . . ?
- What makes . . . funny?

Open-ended tasks are engaging tasks that allow students to show their thinking and learning in explicit ways. An open-ended task contains several levels of difficulty. Theoretically, these tasks benefit all students. Open-ended tasks should allow advanced learners to produce their best products, allow average students to show what they know, and allow struggling students to engage in the same task as everyone else. You can also differentiate so that students are doing various open-ended tasks. Following are some examples of these tasks.

In math:

- Work in a group with two sheets of different-colored paper. Cut the sheets into several pieces. Decide how to demonstrate adding fractions with unlike denominators to another group of students using your colored pieces of paper. If necessary, you may use additional sheets of colored paper.
- Draw a representational picture that includes a three-inch by three-inch rhombus, a two-inch by two-inch trapezoid, a one-inch square, and a four-inch by two-inch rectangle.

In reading:

- Work in a group to create a physical representation of the main character in the story using a set of classroom materials provided by the teacher.
- Create a song summarizing two points of view.

In science:

- Create a picture book for young children that demonstrates the uses of levers, pulleys, and inclined planes.
- Create an imaginary news broadcast that provides an explanation of the scientific forces needed to form hurricanes.

In social studies:

- Interview someone who has recently immigrated to the United States and report on their experiences in a student-created book.
- Create a diagram that shows how the Industrial Revolution changed how people live and work.

In any discipline:

- Create a . . . to demonstrate . . .
- Design a . . . for . . .
- Prepare a . . . to convince . . .
- If you were a . . . , how would you help a . . . ?

Often teachers use open-ended questions and tasks when they are beginning to differentiate. This type of differentiation does not address varied pacing or levels of complexity, but it does encourage varied responses. It gives students an opportunity to create their own answers rather than regurgitate what teachers tell them. Open-ended tasks and questions are good ways for students to see that there can be more than one right response. They lay a foundation for students to take risks and trust their own thinking in a supportive classroom environment.

The downside of using open-ended questions and tasks is that students do not always respond how teachers want or expect them to respond. Let's say a teacher asks students to describe the main character. An advanced student responds, "He is nice." Without a rubric to set expectations, the teacher should accept the response—even though the student could have given a better one. If the teacher asks the student to elaborate, the student learns that the teacher does not actually ask for what she wants. Over time, this can lead to students mistrusting teachers. If you want high-level responses, you should either differentiate open-ended questions and tasks or give students a rubric so they can see how you'll assess their responses. When you give your whole class the same open-ended question or task, you must accept any correct response.

Element 6: Simple to Complex Content

Another important aspect of differentiation is differentiating content. To differentiate content, you shift it from simple to complex. Simple content addresses the facts, details, and rules in a content area. Curriculum designer Lynn Erickson calls this "fact-based" curriculum (Erickson 2008). Elementary and middle school educators teach facts about plants, animals, basic computation, the solar system, westward migration in North America, character, plot, and setting, and the like. At the secondary level, students learn facts about things like cells, genetics, the American Revolution, mythology, and novels. For example, in an invention unit in science class using simple content, students need to know the names of a specific list of inventors, what these people invented, and when they invented it. The teacher asks students to add details to their descriptions and explore the rules—in this case, the patent laws—that allowed these people to move their inventions from creation to mass production.

Once students know the simple content, they can explore more complex content. Complex content

---

TEACHING STRATEGIES THAT PROMOTE OPEN-ENDED THINKING

brainstorming: generating a concept list, map, or web to record many ideas

open-ended word prompts: in what ways might we . . . , what would happen if . . . , think of many . . . , list ways to . . . , elaborate on . . . , create a . . . , devise your own way to . . . , tell new ways to . . .

visualizing: creating images in your mind

transforming: changing from one thing to another literally and figuratively. This could be transforming a two-dimensional drawing from an image of one thing into an image of another thing, transforming a three-dimensional model from a model of one thing into a model of another, or taking an idea and transforming it into a related idea.

symbolizing: representing an idea, concept, or knowledge abstractly

small-group discussion based on case study: working through problems taking various points of view

demonstration: performing a solution so others can see how something is done

independent study: choosing a topic, defining questions, gathering and analyzing information, and creating a product

simulation: working in a group to solve a posed problem and achieve a stated objective within a provided scenario, then present the solution

show and tell: sharing something with the class

graphic organizers: processing information and knowledge in a graphic format

digital storytelling: telling a story using a digital tool

---

addresses principles, concepts, themes, generalizations, issues, and problems. Issues are debatable, and problems are potentially solvable. Themes are global, and generalizations always have been and always will be true.

Themes help students synthesize information so they see the big picture. For example, when a teacher uses the topic of invention as a theme, students study inventors and inventions in science class; they read about them for their literature class; they create invention-related word problems in math class; and they study where in the world these inventions happened in social studies class. Instead of using a topic as a theme, the teacher could make the content more complex by integrating a global theme such as change, patterns, or power (Drapeau 2004). In this case, the teacher chooses the theme of change and connects it to inventions. Now, instead of thinking about inventions through the various disciplines, students think about changes in types of inventions. They think about the changes inventors go through in order to create their inventions and market them. Students consider whether inventions change life-styles. On a grander scale, students consider how future inventions might change civilization as we know it. To drive content deeper, students could discuss issues surrounding the field of invention. They consider whether a universal attitude toward invention exists. They think about the advancement of inventions and technology from the perspectives of economy, sociology (how we communicate and work together as people), environment (effects on the environment), politics (whether inventiveness should advance one political system over another), and philosophy (bettering the world we live in).

To keep going deeper, use a generalization. A generalization is anything that is generally true about the theme. For example, a teacher could ask students the theme-based question "What changes did Cinderella go through in the story?" This question uses the theme word *change*. It is a harder question than simply asking students to describe Cinderella. To differentiate this prompt even more, the teacher could add a generalization, such as "What inevitable changes did Cinderella go through in the story?" The generalization is *change is inevitable*. Or the teacher could ask, "What changes did Cinderella go through that resulted in conflict?" Here, the generalization is *change causes conflict*. These generalizations are statements that are generally true about change. Notice that the generalization is stated within the question. This directs the students' thinking through a particular lens.

When you use a generalization, ask the question in a way that doesn't leave room for interpretation about the generalization. If you imply the generalization instead of overtly stating it, the question will be weak, and your students' responses may or may not be what you are looking for. Do not make your students guess at your expectations. For a list of easy-to-use theme-based generalizations, see the reproducible **Themes and Generalizations** on page 121. Pop these generalizations into your questions to challenge your highly able students.

If you are looking for a way to challenge your high-ability students, themes and generalizations offer a great way to address content complexity. It does take time to tweak questions, but it is worth the effort. The harder it is for you to come up with challenging questions, the harder it is for your students to respond to them. If it takes you seconds to create questions, it will probably take your high-ability learners seconds to respond.

Here are some testimonials from teachers who have tried using themes and generalizations with all their students:

* A fourth-grade social studies teacher said her class time went quickly, and the students were engaged. She felt the lessons were worthwhile.

* A middle school special education teacher said the lessons went better than she had expected. Since her students were poor readers, they were reading stories without much content. Even so, she felt the lessons went well.

* An eighth-grade teacher commented that this technique sparked one of the most mature discussions she has had with her class.

* A high school economics teacher was gleeful. He said he actually got real essays.

* A high school English teacher said 100 percent of her students completed their projects. She said this was the highest set of grades this group had earned.

A final way to differentiate content is using words that elicit philosophical, ethical, or moral reasoning (PEMs). PEMs address concepts such as beauty, justice, truth, idealism, will, purpose, wisdom, and reality. This list is by no means complete, but it is a start. The purpose of PEMs is to prompt students to think about content abstractly. Here are a few examples:

* As students study South Africa and learn about the famous landform Table Mountain, which overlooks Cape Town, they may see it as a beautiful natural landform. The teacher could ask, "What defines that beauty, and is that concept of beauty universal? Is beauty in the eye of the beholder?"

* Another example might be "Should we impose our idea of justice on other cultures?"

* In an invention unit: "Is it idealistic to think that necessity is really the mother of invention? If this

is so, why are there so many kinds of instant coffee when instant coffee, according to *The Oxford Companion to American Food and Drink*, has existed since 1771?" Were all these kinds of instant coffee really necessary?

Another way to target philosophical thinking is to simply use the word *should*, as in the following examples:

* In a first-grade class, the teacher asks the advanced students, "Should the good or bad changes in the town mouse and country mouse's attitude be based on their idea of beauty?"

* In a weather unit, a teacher asks, "Should changes in the cloud formations be inevitable?"

* In a high school example, a teacher asks, "Should changes in Macbeth's personality represent the truth?"

Element 7: Low- to High-Level Thinking

When teachers first learn to differentiate, they often differentiate the level of thinking. This type of differentiation occurs when all students are working on the same skill or concept but thinking about it at varying levels. For example, some students are describing the main character (lower-level thinking), but other students are analyzing the main character (higher-level thinking). Differentiating the level of thinking is a good starting point because it is a simple way to approach differentiation.

One potential problem with this strategy is the temptation to reserve higher-level thinking for above-average and highly able students while providing a constant diet of lower-level thinking for struggling students. Some teachers believe that students should not be asked to think about content at a challenging level until they learn the basics. This will eventually backfire, because no student wants to just regurgitate information all the time. They are stuck in a loop of uninteresting, low-level thinking. When learning is drudgery, it's no wonder that struggling learners need many practices before they learn content.

Higher-level thinking is not the exclusive domain of highly able students. When you differentiate, control the sophistication of both the content and the thinking level. You can ask students to think about simple content at a high level or abstract content at a low level. Advanced students who learn rapidly may move into thinking about abstract content at a high level earlier than their classroom peers.

On the following pages, I address two thinking skill models: the Revised Bloom's Taxonomy and Webb's Depth of Knowledge (DOK) framework.

REVISED BLOOM'S TAXONOMY

The Revised Bloom's Taxonomy connects the level of thinking (or *thinking dimension*) with the type of knowledge (or *knowledge dimension*). The dimensions of thinking are remembering, understanding, applying, analyzing, evaluating, and creating. The dimensions of knowledge are the types of content covered in a unit. These dimensions are factual, conceptual, procedural, and metacognitive (Anderson et al. 2000).

To plan a differentiated unit using the revised Bloom's model, teachers can use a matrix that pairs dimensions of thinking with dimensions of knowledge. Kimberly Joy, a fifth-grade teacher in Sanford, Maine, developed a differentiated unit for her literacy class using the book *Walk Two Moons* by Sharon Creech. She targeted her state's standards for literacy and writing. First, Kimberly identified her essential questions: How does self-concept affect perception and behaviors? How do stories and journeys help us grow? How can journeys be both emotional and physical? What does the novel teach us about how relationships develop and change? Next, Kimberly identified her topics in the unit: genre, character, setting, theme, tone, plot, climax, conflict, symbolism, imagery, foreshadowing, point of view, and literary themes. Finally, Kimberly created a matrix using the Revised Bloom's Taxonomy. (See **figure** 5-7.)

Note a few modifications in Kimberly's matrix. She included multiple rows for factual and conceptual tasks, one row for procedural tasks, and no task for her metacognitive row. This is because she intended to emphasize the conceptual dimension of knowledge in this unit, and she did not plan to address metacognition. She also eliminated the "Remember" column, because she decided to address factual recall through direct teaching and not through the matrix activities. Kimberly modified the matrix by noting product forms at the bottom of each box. This note indicates how she wants her students to show what they know. Kimberly also noted whether the product was written, oral/verbal, visual, or kinesthetic to make sure she provided a variety of types of product forms.

Many teachers who use the Revised Bloom's Taxonomy matrix feel the need to include a set number of rows in their matrix and fill in every box. This isn't

continued on page 109

FIGURE 5-7 Kimberly Joy's Revised Bloom's Taxonomy Matrix

This teacher-created grid provides a variety of questions and activities that review and extend the story content for *Walk Two Moons* by Sharon Creech.

Thinking Dimension	Knowledge Dimension				
	Understand	Apply	Analyze	Evaluate	Create
Factual	This book is a story about the lives of Sal, Phoebe, Gram, and Gramps. Summarize each of their stories and how they relate to one another. **Journal Entry (Written)**		How are Phoebe and Salamanca alike? Different? **Journal Entry (Written)**	Listen to the audio recording of *WTM*. What evidence shows how Sal's father feels about his wife's leaving? **Journal Entry (Written)**	Create a scene that features key elements of the landscape in Bybanks, Kentucky, as described by Sal. Look through the novel for vivid descriptions to capture the scene artistically using whatever media you wish. **Artwork (Visual)**
Factual			Compare and contrast the roles of Mrs. Cadaver and Mrs. Partridge in the book. What purposes do they serve? **C/C Essay (Written)**	*WTM* has forty-four chapters, and each chapter title is carefully chosen and meaningful. Think about the titles and how the author uses imagery to appeal to the reader. Choose three chapter titles and write a persuasive essay explaining why you think the author chose them. **Persuasive Essay (Written)**	Create a map that shows the route the Hiddles take to Idaho. Include important stops discussed in the narrative. Locate approximately where the travelers spent each night. Illustrate maps with pictures or appropriate quotations from the novel. **Map (Visual)**
Conceptual	What do blackberries represent in the book? **Journal Entry (Written)**	How does the idea of journey apply in the book? **Journal Entry (Written)**		What character traits in Sal's mother explain her decision to leave? **Small Group Discussion (Oral/Verbal)**	Role-play the scene in which Sal is stopped by the sheriff after taking Gramps's car to visit the scene of the accident where her mother was killed. One student plays the role of Sal and the other is the sheriff. Work together to develop a script for each role or video record your performance. **Performance (Written/Kinesthetic)**
Conceptual			Read Emily Dickinson's poem "I never lost as much but twice." How is the concept of loss of a loved one in the poem different from or similar to that in *WTM*? Construct a Venn diagram to reflect your understanding. **Venn Diagram (Visual)**	Describe the itinerary for the book. Why does it end where it began? **Journal Entry (Written)**	Choose three characters from the novel. Think about real and metaphorical journeys that each character takes. Using a slideshow or presentation software, develop visuals to accompany an oral presentation that tracks your three characters' journeys and compares the experiences and the lessons each of them gains. **Computer & Oral Presentation (Oral/Visual)**

Conceptual	Sal says that her father didn't trust his own parents to behave themselves on the journey west. Imagine he had asked Sal to write him a letter reporting on what Gram and Gramps were doing. Compose the letter that Sal might have written describing her grandparents' behaviors on the drive from Euclid to Minnesota. Support the letter with incidents from the novel. **Letter (Written)**	Describe Phoebe's best and worst traits. What triggers her acting in the extremes? **Journal Entry (Written)**	Why does the author not reveal what happened to Sal's mother until Sal gets to Lewiston? **Journal Entry (Written)**	Imagine that a movie version of *WTM* is being produced, and you have been chosen to design the advertising poster or a thirty-second commercial. What image would you select to catch the eye of a passerby? What brief description of the book would accompany your visual art? Create a poster or commercial that captures the spirit of the novel. **Poster or Commercial (Visual)**
Conceptual		How are the two sets of grandparents different in the book? How are these differences reflected in their children? **Literature Circle (Oral/Verbal)**	What enduring characteristics do Gram and Gramps show after fifty-one years of marriage? How does the author make these characters memorable? **Journal Entry (Written)**	Create a travel brochure highlighting one of the places visited or mentioned in the book that you would like to visit. Travel brochures may be in digital or paper form but must include pictures or drawings, maps, and information about the place. **Brochure (Visual)**
Conceptual			How do the characters cope with the idea of loss in the book? Describe various losses and the ways the characters deal with them. **Literature Circle (Oral/Verbal)**	Native Americans believe that humans should exist in a harmonious relationship with the spirits of the natural world. Choose a living thing that is special to you—a tree, a flower, or an animal—and celebrate its existence in a poem or model. Try to capture what it is about this life-form that excites your imagination or relates to your life. **Poem or Model (Written)**
Conceptual	Have you ever experienced loss in your life? What coping strategies did you use, and which characters most resembled your way of dealing with loss? **Journal Entry (Written)**		How is the concept of hope kept alive in the book? What significance does it play in advancing the plot? **Think-Pair-Share (Oral/Verbal)**	Create a literature web for *Walk Two Moons*. **Web (Visual)**
Conceptual	Taking on the character of Sal, write a letter to Sal's mom expressing what you think Sal would freely tell her mother. This letter should be three to five paragraphs long. **Letter (Written)**		How is the combined theme of love and death played out in the book? **Think-Pair-Share (Oral/Verbal)**	Create a concept map about how one of the following ideas is explored in *WTM*: loss, journey, identity, memory, or change. Use specific characters and events to demonstrate how the concept is developed. **Concept Map (Visual)**

FIGURE 5-7 Continued

Thinking Dimension	Knowledge Dimension				
	Understand	Apply	Analyze	Evaluate	Create
Conceptual				How does the theme of identity and change work in the book? What characters experience changes from beginning to end? **Literature Circle (Oral/Verbal)**	Both Greco-Roman and Indian symbols are used in *WTM*. What are these illustrations and how do they reflect the philosophy of two cultures? Conduct research and develop an exhibit to display your findings, using an artifact to demonstrate each major symbol and meaning. **Exhibit (Visual)**
Conceptual				Listen to the audio recording of *WTM*. What evidence shows how Sal's father feels about his wife's leaving? **Journal Entry (Written)**	Read Creech's *Love That Dog*. What do you think the two books demonstrate about the author's feelings about poetry? Create your own book of poetry about journeys, including both real and metaphorical ones. Use desktop publishing and graphics software to lay out your book. **Book of Poetry (Written/Visual)**
Conceptual					Research the natural settings of the book (Yellowstone, the Badlands, the Black Hills, cities in Idaho). Create an illustrated map of the journey that highlights these sites, with descriptions of them and paragraphs persuading people to visit them. **Map and Paragraphs (Written/Visual)**
Procedural			The opening line of the book is "Gramps says that I am a country girl at heart, and that is true." Write a persuasive essay arguing the truth of that sentence as revealed in the rest of the book. Follow the steps of the writing process to review and revise. **Essay (Written)**		
Metacognitive					

necessary. You should feel free to decide what works best for each unit and modify the matrix accordingly.

Creating high-quality differentiated curriculum is a laudable goal, but the unit will fall flat if the teacher cannot manage it. Since all students are not doing the same thing at the same time, it is important for the teacher to think about who will be doing what when and whether they can work independently. Here is how Kimberly plans to manage her differentiation in the *Walk Two Moons* unit:

Everyone will read the same book, but I will differentiate how it is read, how students will show what they learned, and the complexity and time commitment of products. The lowest-level group will participate in teacher-led discussions of the text and higher-level questions. The on-grade-level and gifted students will have small-group discussion of higher-level questions.

Lower-ability students will answer one to three questions in their journals. They will also be required to complete a literature web, one persuasive essay, a concept map, and one research assignment with teacher support.

Students working at grade level will complete four to five questions in writing for teacher review. As a small group they will complete a concept map, chapter title or book assignment, and one research assignment with a group presentation. Individually they will be responsible for a literature web, a persuasive essay, and student choice of two other activities.

Gifted students will provide written responses to six or seven discussion questions from the "analyze" or "evaluate" columns in the matrix. Requirements will include one research assignment, student choice of three additional activities from the "create" column (one of which must be a writing piece), and an oral presentation of one of the assignments.

When you understand how the levels of difficulty are organized in the Revised Bloom's Taxonomy matrix, it is easier for you to differentiate instruction. When you design a unit using a matrix, you can preplan and make decisions quickly based on preassessment and formative assessment results. Think of the matrix as divided into quadrants. (See **figure 5-8**.) Decide the distinct entry points for students and how many activities students need to do in each quadrant.

FIGURE 5-8 Revised Bloom's Taxonomy Quadrants for Differentiation

Quadrant One	Quadrant Two
Simple, required content Beginning concepts Basic thinking	Simple, required content Beginning concepts High-level thinking
Quadrant Three	**Quadrant Four**
Complex content Advanced concepts Procedural knowledge Metacognitive knowledge Basic thinking	Complex content Advanced concepts Procedural knowledge Metacognitive knowledge High-level thinking

The top left corner of the matrix (quadrant one) directs learning at a factual level and the beginning of a conceptual level. The thinking level is simplest in this quadrant. This is often where the nonnegotiable learning is listed. Teachers design preassessments that include the skills and concepts addressed in this quadrant. Students who struggle to learn usually begin their learning here. Students who do not have prior knowledge but are highly capable move through quadrant one more quickly than their classmates.

Teachers may begin students who demonstrate prior knowledge in the other quadrants. The top right corner of the matrix (quadrant two) directs students to think more deeply about the simple content. The questions or tasks in this quadrant are a bit more challenging than the ones in quadrant one. Often these questions and activities are more interesting too. The goal is to move the struggling learners into quadrant two as soon as possible. For all the other students, quadrant two works well for a while.

When the average and above-average students are ready for the bottom left corner of the matrix (quadrant three), the content becomes more abstract, but students tackle it with only basic thinking. The highly able students should move into the bottom right corner of the matrix (quadrant four) and work mostly in this quadrant. This is where the most challenge lies, because the content is abstract and the thinking level of the tasks and questions is sophisticated.

DEPTH OF KNOWLEDGE (DOK)

Some districts prefer to use the Depth of Knowledge (DOK) model when they differentiate. DOK is a framework for cognitive rigor in the classroom designed by

Dr. Norman Webb, a scientist at the Wisconsin Center for Education Research. The DOK model focuses more on the setting, the situation, or the scenario in which students produce learning. The levels are not designed as a taxonomy, which means students do not have to master one level before going to the next. DOK analyzes the specifics of assignments in four levels: recall and reproduction (level one), application of concepts and skills (level two), strategic thinking (level three), and extended thinking (level four). You can still use the Revised Bloom's Taxonomy matrix by replacing the Bloom's verb categories across the top with the four DOK categories. However, when you do this, the quadrants are not defined by levels of difficulty. Therefore, you need to make calculated decisions about who will do what.

DOK level one targets knowledge acquisition by focusing on recall and reproduction, locating facts and information, details, data, and ideas that are explicitly stated in print. Some verbs associated with this level are *recall*, *tell*, *name*, *list*, *identify*, *define*, *label*, and *report*.

DOK level two targets concepts and skills that are more complex. This level is referred to as the knowledge application level. It is where students use information or conceptual knowledge. This level focuses on using concepts and skills to show relationships, give examples and nonexamples, summarize results, interpret information, apply organizational structures such as flowcharts, distinguish between relevant and nonrelevant information, and generate predictions. Students identify and solve problems. Some verbs associated with this level are *infer*, *organize*, *modify*, *predict*, *interpret*, *summarize*, *classify*, *compare*, *relate*, and *show*.

In DOK level three—the knowledge analysis level—students use logical, strategic thinking and reasoning to consider why concepts and procedures are used to explain answers. At this level, students connect ideas with evidence, apply word choice and point of view to persuade, use planning and evidence to support inferences, and justify conclusions. Here students are expected to reason, sequence steps, and possibly come up with more than one right answer. Some verbs associated with this level are *critique*, *formulate*, *hypothesize*, *differentiate*, *draw conclusions*, *assess*, *construct*, *develop logical arguments*, *recognize misconceptions*, and *critically analyze*.

In DOK level four, referred to as the knowledge augmentation level, students think about what else can be done, how information can be used, or what they can personally do with the knowledge. This is where students

investigate, use complex reasoning, plan, and develop over a period of time. Some verbs associated with this level are *design*, *synthesize*, *create*, *prove*, *conduct a project*, *apply a model*, *create compositions*, *provide alternative solutions*, and *conduct an investigation*.

A matrix design works well when you want to differentiate, whether you use the Revised Bloom's Taxonomy or the DOK model. Let's look at what would happen to the first row of Kimberly's matrix if she converted it to a DOK matrix. (See **figure 5-9**.)

Element 8: Product Options for Summative Assessment

Products allow students to show what they know. Differentiate products by giving your students a choice among various forms. Be thoughtful about the choices you offer. Think about which products are appropriate for individual students, which products are most applicable to content, which products allow students to express depth and complexity, and which products consider the audience. Also consider whether students have the skills needed for success. If not, find out whether students are willing to learn new skills along with new content.

Students often choose a product because they like it, but it may not be the best choice for the content. **Figure 5-10** offers a table of visual, written, verbal/oral, kinesthetic, and technological product forms that students tend to like (many of which combine multiple types). Students should choose a product form that offers the best match between the content learned and how they best express themselves. Students need to understand their own motives and the purpose of various product forms. Does the student want to evoke awe and inspiration? If so, would a board game be the best product form or would a rap song be better? Students should also think about whether their preferences suit their purposes. For example, a student may like to create posters, but is a poster the most effective way to convey a lot of information to their audience?

Chapter Summary

Although research on differentiation is limited, the research on specific aspects of differentiation confirms the notion that differentiation is sound educational practice. It doesn't really take research findings to confirm this, because good old common sense tells us a one-size-fits-all

FIGURE 5-9 Sample Combined Bloom's-DOK Matrix

Thinking Dimension	DOK Levels			
	Level 1: Recall and Reproduction	**Level 2: Application of Skills and Concepts**	**Level 3: Strategic Thinking**	**Level 4: Extended Thinking**
Factual	This book is a story about the lives of Sal, Phoebe, Gram, and Gramps. Summarize each of their stories and how they relate to one another. **Journal Entry (Written)**	How are Phoebe and Salamanca alike? Different? **Journal Entry (Written)**	Listen to the audio recording of *WTM*. What evidence shows how Sal's father feels about his wife's leaving? **Journal Entry (Written)**	Create a scene that features key elements of the landscape in Bybanks, Kentucky, as described by Sal. Look through the novel for vivid descriptions to capture the scene artistically using whatever media you wish. **Artwork (Visual)**

FIGURE 5-10 Product Options

Visual	Written	Verbal/Oral	Kinesthetic	Technological
Animation	Anecdote	Ballad	Card game	Augmented reality
Banner	Article	Choral reading	Charade	Blog
Billboard	Autobiography	Debate	Clay sculpture	Digital storytelling
Blueprint	Book review	Dialogue	Dance	Editing and publishing sites
Book cover	Commentary	Discussion	Demonstration	Garage Band
Brochure	Critique	Jingle	Dramatization	Google Forms
Caption	Cumulative story	Lecture	Exhibit	Google Maps
Cartoon	Description	Oral report	Experiment	iMovie
Cereal box	Editorial	Public service announcement	Flip-book	Infographics
Chart	Essay	Quiz show	Game	Interactive journals
Coat of arms	Haiku	Radio commentary	Invention	Multimedia presentation
Collage	Headlines	Radio show	Mural	Online games
Concept map	Infomercial	Readers theater	Pantomime	Organizers like Symbaloo
Diagram	Journal	Silly saying	Pop-up book	Podcast
Drawing	Lab report	Soliloquy	Puppet show	PowerPoint
Flowchart	Letter	Song	Recital	QR codes
Graffiti	Limerick	Speech	Relief map	ShowMe app explanations
Graph	List	Tongue twister	Set design	Slideshow with voice
Graphic organizer	Memoir	Travelogue	Simulation	Social media
Illustration	Monologue	Trial	Skit	TED Talk presentation
Map/legend	News report	TV commercial	Theater program	Voice typing
Outline	Paper chain story	Vignette	TV news broadcast	Website
Photo journal	Parody	Warning	Video documentary	Wiki space
Poster	Script			YouTube presentation

curriculum and delivery could not possibly meet the needs of all the diverse learners in our classrooms. You may feel you cannot differentiate for a variety of reasons; however, I encourage you to overcome any limiting beliefs you may have for the benefit of your students.

Knowing and practicing the eight elements of differentiation can empower you as a teacher. Learn who your students are by giving them a survey such as the one in this chapter, by simply talking with students, or through observation. With this knowledge, you can form relationships with your students and find out their interests and preferences. Use preassessments and formative assessments to determine your students' academic needs. Pace the curriculum and provide flexible grouping in order to engage students. Most importantly, you can provide a just-right level of challenge for all students. You can accomplish this by asking students open-ended questions and requiring them to do open-ended tasks, by asking questions that shift content from simple to complex, by shifting students' thinking from low-level to high-level thinking, and by providing students with product options for their summative assessment. Use a tool such as a matrix to proactively plan your differentiation questions and activities.

Differentiation is a sound educational approach that is here to stay. It is a necessary step toward personalized learning. In this chapter, you do the heavy work. You create options, you develop the curriculum, you

orchestrate the learning. Now you are ready to hand over some of that power and control. Teach your students the tools you use to differentiate so they learn how to differentiate for themselves, using the same tools to drive their own learning. When you differentiate, it is likely that you engage your students. When you personalize the learning, you empower them.

Discussion Questions

1. Describe intentional differentiation and how you use it in your classroom.

2. Explain some limiting beliefs about differentiation. Why are these beliefs limiting?

3. Prioritize the top three elements of differentiation in terms of impact. Elaborate on your answer.

4. Think about the various ways you differentiate for your students. Which ones engage students and which ones empower them?

5. It is likely you have been differentiating for years. What new ideas did you gain from this chapter? What changes might you consider in your differentiation practice?

After you've thought about your answers to these questions, visit this website for a video chapter review with the author: freespirit.com/empower-videos.

Learner Survey

Write "yes" or "no" next to each of the following statements. At the end of each section, total your "yes" answers in the space provided.

Group 1

_____ I usually complete my classwork and homework in a timely manner.

_____ I like school and am generally motivated.

_____ I am good at test-taking and usually get good grades.

_____ I sometimes worry about teacher and parent expectations.

_____ I sometimes struggle with open-ended assignments. I prefer to have clear expectations from the teacher.

_____ I enjoy working at my own pace, which is sometimes faster than the rest of the class.

_____ I am organized.

_____ I am a people pleaser. I like to please my teacher and my friends.

_____ **total yes answers from group 1**

Group 2

_____ I do things precisely, down to the last detail.

_____ After I finish an assignment, I often feel like it is not good enough.

_____ When a teacher hands back one of my papers, I look for mistakes before I look for right answers or positive comments.

_____ I am often harder on myself than others are on me.

_____ Sometimes I don't like my work, so I throw it out and start over or I erase so much that I make holes in my paper.

_____ Sometimes I have trouble starting something and I ruminate for a long time.

_____ I constantly check in with the teacher looking for details so I know what to expect.

_____ I regularly ask for help when I really do not need it.

_____ **total yes answers from group 2**

Group 3

_____ I sometimes have ideas others don't seem to understand or appreciate.

_____ I like to choose my own unique way to show my learning.

_____ Teachers sometimes think my questions are off topic or rude, even when I don't mean them to be.

_____ I enjoy art, music, or theater (watching or participating).

_____ I enjoy open-ended assignments more than fill-in-the-blank worksheets.

_____ I have my own unique organization system.

_____ I seek out new things and ideas.

_____ I have less tolerance for inside-the-box thinkers.

_____ **total yes answers from group 3**

Group 4

_____ Most classes and assignments at school are fairly hard for me.

_____ I notice that other students finish their work way before me.

≫⟶

_____ I often feel behind in my work at school.

_____ Other kids seem to "get it" when I don't. I am sometimes frustrated.

_____ I don't really look forward to school, and I don't unusually enjoy it once I'm there because I cannot do what I want.

_____ I don't like to ask for help.

_____ I lack confidence.

_____ I feel different, unlike my peers.

_____ **total yes answers from group 4**

Group 5

_____ I rarely raise my hand in class or speak up, even if I know the answer.

_____ When I work in groups, I tend to take a back seat to other students.

_____ I prefer to work alone or with one close friend, rather than in groups.

_____ I'm a lot different with my friends and at home than I am at school.

_____ Most teachers and kids at school don't know that much about me.

_____ I like to sit in the back of the room.

_____ I have a lot of stomach ailments and headaches or take many bathroom trips.

_____ I do not volunteer in class.

_____ **total yes answers from group 5**

Group 6

_____ I am usually moving, tapping, or fidgeting in class. I have to move.

_____ I enjoy hands-on activities during which I can move around.

_____ I frequently get in trouble at school.

_____ I have trouble following through and completing assignments.

_____ It is hard for me to focus on worksheets and seatwork at school.

_____ I need a lot of stimulation.

_____ I like to sharpen my pencil over and over.

_____ I have the potential to derail the class.

_____ **total yes answers from group 6**

Scoring

Transfer your total from each group to the list below. Note the two groups with the highest totals. These two groups should describe you best. Keep in mind that these groups suggest general learner traits and tendencies. Most people show some characteristics from each group occasionally.

_____ group 1 = academic learner

_____ group 2 = perfectionistic learner

_____ group 3 = creative learner

_____ group 4 = challenged learner

_____ group 5 = hesitant learner

_____ group 6 = high-energy learner

KTW CHART

What I Definitely KNOW and My Source	What I THINK I Know and My Source	What I WONDER About

SCARMA Curriculum Adjuster

Subject/Content Area:

Grade Level:

Standards to Be Covered	Concepts and Skills to Be Preassessed	Assessment Type	Areas Mastered	Replacement Activities, Tasks, or Assignments	Materials and Resources Needed	Additional Comments

PEER FEEDBACK FORM

This form offers guiding questions, cues, hints, and suggestions for writing helpful peer reviews. When you are reviewing a peer's work, use any of the following statements or questions that seem appropriate.

- I'm not sure if this answer is correct because _____.
  Can you clarify this for me?

- If I scored you on this rubric, I would give you a _____ because _____.

- My favorite part was _____.

- I think you did really well responding to _____.

- If I had to choose an area for improvement for you, I'd choose _____ because

  _____.

- How did you figure this out or come up with this answer?

- I like your answer, but it is pretty short. Can you elaborate on it?

- It looks to me like you know, understand, and applied the information. Could you use critical thinking to analyze or evaluate it? Could you think about the information creatively?

- How did you come up with an idea for this?

- I was surprised that _____.

- What assumptions did you make about _____?

- I like the way you _____.

- I think it would be clearer if _____.

- Do you feel good about your responses? Why or why not?

- Do you feel the task allowed you to show what you learned? Would you have preferred to show what you learned in a different way?

SELF-ASSESSMENT FORM

Knowledge and Skills	Not Really	Sort Of	Definitely
1. I can read and understand the information.			
2. I can explain the information to others.			
3. I can remember the information in detail.			
4. I can connect the information to other things I know.			
5. The vocabulary is understandable, not confusing.			
6. I can elaborate on the information.			
7. I can identify a weak area and know how to get help with it.			
8. This information I learned has changed the way I think about _____.			
9. I feel really good about doing this task and showing what I know.			
10. I worked independently or I worked cooperatively with my group.			

Differentiated Pacing Form

Subject/Content Area:

Grade Level:

Student Names	Assignments and Activities							Extra Practice						Extension Activities					

Flexible Grouping Tracker

Unit:

Grade Level:

1. Classify the activities in the unit according to which grouping arrangement would work best.

2. Do the groupings serve the learning objective?

3. Does your teaching plan for the unit offer flexible grouping?

Work alone:	Work with a partner:

Work in a small group:	Work with the whole class:

Work in grouping of choice:

Themes and Generalizations

Theme: Change **Generalizations:** Change can be positive or negative. Change has consequences. Change may make people uncomfortable. Change happens all the time. Change may be threatening.	**Theme:** Patterns **Generalizations:** Patterns allow us to make informed decisions. Patterns build comprehension. Patterns are predictable. Patterns have a discernable order. Patterns are found in the world around us.
Theme: Power **Generalizations:** Power can lead to dominance. Power may be obvious or subtle. Power may consist of opposing forces. Power may be intentional or unintentional.	**Theme:** Order **Generalizations:** Order may be flexible. Order helps us understand. Order organizes complexity. Order creates structures and systems.

Add your own theme words in the chart below.
Then, add your own generalizations, that which you believe to be generally true about the theme.

Theme: **Generalizations:**	**Theme:** **Generalizations:**
Theme: **Generalizations:**	**Theme:** **Generalizations:**

For question 1, write a content question you would ask your students. For question 2, choose a theme and a corresponding generalization and write this generalization into your content question. What does this do to the question? Is the revised question harder than the original question? Would the revised question be more appropriate for your advanced learners?

1. My original content question:

2. My revised question using a theme and generalization:

CHAPTER 6

Personalized Learning: Voice and Choice

Differentiation is meeting more of the learners' needs more of the time. Personalized learning is a natural extension of differentiation; it is students directing their learning more of the time. It empowers learners to drive their own learning. Empowerment, then, is a key element of personalized learning.

Personalized Learning Defined

Scholars and educators use many definitions of personalized learning. For example:

- The nonpartisan think tank RAND Corporation defines personalized learning as "a broad set of strategies intended to make each student's educational experience responsive to his or her talents, interests, and needs" (RAND Corporation 2019).

- Ronald Taylor and Azeb Gebre of the Center on Innovations in Learning say personalized learning is "instruction that is differentiated and paced to the needs of the learner and shaped by the learning preferences and interests of the learner" (Taylor and Gebre 2016).

- The Association of Personalized Learning Schools and Services identifies the following fundamental aspects of personalized learning: putting students' needs first; tailoring learning plans to individual students; supporting students to reach their potential; providing flexibility in how, what, when, and where students learn; and supporting parent involvement (Hanover Research 2012).

- According to the findings from a report by the RAND Corporation (Pane et al. 2015), models of personalized learning include one or more of the following strategies: teachers create individual

goals with students based on their strengths, needs, motivations, and progress; personal learning paths allow students to make choices about the types of strategies and materials they prefer to use; students are allowed to self-pace; flexible learning environments offer resources and time that are responsive to individual needs based on data; and academic and noncognitive skills and competencies are developed to prepare students for college and career readiness.

Although definitions of personalized learning vary, all of them point toward the idea that it involves tailoring instruction to meet individual students' needs and guiding students to become self-directed, autonomous learners. In a way, we can think of personalized learning as differentiation-plus. It encourages learning as a way of being and aims to ignite—or reignite—students' passion for learning. Personalized learning has three objectives: learning content, learning how to learn, and learning about the self.

When teachers use personalized learning, students are aware of the nonnegotiable content—that which they are required to learn—and they connect this content with their interests. When differentiating, the teachers make that connection, but with personalized learning, students learn how to do it for themselves. They feel empowered and more in control of their own learning. However, it is not only important for students to know what they *want* to learn and what they *must* learn. It is also important for them to know *how* they best learn. This is where metacognition comes in.

Metacognition, or awareness of one's own learning or thinking processes, is a key element of personalized learning. Students must understand their thinking and learning so they can determine what their needs are and how they learn best—and then create their own learning path. Metacognition involves both learning how to learn

TECHNOLOGY AND PERSONALIZED LEARNING

Personalized learning is sometimes seen as an instructional method that uses technology to help students learn. Using technology as a teaching tool can encourage students to be self-guided. Teachers often use computer software and websites to help implement personalized learning. For example, the website Khan Academy allows students to move at their own pace through courses consisting of videos that help students learn content. This website, as well as other websites and applications, can supplement personalized learning. But personalized learning is not always e-learning, nor should it be. The use of e-learning alone would isolate students. Along with technology considerations, districts must consider other aspects of personalized learning, such as flexible scheduling, social learning, projects, and opportunities for empowerment.

and learning about the self. For example, many students discover they learn best by using flash cards to review. But some also learn that too many flash cards overwhelms them, diminishing their effort. Knowing this, the students learn to divide the flash cards into small piles and tackle one pile of flash cards at a time. They experience success more often because they have created an attainable goal. Other students like to challenge themselves with bigger tasks and prefer to tackle one set of flash cards, no matter how large the pile is. Some students find they are social learners. For them, it is not about how many flash cards there are—they learn the cards best when working with a partner. With a shift from differentiation to personalized learning, it is no longer just teachers who learn about students and then differentiate for them. The students also begin to learn about themselves and create their own learning paths. Metacognition empowers students to become confident in a dynamic classroom of student-directed inquiry and uncertainty.

When teachers shift from differentiation to personalized learning, their classrooms shift from teachers designing learning experiences for students to students designing learning experiences for themselves with teacher guidance. If students are not aware of how they learn best, they will struggle to make good choices. To direct their learning effectively, students need tools and

support from their teachers before or as they take the following steps:

1. Students identify their interests, strengths, and abilities and use this information to create their own pathways to learning.

2. Students look at their preassessments and formative assessments to determine what to learn next.

3. To achieve their learning targets, students determine what activities and tasks they would like to do and what materials they need.

4. Students schedule conferences with teachers and conduct their own conferences with parents or guardians.

5. Students keep track of their own rate of progress.

6. As students master content and develop their ability to regulate their learning, they truly become self-directed learners.

If you're still confused about the distinction between differentiation and personalization, you're not alone. Differentiation and personalization do share many characteristics. And it doesn't help that researchers, educators, and organizations use these terms to mean a variety of things. For example, a school district may claim to offer personalized learning when what it's really doing is giving students choices—and it is the teachers who come up with the options. The key distinction between differentiation and personalized learning is that differentiation is more teacher-driven (teachers control more of the learning), while personalized learning is more student-driven (students control more of the learning).

In a personalized learning system, teachers often create pathways that move students through individually paced content. A pathway is made up of multiple playlists. A playlist consists of specific activities identified by teachers that help students learn skills and content. But if teachers are creating the playlists and pathways, isn't that differentiation? Of course, it is. Personalized learning means that teachers create playlists less often and allow students to create their own pathways whenever possible. In most cases, teachers should not think that this means a loss of control. Students need to know what they are required to learn and the time frame in which they must learn it, and they create their own activities and projects with the teacher's approval and guidance. A personalized plan needs to work for both students and teachers. Personalized learning does not mean students take charge of their learning 100 percent of the time. Not all students are ready to do that, can do that, or even want to do that. In any personalized learning system, the shift from differentiation (in which teachers model effective instruction) to personalized learning (in which students take control of their learning) is happening all the time. Students need teacher support, need to learn how to make good curriculum-related decisions, and need tools to help them become effective self-directed learners.

Some districts identify themselves as personalized learning districts because they engage in project-based learning or problem-based learning, both of which offer students some autonomy. Other districts identify themselves as personalized learning districts because their students use technology to learn at their own rate or to monitor their own progress. Still other districts use a combination of personalized learning and flipped classrooms. (In the flipped classroom, the direct teaching is given as homework and does not take place during class time. Teachers use videos to introduce and review content. The practice activities take place in the classroom rather than as homework assignments. This gives students opportunities to work with other students and ask the teacher for help when needed. Provisions are made for students with no computers at home or with limited home internet access.) With so many approaches and definitions, it is critical that a school or district define what it means by personalized learning and what initiatives and frameworks it wants to use within this educational approach, decide to what degree it wants students to lead their own education, envision what that looks like in practice, and determine how the district will know if its practices are effective.

Research on Personalized Learning

In 2014, the Bill and Melinda Gates Foundation created the Next Generation Systems Initiative (NGSI) and the Next Generation Learning Challenges (NGLC) Regional Funds for Breakthrough Schools initiative. The districts involved with the initiatives were charged with designing personalized learning pilot schools that could, if successful, become models for other schools. In 2015, as part of these initiatives, the Center on Reinventing Public Education (CRPE) observed the pilot schools.

CRPE found that some teachers flipped their classrooms in order to free up the teacher to work directly with students during class time. Some teachers used independent learning plans, and still others centered their instruction on problem-based learning. Other teachers used "station rotations, adaptive software, personalized learning paths (sometimes referred to as 'playlists'), internships and mentorships, competency-based standards, flexible seating, and explicit socio-emotional learning activities around issues like perseverance and focus" (Gross and DeArmond 2018, 7). CRPE researchers concluded after the one-year period that teachers and students were excited about this way of teaching and learning.

The RAND Corporation carried out a personalized learning study sponsored by the Bill and Melinda Gates Foundation (RAND Corporation 2014) and compared the results of this study, in which teachers were new to personalized learning, with a third study led by John Pane (Pane et al. 2015). The RAND study examined a single year of academic growth composed mostly of secondary students whereas the Pane study looked at two years of academic growth and focused more on elementary schools. Nearly two-thirds of schools in the RAND study had statistically significant positive results in both math and reading. Students in the median comparison group made 3 percent gains in both subjects in one year. Students who started out below national norms made the biggest gains. These results align with the Pane study.

The RAND report indicated that the most common personalized instruction practices included extending practice time and extending time for individual support. A less common practice was competency-based learning, which allows for students to move through the standards at their own rate rather than at an externally designated pace. In a standards-based system, competency is designated as proficient on a rubric. In a grade-based assessment system, competency may be defined as reaching an 85 percent or 90 percent achievement level. The RAND report also showed that personalized learning teachers used more technology, and their students had the ability to make more choices about their learning. The report found that flexible grouping, learning spaces that lend themselves best to personalized learning, and students being aware of data related to their goals had the greatest effects on achievement. Finally, the report noted positive effects for student-driven goal setting, large-group work, and independent study.

Student Voice in Personalized Learning

Student voice goes hand in hand with personalized learning. Giving students voice means allowing them the opportunity to express what they think. When students are empowered, they use their voice to affect themselves and others. Student voice is based on the following convictions (Cook-Sather 2006):

- Young people have unique perspectives on learning, teaching, and schooling.

- Their insights warrant not only the attention but also the responses of adults.

- They should be afforded opportunities to actively shape their education.

To use their voice, students must know what they think and why they think it. Voice may include emotion, but should also take into account sound, rational, critical, and creative thinking. When students use their voice to provide input on their education, they may start out with thin thinking; however, teachers must encourage them to use thick thinking. Thin thinking is surface-level thinking. Thick thinking is reflective, involves multiple levels of knowledge, and is influenced by a variety of inputs. It is often referred to as deep thinking or high-level thinking (Anderson et al. 2000).

Voice allows students the opportunity to influence what they learn, how they learn, and how they are assessed. According to data presented by education researcher Russell Quaglia, "When students have voice, they are seven times more likely to be motivated to learn and four times more likely to experience self-worth in school. . . . These students are also eight times more likely to experience engagement, and nine times more likely to experience purpose in school" (Namahoe 2017).

Student voice is a change agent. It starts with thoughts and feelings that come from the students themselves. With personalized learning, students use their voices to actively make choices about their education—both what affects them personally and what affects the whole school. The teacher's role is to provide opportunities for students to use their voices and to encourage and empower them to do so. Teachers must listen to the student voices and take action. According to youth engagement researcher Adam Fletcher, it is not enough to simply listen to student voice. Educators must get involved with students and get students involved with education if they want to see school improvement (Fletcher 2014).

Voice as a Tool for Student Leadership

Many studies of successful student voice programs have uncovered a common misconception: that an increase in youth leadership means that adults must simply "get out of the way" (Mitra and Gross 2009). On the contrary: in successful leadership programs, teachers and students work together. Teachers prepare students to lead by teaching them problem-solving strategies so they have skills and know procedures to move things forward. Teachers provide students with thick-thinking tools so they are able to address content deeply.

In some schools, students use their voice to help make decisions about teacher hiring. For example, at a high school in Massachusetts, as part of the standard teacher interview process, a group of ten students interviews each candidate. The students generate their own questions, conduct the interview themselves, and make recommendations to the superintendent. Often the interview questions posed by the administrative team or the teachers are predictable. However, the questions posed by the students can be about anything. Candidates often say they are the most nervous about the student group interview.

There are schools empowering students to use their voice to help make changes to codes of conduct. The student council makes recommendations to the administrators or conducts surveys and share the results with administrators. A student council in an elementary school in Wisconsin met to revise an existing teacher-generated list of prohibited bullying behaviors to include some additional ways students feel bullied. They added things like being made fun of when students say the wrong answer in class and students not letting someone sit next to them in the cafeteria because they are saving too many seats at the table for their friends. When students provide input into the codes of conduct, they feel ownership of the school and use their voice to effect change.

Student leaders might use their voice to call meetings, set goals and plans of action, create innovative classroom products such as classroom blogs or student websites, and learn ways to involve their peers to cooperatively achieve their goals. In one elementary school in Maine, students created their own student council. They ran for offices, created campaign speeches based on their platforms, and held elections. Once the student council was formed, it had quite a bit of decision-making power. Students could initiate a new school rule or a rule change by filling out a bill and submitting it to the student council. The student council would discuss the bill, offer the bill's sponsor time to present information to students and to the student council, and then everyone would vote on it. If the bill made it through the general vote, the principal still had veto power. However, the principal could not veto the bill unless it was against district policy, was unsafe or unsanitary, or was hurtful. For example, the students passed a rule that allowed chewing gum in school. Chewing gum is not a safety issue, but it could be a cleanliness issue, so the principal did veto the bill. However, he allowed students to chew gum on an upcoming holiday. The students felt their voice was heard, they understood why the veto was made, and they felt responded to because the principal tried to accommodate the student vote by making a compromise.

In a high school in Harwood, Vermont, students formed a student governance system similar to the one at the elementary school in Maine. Students or faculty members proposed bills that were circulated, discussed, and voted on. A bill was proposed to add an eighth period to accommodate the school's newly adopted proficiency-based approach. When the students presented their suggestion, they learned about the many factors, such as bus schedules and fixed budgets, that affect the school day. Even though it was determined that the additional period would not work, the students felt like their voices were heard and considered (Gewertz 2016).

Developmental psychologist Shepherd Zeldin studied several community-based programs in which students and adults shared governance responsibilities and found that when student leadership was part of the program, young people showed deeper commitment to their communities, greater self-confidence, increased ability to take on governance roles and responsibilities, and a strengthened sense of organizational commitment (Zeldin 2004). These benefits are just as applicable for school-based initiatives as they are for community involvement. For example, one group of elementary students (not part of Zeldin's study) decided that their community should ban the use of polystyrene (Styrofoam) because it is bad for the environment. The students did research and brought their request to the town council. As a result of their research and the information they presented, the town council voted to ban the use of polystyrene. Stores and restaurants in town complied with the new ordinance and started packaging their food in cardboard boxes. The students' voices were heard, and they brought about change.

Voice as a Tool for Communication

Students can use their voice and thick thinking to express their thoughts about their learning goals. Students should have an opportunity to think about what works best for them and about their strengths and weaknesses and their likes and dislikes. They increase their level of self-awareness and understanding about their learning needs. Students consider what support and feedback they may need in order to accomplish their goals. When students set goals with their teacher, the cooperative process gives teachers a window into their students' thinking. Teachers help students fine-tune their learning goals to better suit their individual needs. Teachers also gain insight into how they may provide appropriate coaching to help students reach their goals.

When teachers ask students for their point of view, students can use their voice to offer their opinions, make suggestions, discuss any confusing points, and identify areas of personal disconnection. This conversation allows students to provide input into their instruction. For example, a sixth-grade teacher was thinking about redoing a science unit. In the past, the unit had seemed sort of flat and boring, though students were moderately engaged in it. The teacher wanted to change the instructional format, but she wanted students' input before she spent time redoing the unit. She had heard about the Follett Challenge (page 75) and was excited about this game-based learning format, but she did not really want her classroom to compete in the challenge. She thought she might use it as a structure for her energy unit, creating a game based on a mystery that the students needed to solve. The teacher shared this game idea with her students, and their enthusiasm inspired her to create the unit. The students appreciated that the teacher not only asked for student input, but also followed up on it. If she'd decided at the last minute that the game would take too much time, the students would have felt their voices were not heard.

When students work with a partner or in a small group, they have opportunities to listen to peers, hear varying perspectives, and use their voices respectfully. Students can enhance their group discussions by designing a process. Structured group discussions can pull in learners who might otherwise silently do nothing. Students must work out what structure—if any—would best serve their needs. They might want to consider the answer to these questions before they begin their discussion:

- Is each person expected to contribute to the discussion?
- Do group members take turns sharing responses?
- Are roles (group leader, secretary, timekeeper, questioner, clarifier, summarizer) necessary?

When students use their voice to influence or share ideas with a broader audience, their engagement in learning shifts to empowerment. Often students feel empowered when they publish something in a local newspaper or a blog. They feel empowered when they present their point of view at a school committee meeting or stand up for a program that might be cut from the budget. Using their voice to perform or broadcast their work is also empowering.

The Role of Voice in Assessment

Student voice plays a role in assessment when students are allowed to assess their own work. Students often assess themselves more harshly than teachers assess students. But note that if the student self-assesses the work and then the teacher assesses the work—and the teacher assessment is all that counts—then the student will likely view the self-assessment as a waste of time.

You can turn any rubric that you commonly use into a teacher-student combo rubric. You and your student fill out separate copies of the same rubric. If you and your student score the student's work differently, then meet with the student to discuss the discrepancy. **Figure 6-1** shows an example of a student rubric. The student filled out the rubric by checking each appropriate box and writing comments in the far-right column. **Figure 6-2** shows an example of how a teacher might fill out the same rubric.

Figure 6-1 Sample Combo Rubric (Student)

After reading *An Orange for Frankie* by Patricia Polacco, imagine half the people in your town are homeless and your family is not. What problems will arise, and how might you help those in need? Create a presentation and share your solutions with the class.

	Developing	Proficient	Advanced	Comments
Content	☐ Content is confusing and may contain misinformation.	☐ Content contains basic, required information.	☒ Content contains abstract, sophisticated information that goes beyond required information.	I added three more references.
Thinking Process	☐ Content presented is a rehash of ideas and demonstrates little attempt at advanced thinking.	☒ Content presented demonstrates analysis or synthesis and/or makes multiple connections.	☐ Content presented shows considerable originality, inventiveness, or innovative thought.	I connected the information to economics.
Product: Presentation	☐ Spelling and punctuation are somewhat accurate. Information is not well organized. Graphics detract from the information. Font formatting is distracting.	☐ Spelling and punctuation are mostly accurate. Information is organized. One slide or item seems out of place. Graphics are attractive but a few do not support the text. Font is readable.	☒ Spelling and punctuation are accurate. Information is well organized. Graphics enhance the information. Font formatting enhances the readability and content.	My PowerPoint is very good.
Presentation: Voice and Choice	☒ Body language is distracting. Voice sounds monotone. No choice of items that were elaborated on. All information presented as of equal worth.	☐ Body language does not distract from presentation. Voice changes throughout presentation. Few choices of items that were presented as more important points.	☐ Body language enhances certain information. Consciously uses voice to excite the audience. Clearly emphasizes certain information to draw attention to most important points.	I was nervous, and I know I need to work on my voice and less moving around for next time.

Figure 6-2 Sample Combo Rubric (Teacher)

After reading *An Orange for Frankie* by Patricia Polacco, imagine half the people in your town are homeless and your family is not. What problems will arise and how might you help those in need? Create a presentation and share your solutions with the class.

	Developing	Proficient	Advanced	Comments
Content	☐ Content is confusing and may contain misinformation.	☒ Content contains basic, required information.	☐ Content contains abstract, sophisticated information that goes beyond required information.	You had additional references, but you basically just restated the information.
Thinking Process	☐ Content presented is a rehash of ideas and demonstrates little attempt at advanced thinking.	☒ Content presented demonstrates analysis or synthesis and/ or makes multiple connections.	☐ Content presented shows considerable originality, inventiveness, or innovative thought.	You connected the points in the story to money.
Product: Presentation	☐ Spelling and punctuation are somewhat accurate. Information is not well organized. Graphics detract from the information. Font formatting is distracting.	☐ Spelling and punctuation are mostly accurate. Information is organized. One slide or item seems out of place. Graphics are attractive but a few do not support the text. Font is readable.	☒ Spelling and punctuation are accurate. Information is well organized. Graphics enhance the information. Font formatting enhances the readability and content.	Your PowerPoint was well done.
Presentation: Voice and Choice	☐ Body language is distracting. Voice sounds monotone. No choice of items that were elaborated on. All information presented as of equal worth.	☒ Body language does not distract from presentation. Voice changes throughout presentation. Few choices of items that were presented as more important points.	☐ Body language enhances certain information. Consciously uses voice to excite the audience. Clearly emphasizes certain information to draw attention to most important points.	Your presentation voice is improving from last time. You are also getting better at identifying most important points.

In **figure 6-3**, you will see an example of a student self-assessment tool. (For a blank version of this tool, see the **Student Self-Reflection** reproducible form on page 137.) In a standards-based classroom, this student would receive a proficient rating. Teachers fill in the grid with the task-specific elements: required knowledge, level of thinking, any additional requirements, and product. Students reflect on their work, check the appropriate boxes, and write comments at the bottom of the form. Self-reflections can also be shared with peers as a guide for discussion. Such discussion can be a powerful opportunity for students to learn the skills of critique. On page 138 you'll find a reproducible list of starter phrases students can use to guide their critiques. The starter phrases offer a way for students to use their voice to give their peers meaningful feedback.

Choice: Giving Students Control

When educators talk about choice, they often equate it with personalized learning. However, teachers usually provide the choices, and when they do, they are applying differentiation. Differentiation is when the teacher offers a choice of activities or products. Personalized learning is when the teacher identifies the standards students need to cover and leaves it up to them to decide how to learn the content and show what they know.

Providing choice is a way to increase engagement and empowerment, promote ownership, and boost learning. Choice helps students feel personally invested in doing high-quality work. It increases happiness and lowers stress and anxiety (Ronan 2015) while at the same time positively affecting achievement. Researcher Alfie Kohn cites a study of second graders who, as a result of choice,

Figure 6-3 Sample Student Self-Reflection

Task: In a persuasive essay, evaluate the nebular theory of the formation of the solar system based on the characteristics and properties of Mars and Venus.

	Could Use Improvement	Covers It	Super
Knowledge of required content: Nebular theory Properties of Mars and Venus	☐ Facts are lacking regarding nebular theory or properties of Mars and Venus.	☒ Essay includes important facts regarding nebular theory and properties of Mars and Venus.	☐ Knowledge of nebular theory and properties of Mars and Venus is comprehensive and goes well beyond the required content.
Level of thinking: Evaluation	☐ Evaluation is weak and lacks justifications. Few and obvious conclusions are made.	☒ Evaluation demonstrates conclusive analysis with justifications. Common and logical conclusions are drawn.	☐ Evaluation is in-depth and makes logical, unique connections. Sophisticated, abstract, defensible conclusions are drawn.
Additional requirement: Text evidence	☐ Text evidence is superficial.	☐ Thorough text evidence is drawn from required texts.	☒ Text evidence goes beyond required texts.
Type of product: Persuasive essay	☐ Essay is not very persuasive. Makes one or two points.	☒ Essay is persuasive and well written. Includes many defensible points.	☐ Essay is persuasive and in-depth. It could be presented to scientists.

Comments:

For this assignment, I think I covered what was required of me in all areas except for the text evidence category. I did use a few more references than what was required. I scored myself super in this area. You will see I cited additional research at the end of my assignment.

Next time:

I think for next time, I would like to improve my evaluative thinking. I think I can do this by focusing on specific evaluation skills.

completed tasks in less time than those students who did not have choice (Kohn 1993).

Some teachers—particularly new teachers—are not comfortable handing over control of what they teach and how they teach it. Other teachers feel more comfortable giving students choice, because they trust that the students are learning, and they want to encourage students to be more responsible for their own learning. In a study by education researchers John Guthrie and Marcia Davis, an increase in teacher control and a decline in student choices led to a large decline in motivation of upper elementary students (Guthrie and Davis 2003). Research also indicates that teachers and students may not have the same perceptions about student choice. Student empowerment advocate John Spencer confesses that at one time, he was hesitant to provide choice to his class because it was a challenging group of students. When he eventually incorporated choice, he found it to be the solution to the difficult classroom behavior. Students who had been making trouble became engaged and even empowered (Spencer 2016).

Benefits and Challenges of Student Choice

Choice empowers students. When students make their own decisions and teachers listen and honor these choices, students feel important and valued. They become invested in their learning, and as a result, they are likely to have meaningful conversations with their teachers and classmates. These conversations build a positive, open relationship between the teachers and students. Students' self-esteem increases, and their self-concept improves. They feel in control of their learning, and they are often proud of their actions. This increase in self-esteem can lead to an increase in student independence.

A potential drawback is that choice can feel overwhelming to students. When students say they don't know what to choose, it might mean they are afraid of making the wrong choice. They may be unsure of expectations or afraid of taking a risk. Some might be afraid that their peers will make a different choice. Here are a few ways to minimize students' fears about choice:

1. Ask students to list two strengths they possess. Post the names and strengths on a bulletin board so that all students can see whom they might go to for help with drawing, writing, and so on. This strategy helps students see that their classmates have a variety of strengths, and they can use their strengths to help one another.

2. If possible, classrooms, schools, or districts could use standards-based grading. Students should be able to move at their own pace in a standards-based grading system. They do not need to worry about mastering content at the same time as their classmates. Depending upon how the standards-based grading system is set up, advanced students could work at a proficient level and not feel pressured to always work at an advanced level.

3. Make sure the options you offer are all valid. Students want to know that their choices count. A student once asked her teacher, "Is this a real choice or one of those choices where there really is only one right choice?" If students think teachers prefer one option over another, they will try to figure out which choice that is.

4. Let students know that it is okay to make mistakes. If their choices do not work out, they will learn from their mistakes. Allow students to redo or revise their work.

5. Sometimes it helps to give students a decision-making process so the freedom to choose is not so intimidating. See **figure 6-4** for an example. In the left column, students list their product options. Teachers help generate evaluation criteria or students create their own. (Criteria should always include depth of content.) Students respond to the criteria with yes, no, or maybe. When students respond with a no, the option is eliminated. In this example, the report and the rap song are eliminated. The two best options appear to be the poster and the game. Analyzers like this one can help students think logically about their decisions. Once they internalize this process or learn to apply criteria when making a logical decision, they don't need to use a form.

Student-Driven Choice

Student choice moves along a continuum from fully teacher-driven to a combination of teacher-driven to student-driven to fully student-driven. (See **figure 6-5**.) This continuum also moves students from differentiation

Figure 6-4 Sample Decision-Making Analyzer

Should I create a poster, write a report, create a game, or write a rap song?

Options	Can I complete this on time?	Do I have the materials?	Do I want to do this?	Justify or clarify.	Check for depth of content.	Decision
Poster	Yes	Yes	Yes	I like to do art.	May need to supplement with either written or oral information	The poster looks like my best option because I want to do it and I can finish it on time, but I probably will need to add written or present oral information to go along with the poster.
Report	Yes	Yes	No	I do not like to write.	This will work.	Eliminate
Game	Yes	Yes	Maybe	I'd like to make the game, but I think it will be a lot of work.	This will work.	The game is a possibility that could work, but I'm not sure if I really want to make a game.
Rap song	Yes	Yes	Maybe	This could be fun, but I do not want to perform the song in front of the class.	No. I probably will not be able to fit all the content into a rap song.	Eliminate

Figure 6-5 Student Choice Continuum

Differentiation		Personalized Learning	
Teacher-driven options	Teacher-driven options with student additions	Student-driven options with teacher approval	Student driven options
→			
Potentially engaging	Generally engaging	Generally empowering	Empowering

to personalized learning. Educational leadership professors Douglas Fisher and Nancy Frey call this the "gradual release of responsibility" (Fisher and Frey 2013). With teacher-driven choice, students choose among options that teachers provide. With teacher-driven combination choice, teachers provide most of the options, but students may add their own options with teacher approval. With student-driven combination choice, students consult with teachers before making a decision. With student-driven choice, students generate multiple options and choose from these. No teacher approval is necessary.

When students understand their strengths and use logical reasoning to make decisions, they make choices that excite and motivate them. These exciting choices can make learning feel playful to students. Play positively affects the development of the prefrontal cortex, which is where high-level thinking occurs. Playful activities that use imagination and creativity engage the brain and encourage long-term learning. Teachers should empower students with the knowledge that play is a positive thing not just because it is enjoyable, but also because it drives learning. Self-directed learning, whether it involves play or not, is engaging because it releases dopamine, a neurotransmitter associated with pleasure. Students with high levels of dopamine are usually go-getters, focused and motivated. They have good concentration and judgment and low impulsivity. We want to encourage students to search out positive ways to learn what drives, motivates, and excites them so they make good decisions about how to direct their own learning.

Guiding Students to Make Good Choices

Giving students choice is just the beginning. It is also important for students to know how to make good choices. Before students make a choice, they should be

aware of what they need to know, how they learn best, and to what degree they need to learn content. Since most districts are required to meet standards or learning targets, students must consider how they might connect their choice to learning targets.

Students know their own interests and strengths. If their strength is in art or they have an interest in visuals, students might want to consider making a poster to show what they know instead of a written report. However, a good choice must also align with the students' academic abilities—if students choose to read an article, they should make sure the reading level is something they can handle but also not overly simple. Students also need to consider choosing a product that allows them to show the degree of content they learned. For example, in a sixth-grade class, students chose to read *Holes* by Louis Sachar. One student decided it would be interesting to summarize some of the issues the story touched on, such as racism, illiteracy, and incarcerated youth. For a product form, the student chose to draw a picture of what she thought the main character looked like. She chose this product form because she likes to draw. However, a drawing of one character is not a very effective way to demonstrate knowledge about how complex issues were dealt with in the novel. A better choice would be to create a debate or editorial review of the issues in graphic novel form. This allows for a more in-depth review of issues while using the student's affinity for drawing. Students should also consider the resources available to them. Do they have the time, materials, and space they need to accomplish the task? For example, should students choose a product like a multimedia presentation that includes multiple resources and a variety of videos, quotes, and visuals when the product is due in two days?

Students make good choices according to the support that is available to them. Moving from engagement to empowerment and from differentiated learning to personalized learning does not mean students have to learn and produce products entirely on their own. Teachers still need to coach and help students in any way they need so that students experience success.

Types of Choices

Differentiation allows for some student choice; the teacher offers two or three choices to the student. But these are choices teachers have already made for their students . . . even if they are open-ended choices. When teachers offer two choices and allow students to create a third if they prefer, this moves along the continuum from differentiation to personalized learning. Finally, when teachers allow students to make their own choices and provide none, teachers have released students from depending upon the teacher to drive learning. You must decide for yourself how far you are willing to go with student-driven choice. To make student-driven choice work, teach your students to consider the consequences of their choices. In other words, advise them, "Think before you choose."

CHOICE OF CONTENT

You may allow students to choose topics or subtopics based upon the required content. This type of choice empowers students and leads to their sense of ownership in the course content (Flowerday and Schraw 2000). It is unlikely that students will have completely free choice when it comes to topics and subtopics. You will need to talk about the standards and show students how the standards drive the expected outcomes in learning content. Model how to anchor topics and subtopics to standards or learning targets by unpacking the content with them.

CHOICE OF PROCESS

Foster choice through a variety of instructional activities. One common type of activity is a choice board from which students choose which activities or products they want to do. The choice board is arranged in a square grid. Students must to do all the activities in a row, in a column, or on a diagonal, as in tic-tac-toe. You can create choice boards in three-by-three, four-by-four, or five-by-five grids. See **figure 6-6** for an example of a math choice board.

An alternative to the choice board is the choice wheel. In **figure 6-7**, see the math choice board converted to a choice wheel. With a piece of cardboard or card stock, build a wheel divided into wedges. In each wedge, write an activity, question, or product. Make a

spinner from cardboard or card stock and attach it to the wheel with a brad fastener. Let students spin three times and then choose. You can adapt this activity by letting students fill in one or more of the wedges. You may need to approve students' ideas to ensure they fit within the content parameters. Instead of a choice board or wheel, you can simply create a list of options and let students choose one. You may include a free-choice option. With personalized learning, students create their own choice boards and choice wheels.

Here's another strategy that includes an element of choice: Students generate their own questions about the content and write each of their questions on an index card. For example, after reading a book, a student writes, "Why did the main character react the way he did?" or, "What would happen if the story took place in a different country?" Students put all their questions together in a list and choose which ones to answer. Alternatively, the teacher collects the index cards, turns them facedown, and has students come to the front of the room one by one, choose a card, and answer the question on the chosen card.

Once you have shown them how these instructional strategies work, students can create their own choice board, wheel, or list. These are no longer teacher strategies to use with students. They are now student strategies that students can choose any time they want when they are deciding how they want to review content.

CHOICE OF ENVIRONMENT

Students can also choose their groupings at least some of the time. It is helpful for students to know how they work best. Do they do their best work alone or with a partner? Do they prefer to work in a small group or as part of the whole class? Along with the type of grouping, you may or may not have students choose who is in the group. For example, students might want to work with their friends, but that may not be the most productive grouping arrangement. If a group meets based on interest, and the group is discussing medical practices during World War I, all students in the group should be interested in medical practice. It wouldn't work to place a student in the medical group who is interested in who fought which battle and why. If a group is doing research, it does not always work well if the group consists of students with a wide range of ability. Often the high-ability students feel as if they are doing all the work. If students who need help researching are placed together in a group, the teacher can do some direct teaching of

Figure 6-6 Math Choice Board

Why is manipulating decimals easier than manipulating fractions?	From your point of view, what is the easiest way to explain fractions?	Numerators are to denominators as percents are to . . .
What is the purpose of using percents?	What patterns do you find in the places in the decimal?	Define five skills or concepts you need to understand when using decimals to solve a problem.
What happens to a percent when you divide it by one hundred?	What would happen to the percent if you multiplied it by one thousand?	Would you rather convert a fraction or a decimal to a percent? Why?

Figure 6-7 Math Choice Wheel

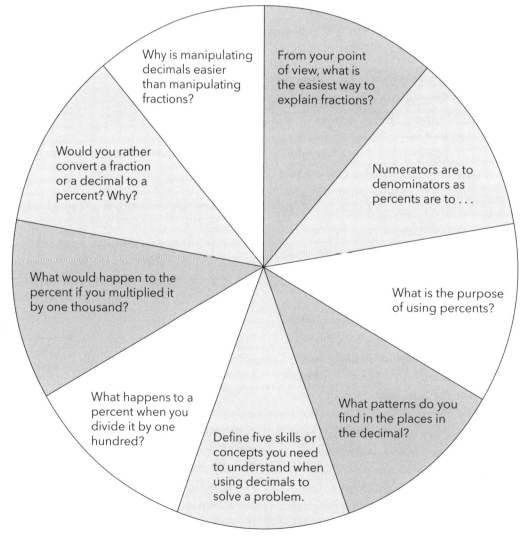

research skills with this group. It takes a while for students to learn and accept who should be in their group to create the most productive group.

CHOICE OF PRODUCT AND ASSESSMENT

Once students understand there are many types of products that are more or less effective in various contexts for various reasons, you may allow them to choose their product type. Remind students that there are visual products, such as graphic organizers, timelines, flowcharts, cartoons, graphs, and charts. There are verbal products, such as discussions, debates, interviews, and podcasts. There are written products, such as summaries, reports, essays, and journal entries. There are kinesthetic products, such as skits, videos, demonstrations, and games. Point out that students' favorite products may or may not be the best way to show what they know or the best product form for a particular audience. If you are

concerned that students will choose the same product over and over again, keep a running list of students' product choices—or better yet, have students keep track of their own product choices—and don't allow repeats (or allow only a few). If you want to empower students, allow students to choose their audience.

You can incorporate choice into assessment in a variety of ways. For example, ask students to generate their own questions about the content, then use their questions to create a quiz. The students will not know which questions you will choose for the quiz. Another approach is to let students choose which questions they want to answer. Create a quiz with ten of the student-generated questions, then tell students they must answer five of the ten questions. Or, students could choose which questions to answer on a test or a quiz with questions worth varying amounts of points. This would empower students

CHOICE, ENGAGEMENT, AND EMPOWERMENT IN ACTION

As students become more self-directed learners, they become truly empowered learners. Rachel Sugarman's gifted and talented students in Wiscasset, Maine, exemplify empowered students who are engaged in personalized learning. She shares four choice projects that her students participated in:

- Lucas, a seventh grader, is a highly creative overall academic learner with gifts and talents in both the visuals arts and technology. Lucas's ELA class was focused on narrative writing in quarter two. Lucas's creativity took over, and he brought the entire group with him. The narrative story he collaborated on writing ended up becoming a podcast with digital graphics to accompany it.

- Brandon, a passionate third grader, is an overall academic learner with a huge interest in and zest for technology. As part of a unit on inventing, Brandon created an iMovie that he solely recorded and edited, as well as inputting sound effects and graphics himself. He has a private YouTube channel where he posts all the documentation of his work completed in his gifted and talented class (his decision). Brandon has taken it on himself to be our class videographer and filmmaker, helping other students to make videos and movies that document their personalized studies.

- Maize, an eleventh-grade visual artist, is passionate about digital animation. As part of her gifted and talented program, local animator Christina Prescott was hired as a mentor. Through Christina's mentorship, Maize was able to learn the basics of computer animation, demonstrating the use of anticipation through the digital drawing of a simple figure, and focusing on staging—in other words, using a storyboard for her scenes.

- Naomi, a ninth grader, worked on a passion project as part of her gifted and talented accommodation this school year. A school-based health project sparked her interest in designing her own line of healthy and natural cosmetics. Naomi has been investigating common ingredients in cosmetics made by various cosmetics companies, has been meeting with professionals in the cosmetic world, is developing a makeup brand of her own that will include both logo and letterhead, and plans on marketing her own cosmetics and participating in the Youth Enterprise Zone at the Common Ground Country Fair in Union, Maine.

to think about which questions they want to answer in order to receive a particular grade.

The issue of grading always comes up with product choice. You can deal with it in a variety of ways. One way is for students to create their own rubric and submit it for your approval, then you use the rubric to grade the work. This helps you see exactly how students envision the product. If your students are unable to create their own rubrics, you can give them old rubrics to modify or use as a guide to create their own. Students can also choose to self-reflect, as in **figure 6-3**, or complete a combo assessment as in **figures 6-1** and **6-2**.

One concern you may face when you allow student choice is managing due dates. As mathematics professor Samantha Bates Prins points out, it can be very difficult to cover the necessary content in a completely student-choice-driven course (Bates Prins 2009). Students need to master content within a set time frame. To help foster an honest relationship with your students, share with them the district expectations about required content, mastery, and timelines. Together, you and your students should set realistic deadlines for activities, assignments, formative assessments, and summative assessments. These can all be managed in a spreadsheet.

Chapter Summary

Differentiation is teacher-driven, and personalized learning is student-driven. Both differentiation and personalized learning are multifaceted concepts. With personalized learning, students create goals and pathways to their learning. They decide what they want to learn, how they will learn it, how they want their learning assessed, and what products they will produce to demonstrate their knowledge. However, it is unreasonable to expect students will drive their own learning 100 percent of the time.

The research on various aspects of personalized learning shows that voice and choice have a significant impact on learning. The research can be confusing, though, because what some call personalized learning others call differentiation. For example, choice is often equated with personalized learning even when the teacher creates the options. According to the definitions presented in this book, this type of choice is teacher-directed and falls more in line with differentiation.

When students create their own choices, they experience personalized learning. Teachers can give students choices of content, process, environment, products, and assessments. Choice can empower students, but it can also overwhelm them. When this happens, students need a strategy to rely on that helps them know how to make good choices. This is where teachers step in to provide students with tools to help students with their decision-making. Personalized learning is not hands-off learning. The teacher still is responsible for modeling good teaching practices and helping students by supporting them with structures and strategies so that students have the tools they need to be independent and self-confident learners.

Discussion Questions

Decide whether each of the following statements is true or false and think about why:

1. Student voice is important only for high school students. Primary and elementary students should focus on learning other skills before they need to experience finding their voice in school.

2. Teachers can let students make decisions, but adults should take responsibility when the consequences don't work out.

3. Personalized learning is not realistic because teachers have too many students with too many needs. Teachers cannot possibly provide voice and choice for all students.

4. Listening is not that important a skill when we are talking about student voice. Voice is more about expressive language and being a good communicator.

5. Open-ended choice (or free choice) is always effective.

After you've thought about your answers to these questions, visit this website for a video chapter review with the author: freespirit.com/empower-videos.

Student Self-Reflection

Task:

	Could Use Improvement	Covers It	Super
Knowledge of required content:	☐	☐	☐
Level of thinking:	☐	☐	☐
Additional requirement:	☐	☐	☐
Type of product:	☐	☐	☐

Comments:

Next time:

Critique Starter Phrases

I Like	I'm Not Sure About	Suggestions for Improvement
My favorite part was . . .	I didn't understand . . . because . . .	I think it would be clearer if . . .
Absolutely don't change . . .	I was confused when . . .	What would happen if . . .
I like the way you . . .	Can you explain why . . .	I'd like to learn more about . . .
I like how you said . . .	Am I right in thinking . . .	Some people might think . . . but . . .
You include . . . that helps me understand . . .	I'd like to hear more about . . .	You need to include . . .
The things you did well . . .	Why did you include . . .	You still need to explain . . .
I was interested in what you were saying when . . .	I don't see how . . . connects to . . .	Can you provide examples of . . .
I could really feel the emotion when . . .	I'm a bit critical of . . . because . . .	The opening would be stronger if you . . .
This reminded me of . . .	I do not see where you addressed . . .	You could wrap things up by . . .
I could really relate to what you were saying when . . .	I found . . . challenging.	Your point of view would be stronger if you included . . .
Your evidence to support . . . is strong because . . .	Why will . . .	Your argument would be stronger if you added data to . . .
. . . was powerful.	How will . . .	I wanted to know about . . .
. . . was inspiring.	Should you . . .	I was wondering if . . .
. . . sparked my curiosity.	Can I make the inference that . . .	One suggestion would be . . .

CHAPTER 7

Putting It All Together: Empowering Students to Design Their Own Instruction

When teaching practice shifts from differentiation to personalized learning, opportunities for students to experience student voice and choice increase. Students become empowered to use their voice to express themselves and influence others, to engage in leadership roles, and to make decisions about their own learning. Teachers provide students with tools and resources to help make this happen. As choice increases, ownership increases. When you inspire student empowerment, students feel in control of their learning, and they develop a sense of what it means to become independent, self-directed learners. They feel more capable to design their own instruction.

Competency-, Mastery-, and Proficiency-Based Education

Competency-, *mastery-*, and *proficiency-based education* are terms that are often used interchangeably, although their definitions address distinct elements within an educational system. Competency-based education is a system of instruction, assessment, and grading that measures learning at the learner's own pace, as opposed to a traditional educational system in which learning is organized around seat time. States and/or districts define competencies (or knowledge and skills) that students must master. Proficiency describes the level of skill the students demonstrate. Students demonstrate proficiency in the competency areas, which results in subject area mastery.

Competency-Based Learning

Competency-based education allows students to move through instruction at a rate that is appropriate for each learner (Anand and Schimke 2015). For example, when

students in a math class demonstrate they know how to add decimals, they move on to the next skill (such as multiplying decimals), as opposed to a traditional system in which all students add decimals for the designated time period—whether they master the skill on the first day, the second day, or not at all—and then move on together to multiplying decimals. Competency-based education is anchored in a standards-based educational system that identifies what students need to learn and is dependent upon effective use of preassessment and formative assessment. Through assessment, students demonstrate whether they are competent to move on or need additional practice. Competency-based education empowers students to master content and progress at their own pace. This shift away from grade-level groupings is "the single most significant policy enabler for personalized learning" (Wolf 2010). Competency-based education works well when teachers are looking to differentiate instruction, individualize instruction, or provide more student-directed personalized learning and empowerment.

Teachers' relationships with their students matter in a competency-based education system, because teachers must know enough about their students to help them create appropriate pathways. In some schools, teachers build relationships through daily meetings and home visits. In other schools, teachers ask students what courses they would like to take, then create the courses and embed competencies and essential skills into them. Competency-based education provides opportunities that enable personalized learning and reduces seat time, which can be replaced with activities outside the building.

Competency-based education offers an alternative way to plan and deliver instruction and to learn information and skills. Teachers do not just cover the content. Students do not just sit and receive information. They do not receive scripted lessons, nor are they expected to complete lessons at the same time on the same day. Instead, students work at their own rate toward their own outcomes at their appropriate instructional level. They seek help from their teachers or their peers. Group work is emphasized at all grade levels. Teachers and students use information from formative assessments to determine next steps. When students test out of a level, teachers can use digital and in-person blended learning options.

A competency-based learning system lends itself naturally to a shift from differentiation to personalized learning. Competency-based learning used with differentiation or personalized learning means that teachers and learners respond to the learners' needs. Since not all students learn in the same way, it is important to identify the way in which competency will be achieved for each learner. Once standards are identified, students are preassessed, and then, in a personalized education system, students determine their own pathway and playlist to get to the formative assessment. If they do well on the formative assessment, they move forward again. In a personalized learning approach, some teachers are more comfortable developing preassessments and formative assessments but are willing to let students determine their own summative assessment.

Mastery-Based Learning

The term *mastery-based learning* is sometimes used synonymously with *competency-based learning*. Mastery learning was first named in the 1960s by Benjamin Bloom and John Carroll. The notion, as explained by education researcher Vahid Motamedi, was that a student had to achieve a certain percentage of knowledge mastery before moving on (Motamedi 2011). Today, districts determine the percentage, usually between 85 to 95 percent of the subject content, that students must master. Bloom noted that aptitude was a matter of the time it took a student to learn material—the student's rate of learning—not necessarily a matter of ability. This suggests that all students can achieve at a high level if given enough time (Bloom 1968). Mastery learning is still a strategy used with differentiation (Wiggins and McTighe 2005) and continues to be emphasized in some districts. Differentiation is not only used but necessary in a mastery learning system, because not all students are learning the same thing at the same time and some students need extra explanation and support. "When compared to traditionally taught education classes, students in

mastery learning classes have been shown to learn better, reach higher levels of achievement, and develop greater confidence in their ability to learn and in themselves as learners (Guskey 1997, 2001, 2009).

Mastery-based education continued to grow, especially when the US federal education bill passed in 2015. The bill said that states could forgo end-of-year subject tests; this empowered districts to switch to mastery-based instruction. Because the mastery approach focuses on growth rather than having specific knowledge and skills at a specific time, it's a valuable approach for schools with high immigration populations, because immigrant students typically need time to learn English.

As with competency-based learning, the mastery-based teaching process begins with explaining to students what needs to be learned, and then a formative assessment is given to students to determine what was learned. Students who do well on the formative assessment may engage in enrichment activities or move forward to the next unit. Students who do not do well in the formative assessment participate in remedial activities, take another formative assessment, and then move into the next unit when they are ready.

Educators may have concerns about mastery-based learning. Some feel the system is set up for students to work on the computer, thus eliminating the need for staff, in order to save costs. Some think mastery learning works well with skill-based, sequential instruction and curriculum design, such as for math and foreign-language courses, but worry that it is not effective in the humanities because the discipline is not linear in nature. In these types of subject areas, it is more difficult to move sequentially from one standard to the next. Some educators fear that students who need many repetitions to learn will forget information in a mastery-based system. Since the system is designed for students to attain knowledge and move on, students who flourish with a spiraling curriculum may find themselves floundering.

Often families have difficulty understanding or accepting the system of assessment in mastery-based education. Students may not receive grades on their formative and summative assessments. The rubric is the most common type of assessment tool in mastery learning. The language in a rubric is something like *not yet reaching the standard*, *approaching the standard*, *meeting the standard*, and *exceeding the standard*. Rubrics vary in wording, but most use some sort of four-point scale to identify where students are in the learning process. Some schools find it necessary to or choose to translate the four-point scale into grades when reporting to parents.

Proficiency-Based Learning

Competency-based learning and mastery-based learning are aligned with proficiency-based learning. A competency-based learning system defines what students need to be competent in. A mastery system defines the level at which students need to know something. A proficiency-based learning program describes how well students know the content. As districts started to explore proficiency-based learning, some states, such as Maine, New Hampshire, Vermont, Idaho, and Illinois, jumped on board with competency-based, mastery-based, and proficiency-based programs. These programs varied, but they all focused on a standards-based continuous progress approach.

In 2012, Maine's state legislature passed a law called An Act to Prepare Maine People for the Future Economy, which required all students to graduate from high school with a proficiency-based diploma. While forty-eight states had adopted policies to promote competency-based education, Maine took it a step further and tied proficiency to graduation requirements (Barnum 2018). The new law left implementation up to individual school districts. Districts unpacked standards, identified scope and sequence of content and skills anchored in the standards, and created four-point rubrics that identified three as proficient and four as advanced. Once a student reached a three on a rubric, the student had achieved proficiency for the standard and could move on. As with competency- and mastery-based learning, it did not matter how long it took a student to reach proficiency.

In some Maine schools, teachers significantly changed their teaching style. Maine saw more flipped classrooms and more personalized learning. This resulted from the change to proficiency-based education along with a longtime relationship with statewide one-to-one computer technology initiatives.

Some Maine schools struggled to make proficiency-based education work. A 2018 study of Maine's new system found that in eleven Maine high schools, there was little personalized instruction. The study found a higher level of engagement among students, but they also had slightly lower SAT scores (Shakman et al. 2018). Only 18 percent of high school teachers surveyed felt the new system increased rigor (Johnson and Stump 2018). Parents were confused and worried. They wondered if proficient

MASTERY COLLABORATIVE

The New York City Department of Education has established a program called Mastery Collaborative (MC). In MC's member schools, learning is student-centered, mastery-based, and implemented with a culturally responsive lens. The schools in this collaborative have increased achievement scores among their low-achieving students. The program grew in popularity in struggling schools, high-achieving schools, schools for the gifted and talented, and among schools with high ELL populations. The MC approach has transformed many schools, one of which is the New York Middle School 442. In two years, reading proficiency levels among the student body increased 22 percentage points, and math proficiency increased 21 percentage points (Spencer 2017).

meant a B or an A. They worried that colleges would not be able to make sense of the proficiency-based reporting system. Parents and teachers worried that this type of educational system enabled struggling students to take so much time to learn content that they would be unable to graduate with their class. Teachers worried that students would not progress fast enough and would become discouraged (Barnum 2018).

In July 2018, Maine lawmakers repealed the proficiency-based diploma requirements. They left it up to districts to choose between a traditional diploma and a proficiency-based diploma. In some districts, educators breathed a sigh of relief. Meanwhile, in other districts, educators who were invested in the new system decided to keep going.

Beginning (or Refining) Your Personalized Learning Practice

All schools that address standards address competency skills that students must master—at least to some degree. Differentiation comes into play when teachers provide students with specific strategies to help them become proficient in the identified skills. Personalized learning comes into play when students set their own goals, know how they learn best, apply their own techniques to learning, manage their own time, and choose effective products to show what they know. Once teachers or a district determine what constitutes competency, mastery, or proficiency, teachers can shift from differentiation to personalized learning by sharing these nonnegotiable competencies, levels of mastery, and proficiency with their students.

Avoiding Pitfalls

When a district shifts from a differentiated approach to a personalized learning approach, it is helpful to plan ahead for potential pitfalls that other districts have experienced. Often districts research how various schools shift to personalized learning, but in the end, teachers must make their own decisions based on what works best for them and their situation.

PEDAGOGY

One critical issue to consider is pedagogy, or knowledge about the science of teaching and learning. Are all students capable of knowing enough about their learning to drive their own learning? After all, educators go to school for years to learn how to teach. Teachers learn about types of assessment and how to use results to develop appropriate lessons. They learn about the content they are teaching and how knowledge is constructed. Through education and training, teachers gather instructional tools and techniques that motivate, engage, and inspire students. Students are not trained teachers. Therefore, in a personalized learning classroom, it is critical for students to have access to pedagogical information so they can direct their own learning. Without such information, students would be like drivers who know their destination but not how to get there. You do not want your students driving around aimlessly, enjoying the ride but getting lost—so give them a map.

ASSESSMENT

Assessment can be a concern for teachers, students, and parents. With personalized learning, how do we determine proficiency and define the process of moving forward? Who decides when students can advance? Do highly capable students move forward if they are proficient, or is the grade-level standard differentiated for them? The same goes for struggling students. How long do they stay at the same level? Can they move forward if they are not proficient? How is growth described on report cards? How will educators help parents understand

the reporting system? Who decides what formative and summative assessments to use? Do students just do periodic check-ins with the teacher? Do students decide how they will learn something and then how they will show what they know? Educators must spend time agreeing upon what performance indicators students need to reach and how they will communicate results.

STUDENT CHOICE

Teachers may find it difficult to give timely, specific feedback when they allow students to choose their products. They may feel overwhelmed by the number of projects going on in the classroom at one time. You can often address this problem by generalizing feedback that can be used in many contexts. Develop generic rubrics and generic responses that you can tweak by substituting various adverbs and adjectives. Comment on work completed as well as ways to improve the work for next time. When you provide choice in assignments and assessments, you need a way to make your feedback doable and as timely and as helpful as possible.

Figure 7-1 offers a filled-in example of a teacher-created rubric that the teacher uses with students who read any book. In this personalized classroom, the reading assignment is not required, but if students choose it, they also choose to use the formative assessment rubric. This generic rubric describes levels of performance for students' reading response journals. In this assignment, students are asked to summarize the information in each chapter. The summaries help students remember story details. They can use their chapter summaries to review for their summative assessment. In this example, the teacher has checked the appropriate indicators within the rubric and has made a generalized comment. Notice that the teacher did not name the characters or any plot points. This is intentional, because the teacher plans to use the comment with other students who may or may not read the same book. (For a blank reproducible version of this rubric, see page 153.)

To shift from teacher-created assessments to student-created assessments, you must first show your students how to create high-quality rubrics. Start by creating rubrics yourself, then shift to creating rubrics with students, then let students create rubrics independently. When older students are ready to make their own rubrics, you can direct them to websites such as rubric-maker.com. Some teachers allow students to create their own formative assessments, but teachers and

Figure 7-1 Sample Reading Response Rubric

Assignment: As you read the book, summarize the information in each chapter in your reading response journal.

Assignment	Okay	Very Good	Fantastic
Reading responses to: *The Outsiders* by S. E. Hinton	☐ Responses are on time. ☐ Responses cover the basics. ☐ Responses are obvious. ☐ Responses provide minimal detail.	☒ Responses are on time. ☒ Some responses are in-depth. ☒ Some responses are thought-provoking. ☒ Some responses are elaborative, expressive, and sophisticated.	☐ Responses are on time. ☐ Responses go beyond the readings. ☐ Responses are thought-provoking. ☐ Elaboration provides new insights.

Comments: Your responses are quite detailed and reflect critical and creative thinking. You demonstrated inferential reasoning when you described the main character's actions. I think your responses were very good. If you are interested in improving your responses for next time, try connecting the main character's actions and behaviors to another character that you read about in a different story. Next time, you could also elaborate on some "aha" moments in the story that provided you with some rich insights.

students together create the summative assessments. These teachers like to maintain some control over the components included in the summative assessment.

The rubrics used with formative assessment indicate what to do next. With personalized learning, this information is important to both the teacher and the student. It helps them know whether to move on or not. Formative assessments prepare students for the summative assessment. Educators need to decide if formative assessments "count," and if so, how much they count.

TEACHER MODELING

Personalized learning and student choice may limit the use of teacher modeling, which can be problematic. It takes more time for teachers to model skills with small groups and individuals than it does to model a skill in a whole-class lesson. But teachers should continue to model techniques for students. Modeling helps students understand how resources and time constraints impact choices. It also helps students learn how to set goals, plan, and execute their plan. Teachers can model the use of goal-setting and the use of planners that help direct and organize learning. In a successful personalized learning environment, the teacher plays an "integral role in student learning: designing and managing the learning environment, leading instruction, and providing students with expert guidance and support help them take increasing ownership of their learning" (Pane et al. 2015)

Getting Started

Let's assume you and the administrators in your districts have done some hard work. You know the nonnegotiable standards that must be addressed, and you have unpacked the standards to determine specifically what content and skills are to be taught when. You apply this information in your up-front unit planning. You can use a couple of helpful tools to organize instruction in this preplanning stage.

One such tool is the 4S planner, which helps you organize the scope, sequence, and schedule for standards to be learned. In **figure 7-2**, you'll see a sample 4S planner in which a first-grade teacher identifies the parts of the anchor standard as well as the parts of the standard key details in text. The teacher sets goals for all students by listing mastery dates. She knows not all students will hit these target dates, but she needs to organize in her own mind the scope and sequence. (For a blank reproducible version of this planner, see page 154.) If you are an upper elementary or middle school teacher, you can fill out the 4S planner together with your students. Assist students so they list realistic mastery dates. High school students can fill out this chart themselves—especially if they have been using an organizer like this in previous grades. For struggling or anxious students of any age, the list of standards may seem overwhelming. Work with these students to minimize the number of standards listed. As students master three or four skills, you can add three or four more.

Figure 7-2 Sample 4S Planner: Standards, Scope, Sequence, and Schedule

Reading Standard: CCSS.ELA-Literacy CCRA.R.1 Anchor Standard	Target Mastery Date	Actual Date Mastered
(anchor standard) logical inference	March	
(anchor standard) textual evidence	October	
(anchor standard) conclusions drawn from text	October	
Key Details in Text		
Story retelling	September	
Feeling words	September	
Compare and contrast books	October	
Narrator at different points in the story	January	
Illustrations, details to describe character, plot setting	November	
Compare and contrast adventures/experiences of characters	December	
Read prose and poetry for grade one with support	March	

The next step is for students to consider their learner profile. On page 155, you will find a reproducible **Right-Now Learner Profile** form for students. Knowing their learner profile will help students make informed decisions about what will work best for them. Help your students understand that this profile reflects their interests and needs *right now* and that these may change over time for a variety of reasons. For example, as students become more comfortable with you and their classmates, they may be more willing to ask for help or to work with others. You can decide how often you want your students to complete this profile. (I recommend that you have students fill it out at the beginning of the year and at least one more time, preferably halfway through the year.) If your students are in the primary grades, you can simplify the form by limiting the top questions to numbers 2, 4, 7, and 8. You can shorten or modify the table as well. As with any questionnaire or survey, some students will not fill out this form realistically. Even an unwillingness to fill it out seriously should tell students something about their learner profile.

Using the Instructional Design Planner for Personalized Learning

You can use the reproducible **Instructional Design Planner for Personalized Learning** on page 157 to determine how much control you want to give your students over the following instructional design steps:

1. Determine nonnegotiable content based on standards.
2. Connect content to students' interests.
3. Create a preassessment.
4. Use data to inform instruction.
5. Determine grouping.
6. Differentiate the content depth and complexity.
7. Differentiate the thinking process.
8. Differentiate the product.
9. Decide on materials to use.
10. Devise instructional strategies and learning opportunities.
11. Share memory techniques.
12. Make modifications.
13. Create formative assessments and feedback.
14. Create summative assessments.

The instructional design steps are listed in the left column of the planner. For each step, consider who should be in control: you, the student with your assistance, or the student alone? This planning may seem like a lot of work at first, but over time, you'll be able to think through all the steps in your head, and you'll no longer need to fill out the form. Why would you want to use the instructional design planner in the first place? It can help you see how much personalized learning you are actually doing. As you become more comfortable with personalized learning and your students take on more and more responsibility, you may see marks shifting from left to right across the columns.

STEP 1: DETERMINE NONNEGOTIABLE CONTENT BASED ON STANDARDS

For the first step in the instructional design planner, you will likely always determine the content and skills, because these are nonnegotiable learning based on standards. There is not a lot of wiggle room in this step. You can identify topics, subtopics, and skills with students, but these will all likely be nonnegotiable as well.

STEP 2: CONNECT CONTENT TO STUDENTS' INTERESTS

For the second step, you and/or the students connect content to students' interests. If you plan to control this step, you might identify what students at a certain age are usually interested in. For example, you might say most students are interested in sports. Let's say the unit is about decimals. You decide to connect the decimal unit to sports data and mark the "teacher" column. If you decide to generate ideas with students or sit one-on-one with students who claim they have no interests, mark the "student with teacher assistance" column. Some students see connections easily. They know what they are interested in and can readily connect the content with their own interest. If you know they can do this independently, mark the "student" column.

STEP 3: CREATE A PREASSESSMENT

You will usually come up with the preassessment, not your students. You may create more than one type of preassessment, but even if students choose which one they want to complete, you would still mark the "teacher" column.

STEP 4: USE DATA TO INFORM INSTRUCTION

When students use commercial programs, it is easy for them to know what to do next. For example, with leveled readers, students take an assessment and then move on to the next level reader. It can be a little trickier for students to use data when they are doing an independent study or a long-term project. At certain points, you and your students will need to review data together and decide what is the next step forward. Over time, students get used to looking at scores and feedback and can determine for themselves what to do next.

STEP 5: DETERMINE GROUPING

The next element in the instructional design planner is grouping. In some instances, you will determine the groups by ability, by students' strengths and interests, or randomly. Other times, students will choose groups with your assistance. For example, you require all groups to include both critical and creative thinkers as well as an on-task manager, and students choose groups that fulfill your requirement. If you mark the "student" column, that means your students may form groups any way they like.

STEP 6: DIFFERENTIATE THE CONTENT DEPTH AND COMPLEXITY

Like Kimberly Joy on page 106 in chapter 5, you might create a Revised Bloom's Taxonomy matrix and allow your students to choose from the tasks on the matrix. This is an excellent example of high-quality differentiation, but if you control the options, you would mark the "teacher" column. If you want to move to more personalized learning, you can work with students to complete the matrix and give students the power to create some of their own activities. In this case, you would mark the "student with teacher assistance" column. Once students understand how the model works, they can work in a group to create their own matrix, and you would mark the "student" column. Creating a matrix takes quite a bit of time and skill and may not appeal to all students. For students who do want to drive their own learning, the matrix provides a structure that might make it easier. You can share the idea of developing questions and activities based on simple to complex content and basic to abstract thinking as described in chapter 5.

STEP 7: DIFFERENTIATE THE THINKING PROCESS

You will want to ensure that your students are engaging in rigorous thinking. Students may have a hard time differentiating the thinking process without a list of skills (verbs and phrases) to help them direct their thinking. When students direct their own learning, they learn to pay attention to the verb. They can substitute the verb to make thick or thin thinking, depending upon their preference. They can also assess the types of thinking skills they plan to use. This helps them see if they are focusing mostly on recall and comprehension or more on analytical and evaluative thinking. **Figure 7-3** classifies several questions and commands according to thinking skills.

Figure 7-3 Thinking Skills Classification

Remember	Understand	Apply	Analyze	Evaluate	Create
How is . . . ?	How would you compare.. . . . ?	What facts would you select to show . . . ?	How is . . . related to . . . ?	Do you agree with the actions of . . . ?	How would you improve . . . ?
When did . . . ?	How would you rephrase the meaning of . . . ?	Can you use the facts to . . . ?	How would you categorize . . . ?	How would you prioritize . . . ?	How could you change the . . . ?
How would you explain . . . ?	State in your own words . . .	What would result if . . . ?	Can you identify the parts of . . . ?	How would you justify . . . ?	Can you think of an original way for . . . ?
Why did . . . ?			What is the relationship between . . . ?		
Can you list three . . . ?					

STEP 8: DIFFERENTIATE THE PRODUCT

Students can also classify the product forms they plan to use (see **figure 7-4**). Provide students with a list of possible products, which students may or may not use. In the Instructional Design Planner, you might mark that you will assign products, that students will choose product forms with your assistance, or that students will decide for themselves which product to use.

STEP 9: DECIDE ON MATERIALS TO USE

The planner indicates who decides what materials to use for instruction and for product production. With personalized learning, students usually determine what they need for materials, but it helps for teachers to check out the list before students proceed. Sometimes, teachers will think of additional materials that a student may need.

STEP 10: DEVISE INSTRUCTIONAL STRATEGIES AND LEARNING OPPORTUNITIES

Teachers use instructional strategies all the time, but students do not usually think much about what strategies teachers use to teach them. Students only consider whether they like a strategy. For a list of learning strategies you can share with your students, see the reproducible on page 158. When students encounter an unlisted strategy that they like and that helps them learn, they can add it to the list.

Creating Tiered Questions

One instructional strategy you can use to help students learn is developing tiered questions. You can use tiered questions to create easy, medium, and hard levels of challenge. Coming up with many and varied ideas might seem daunting, but it can be easy and quick if you use

Figure 7-4 Product Forms Classification

Written	Oral	Visual	Kinesthetic
Journal entry	Debate	Bulletin board	Skit
Worksheet	Discussion	Storyboard	Demonstration
Letter	Speech	Graphic organizers	Construction
Questionnaire	Joke	Book jacket	Model
Poem	Complaint		
List	Game		
Headline			

a system. By putting together combinations of content and thinking levels, you can teach your students how to create three levels of tiered questions.

The Drapeau Tiered Questioning Student Guide (**figure 7-5**) helps students understand tiering and provides them with a formula to generate their own high-quality questions. They can also use this guide to assess what level of questions drives their learning. Students choose from a list of tiered questioning options to create an easy, medium, or hard question. In option 1, students pay attention only to the verbs. The first question includes a low-level verb, the second a high-level verb, and the third two high-level verbs. Students can use this option to learn how to generate a set of three questions from easy to hard, or they can take a given question from a worksheet or textbook and classify the question, according to its verb, as level one, two, or three. Students then simplify the verb or make it more complex in order to create multiple levels of difficulty for the same question. Then students reread their questions. Which question do they like better? Some students choose more complex questions because they are more exciting. Which one challenges them? Students do not always have to choose the highest level of challenge, but they should do so at least some of the time.

Students have the option to use the same question or create a new question and try out option 2. This time they pay attention to the verbs again, but in tier three they must overtly embed a theme and generalization. (See page 103 in chapter 5.) The theme and generalization should not be implied; the wording should be identifiable within the sentence itself. Notice that the third-tier question includes the theme and generalization that change may take place over time. Students often won't choose option 2 because it is hard to come up with a question that uses the theme and generalization. It is easier to just change verbs. However, the third-tier questions in option 2 are often more interesting. They also make the focus more specific and drive students' thinking deeper.

In option 3, there is a slight variation that makes an important difference. This time there is a low-level verb, a theme word with no generalization, and a theme word with a generalization. Option 3 shows the power of the generalization. Notice the difference between the second-tier and third-tier questions. The generalization is that change is inevitable, which asks students to think about the changes through the lens of inevitability. Which question do students like better?

Option 4 changes things again by asking students to think about philosophical, ethical, or moral (PEM)

reasoning. (See page 104 in chapter 5.) The theme and generalization are targeted at the second tier, and the PEM—in this case, universal truths—drives students' philosophical thinking. Additionally, the word *should* drives ethical and philosophical thinking as well. The PEM questions are hard to think of unless students are generally philosophical thinkers and they like to think this way.

If you are differentiating, you can create the tiered questions using the guide yourself. If you want to personalize instruction, model the system so students know how it works and then have students create their own questions at whatever level of complexity they want to target. Students may generate all three levels of a question or not, but best of all, students now know how to control questioning that drives their learning.

Using Pathways and Playlists

Pathways and playlists are a way to organize instructional strategies and learning opportunities. Pathways are routes to learning outcomes. Playlists consist of the specific activities that take place along a pathway. Teachers usually create the playlists, but in a personalized learning classroom, students could create their own.

Figure 7-6 offers examples of three teacher-created pathways for a math unit from which students choose. The pathway headers are not static. There is not always a textbook/technology path, graphic representations path, or social pathway. These may change when students embark on a new unit. The teacher notes whether each activity is a group activity, a pair activity, or an

Figure 7-5 Drapeau Tiered Questioning Student Guide

	Tiering Strategies	Examples
Option 1	1. Low-level verb	Describe Cinderella's personality.
	2. High-level verb	Analyze Cinderella's personality throughout the story.
	3. Two high-level verbs	Compare and contrast changes in Cinderella's personality in relation to pre- and post-assertiveness training and evaluate her potential for long-term happiness.
Option 2	1. Low-level verb	Describe Cinderella's personality.
	2. High-level verb	Analyze Cinderella's personality throughout the story.
	3. Theme and generalization	Predict what changes in Cinderella's behavior may take place over time.
Option 3	1. Low-level verb	Describe Cinderella's personality.
	2. Theme word	Predict changes in Cinderella's behavior after she marries the prince.
	3. Theme word and generalization	Predict inevitable changes in Cinderella's behavior after she marries the prince.
Option 4	1. Low-level verb	Describe Cinderella's personality.
	2. Theme and generalization	Predict inevitable changes in Cinderella's behavior after she marries the prince.
	3. PEM	Should Cinderella's actions represent universal truths?

Figure 7-6 Sample Pathways and Playlists

Pathway 1: Textbook/Technology		
Playlist 1	**Grouping Arrangement**	**Formative and Summative Scores**
Activity 1.1: textbook page 35 odd numbers	Individual	85%
Activity 1.2: textbook page 37 last 10 examples	Individual	90%
Activity 1.3: textbook page 38 all examples	Individual	90%
Activity 1.4: video 1–"Adding Fractions with Different Denominators"	Individual	
Activity 1.5: video 2–"Adding Fractions with Unlike Denominators"	Individual	
Pathway 2: Graphic Representation		
Playlist 2	**Grouping Arrangement**	**Formative and Summative Scores**
Activity 2.1: graphic representation packet pages 1–4	Individual	75%
Activity 2.2: graphic representation packet pages 5–8	Individual	65%
Activity 2.3: activity math with everyday objects page 9	Individual	Proficient
Activity 2.4: math around the room 1	Individual	Proficient
Activity 2.5: math around the room 2	Individual	Proficient
Pathway 3: Social Learning		
Playlist 3	**Grouping Arrangement**	**Formative and Summative Scores**
Activity 3.1: team-based solving word problems 1	Small group	Proficient
Activity 3.2: team-based solving word problems 2	Small group	Advanced
Activity 3.3: team-based solving word problems 3	Small group	Proficient
Activity 3.4: team-based solving word problems 4	Small group	Advanced
Activity 3.5: team-based solving word problems 5	Small group	Advanced

independent activity. There is also a place to record scores. For a blank reproducible you can use to create your own pathways and playlists, see page 159.

In pathway 1, the textbook/technology pathway, the playlist includes textbook pages with specific exercises students must complete as well as videos that students must watch. In pathway 2, graphic representations, the playlist directs students to complete a packet of graphic representations and use everyday objects to represent the new learning. In pathway 3, the social learning pathway, the playlist specifies that students work in teams to solve word problems that incorporate specific number concepts. The playlist consists of various types of word problems the team will solve.

Using an Instructional Activities Planner

Another planning tool you might consider using is the **Teacher and Teacher-Student Instructional Activities Planner**. It gives the teacher an overview of the activities or playlist that will occur in the unit, who will create or control the activities (the teacher, the student with the teacher's assistance, or the student alone), the grouping

arrangement, when the activity will occur (in the beginning, middle, or end of the unit), the type of assessment, and whether specific time will be spent on student reflection. Much of the information from the other planning tools is transferred to this tool with some added details.

In the sample unit shown in **figure** 7-7, the teacher assigns a science experiment. She will group students in pairs for this activity. The science experiment will take place in the middle of the unit; students will record and reflect on their findings. The students work in small groups to create tiered questions that they will answer throughout the unit. The tiered questions require a variety of products, because students do not want to just ask and answer questions. The next activity listed is a YouTube link for students to watch individually at the beginning of the unit. There will be no assessment of this activity, but the teacher is expecting student reflection through discussion. Next on the planner, there are four blank activities that are not named. This is because students will decide what they want to do at this stage. Below that is the teacher-created Jeopardy game that students play in teams at the end of the unit. The teacher observes who answers which questions. Finally, the teacher assigns a presentation as a summative assessment. Students work individually on it and present it to the class. They reflect on how they did.

STEP 11: SHARE MEMORY TECHNIQUES

Support your students by teaching them memory techniques. All you need to do is share these techniques with students and ask them to identify which are most helpful to them. This knowledge empowers students because it gives them a way to help themselves. Common memory techniques include:

- speaking out loud
- forming associations
- drawing pictures
- visualization
- learning by doing
- chunking and categorizing information
- physical movement
- using flash cards
- writing out
- discussing in groups
- using mnemonics
- creating a song
- using senses
- using metaphor and analogy
- acronyms and acrostics

- repetition, review, practice, rehearse
- attaching emotion
- organizing information
- outlines and flowcharts
- highlighting
- sticky notes
- real-life examples
- color coding
- paraphrasing

STEP 12: MAKE MODIFICATIONS

Teachers usually make modifications for struggling learners, ELL students, gifted and talented students, and students with IEPs. Personalized learning does not mean that teachers expect students to teach themselves. If that were so, neither teachers nor students would bother to come to school. Teachers support students when they need help. When your students need help remembering vocabulary words, ask them to create vocabulary index cards, create word games with vocabulary words, or find characteristics of words within words. Show students comprehension strategies such as using a cognitive graphic organizer that helps them build comprehension skills. Students can learn how to identify the most important words by highlighting, underlining, listing, or marking them with sticky notes. You may assign partners to read together. You can scaffold assignments for struggling students by modifying reading assignments or by choosing only the most important reading assignment

Figure 7-7 Teacher and Teacher-Student Instructional Activities Planner

Playlist Activities or Tasks	Teacher Assigns	Teacher and Student Assign	Student Creates	Grouping	When	Type of Assessment	Student Reflection
Science experiment	✓			Pairs	Middle of unit	Science log	✓
Tiered questions			✓	Groups	Throughout unit	Varied	✓
YouTube	✓			Individual	Beginning of unit	None	✓
			✓				
			✓				
			✓				
			✓				
Jeopardy	✓			Teams	End of unit	Observation	
Summative assessment: presentation	✓			Individual	End of unit	In-class presentation	✓

and eliminating the others. You could minimize the length of an assignment by asking students to answer every other question or answer the three most important questions. You might give students extra time or allow some students to make grammatical errors. You can learn about general as well as specific modifications from your literacy and math specialists, special education teachers, gifted and talented teachers, and curriculum coordinators. Share these ideas with your students, who will then have the tools to make modifications for themselves.

STEP 13: CREATE FORMATIVE ASSESSMENTS AND FEEDBACK

With personalized learning, students determine which assessment to use when, and self and peer feedback are used more often than with differentiation. When you use the instructional design planner for personalized learning, either you or your students can create formative assessments. Either way, it is helpful to have a handy generic form that can be used with any content. On page 160 you'll find a reproducible **Formative Assessment Questions** form with seven general questions that assess what students have learned so far. The questions do not target recall and regurgitation; rather, they target high-level thinking. Instead of asking students to make a definition, the first question asks about the purpose of the topic. The second question has students make connections between topics. The third and fourth questions target critical and creative thinking. The fifth question directs the student to synthesize information by summarizing. The sixth question asks students to make personal meaning, and the seventh question sparks students to wonder about the topic. **Figure 7-8** shows how this form might be applied in math and science.

If a teacher uses the form as a guide, students begin to learn about the content with this structure in mind. They know at some point they will have to answer questions based on these seven organizing thoughts. Once students answer the seven questions, they are asked to reflect on how they feel about their answers. If they can answer the questions and feel good about their answers, they are ready to move on. If they hesitate and are not sure about some of their answers, they may need a little more practice. If they do not feel good about their answers, it might be that they are unable to answer such advanced questions. The teacher can modify the questions to target a lower level of knowledge and application, and if students do okay with the simpler

questions, they can move on. If students cannot answer basic questions, they should review the information again. Notice that the "reflect" section asks students what activities they plan to do to review. They use study skills to help them remember the content, or they may need to go back to the basics and start again if at some point they were confused and did not understand the information. If students need help coming up with review activities, they can meet with their teachers, who can brainstorm ideas with them.

STEP 14: CREATE SUMMATIVE ASSESSMENTS

Summative assessments often culminate in some sort of presentation. Students know what knowledge they must demonstrate because some content is nonnegotiable. Students decide how they will show what they know, whom they will present the information to, and when they will present it. This is all usually based upon teacher approval. They must think about presenting within the confines of a designated location. They need to consider who will be their audience and when is an appropriate time to present the information to the audience. This process involves a lot of decision-making and organization.

If students begin learning the process at a young age, and they begin with making a few small decisions, they build the skills necessary to plan and execute presentations. It is much harder for students to begin to do this type of summative assessment for the first time in middle school or high school. For some students, just learning the content is hard enough. When we add planning and carrying out a presentation, students need to employ many additional skills. There will be times when teachers choose the summative assessment and plan for the presentations. There will be times when students will need assistance from teachers to move from decision-making to presentation, and there will be times when students are capable and ready to do this on their own. We often see these skills come together in the senior year of high school, when students plan and organize capstone projects, but in a personalized learning system, these skills come together earlier than in a traditional system.

Feedback on Instructional Design for Personalized Learning

When you are using the instructional design planner (page 157), it is often best for you to control nonnegotiable content and preassessment. The rest of the

Figure 7-8 Sample Formative Assessment Questions

Student name: Madeline Zaccha   **Date:** May 17, 2020

Topic: Math and science

Formative Assessment (Math)

1. What is the purpose of decimals? Give as much detail as possible.

2. Describe the link between decimals and fractions.

3. Analyze the causes and effects of using decimals. Elaborate on your answer.

4. What if there were no decimals? Could you predict what might happen?

5. Summarize what you have learned so far about decimals.

6. Why is it important to know about decimals?

7. Generate a list of your unanswered questions about decimals.

Formative Assessment (Science)

1. What is the purpose of gravity? Give as much detail as possible.

2. Describe the link between gravity and you.

3. Analyze the causes and effects of gravity. Elaborate on your answer.

4. What if there was no gravity? Could you predict what might happen?

5. Summarize what you have learned so far about gravity.

6. Why is it important to know about gravity?

7. Generate a list of your unanswered questions about gravity.

Reflection

1. How do you feel about your responses to the questions above? Check one:
   ☐ good   ☐ bad   ☐ so-so

2. Do you feel ready to move on, or do you think you need more review? Check one:
   ☐ move on   ☐ not ready   ☐ not sure

3. If you want to review, what activity or activities will help you?

Manage

1. Record your progress on your management tracker and date it.

2. Begin your next subtopic exploration or let the teacher know if you are ready for your summative assessment.

---

elements on the chart can move from teacher-directed to student-directed. But even when students are capable of determining materials, there are times when you will limit the use of materials (such as calculators) or require materials (such as a compass). You must use common sense to determine who drives the learning when. Consider where you can give more student control.

If you want your students to give you feedback on this issue, ask them to complete the reproducible **Student Feedback Form** on page 161. If you are concerned that some students might be uncomfortable saying anything that might seem to criticize you, ask students to fill out the feedback form but not put their name on it. You can also ask them to work with a partner or in a small group to complete the form. This tool gives students voice and empowers them to make a difference.

The instructional design process consists of identifying standards along with the nonnegotiable content. This content includes topics, subtopics, and skills that range from simple to complex. Next, pathways are determined according to students' interest, readiness, and competencies. Playlists are made up of specific activities, tasks, products, and exhibitions. Assessments involve rubrics, performance indicators, grading, portfolios, and feedback. The last component in the system incorporates ways to manage personalized learning.

All the information can be synthesized in the student's personalized learning plan (PLP). See page 162 for a reproducible **Student Personalized Learning Plan (PLP)**. This form includes the major areas of student strengths and weaknesses in the academic, skill, executive function, and work habit areas. There is a place to note specifically what goals will be addressed in each area. Teachers, students, and parents all comment on each of the goals at conference time.

In a personalized learning classroom, students lead the parent/guardian conferences. When they schedule the conference, they check with the teacher to make sure the time slot is available. They must create a formal invitation that they send to their parents/guardians. Parents/guardians are also expected to reply formally to the invitation. Once the acceptance is received, students check off the time slot on the teacher's schedule so that others know that the time is taken. Finally, students organize the information they want to share. They use the PLP to guide their discussion, and they may also use the Student-Led Conference Prep form (see reproducible on page 163). Students share a working portfolio with a collection of their work. This work provides evidence that supports their comments.

Chapter Summary

The forms and figures included in this chapter are meant to serve as support material both for teachers who are just beginning to personalize learning and for teachers who are looking to refine their personalized learning practice. This chapter focuses on an instructional design for personalized learning that you can use for everyday instruction. All aspects of the instructional process are broken down into small pieces so you can assess for yourself where and how you might shift their instruction from teacher-led to student-led. If you have a strong differentiation background, this shift naturally flows from you directing the high-quality instruction to teaching students what high-quality instruction looks like so they can direct their own high-quality learning.

Personalized learning may begin with one lesson, a unit approach, a classroom design, a school-based directive, or a district initiative. It may be instituted through state or district policy or simply through state or district support. What matters most is that if you believe personalized learning is a worthy approach to education, you continue to move your practice forward.

Personalized learning empowers students to take control of their learning. It empowers them with knowledge of their strengths, weaknesses, and interests, with knowledge about how they learn best, and with an opportunity to make a difference in the world around them.

Discussion Questions

1. What is your vision of personalized learning?

2. Why should you personalize learning?

3. What are some instructional shifts that you plan to make as a result of reading this chapter?

4. The Bill and Melinda Gates Foundation identifies four personalized learning elements: learner profiles, personalized learning paths, individual mastery, and flexible learning environment. Do you agree with these four elements? Why or why not?

5. Evaluate the role competency-based, mastery-based, or proficiency-based education plays in personalized learning.

After you've thought about your answers to these questions, visit this website for a video chapter review with the author: freespirit.com/empower-videos.

Reading Response Rubric

Assignment: As you read the book, summarize the information in each chapter in your reading response journal.

Assignment	Okay	Very Good	Fantastic
Reading responses to:	☐ Responses are on time. ☐ Responses cover the basics. ☐ Responses are obvious. ☐ Responses provide minimal detail.	☐ Responses are on time. ☐ Some responses are in-depth. ☐ Some responses are thought-provoking. ☐ Some responses are elaborative, expressive, and sophisticated.	☐ Responses are on time. ☐ Responses go beyond the readings. ☐ Responses are thought-provoking. ☐ Elaboration provides new insights.

Comments:

4S Planner: Standards, Scope, Sequence, and Schedule

Standard	Target Mastery Date	Actual Date Mastered

Right-Now Learner Profile

Right now, I would describe myself as a learner in the following ways:

1. I would describe myself as the following type or types of learner (check one or two):
   - ☐ Academic learner: I like to learn and I usually learn easily.
   - ☐ Perfectionist learner: I like to do the best work I can and I want my work to be right.
   - ☐ Creative learner: I like to come up with unusual ideas and different ways of doing things.
   - ☐ Challenged learner: It's hard for me to learn and it takes me longer to learn than it takes others.
   - ☐ Hesitant learner: I dislike speaking out loud in class and I don't like being called on.
   - ☐ High-energy learner: I can't sit too long and I like to do active things.

2. My interests are:

3. I really dislike the following subject areas:

4. I am happy when:

5. I am proud of the work I do in:

≫——→

6. I get nervous when:

7. I am really good at:

8. I sometimes need help with:

Place an X in the appropriate box for each learning behavior.

Learning Behaviors	Not Really	Some of the Time	Definitely
I am a social learner.			
I have a can-do attitude about schoolwork.			
I like to help others.			
I am excited to learn.			
I wait for someone to show me what to do.			
I ask for help.			
I work hard.			
I like to do hands-on things, and I like projects.			
I like projects that make me feel that I am doing something that matters.			
I'd prefer teachers just tell me what to do than have to decide for myself.			

Instructional Design Planner
for Personalized Learning

Unit:

Place an X in the appropriate box for instructional design element.

Instructional Design Steps	Teacher	Student with Teacher Assistance	Student
1. Determine nonnegotiable content based on standards.			
2. Connect content to students' interests.			
3. Create a preassessment.			
4. Use data to inform instruction.			
5. Determine grouping.			
6. Differentiate the content depth and complexity.			
7. Differentiate the thinking process.			
8. Differentiate the product.			
9. Decide on materials to use.			
10. Devise instructional strategies and learning opportunities.			
11. Share memory techniques.			
12. Make modifications.			
13. Create formative assessments and feedback.			
14. Create summative assessments.			

Learning Strategies

Here are many strategies you can use to help you learn and practice your new learning.

1. Brainstorm ideas about . . .

2. Use notecards or flashcards to review.

3. Cut and paste pictures and label them.

4. Match different aspects of something.

5. Write in your journal about . . .

6. Use the ShowMe app to explain . . .

7. Generate questions and trade with a friend.

8. Make games such as bingo, concentration, and "are you smarter than a fifth grader?"

9. Once you know the content, you can play with it by using SCAMPER: **substitute** ideas, **combine** ideas, **adapt** ideas, **modify** ideas, **put** ideas to other uses, **eliminate** ideas, or **rearrange** ideas.

10. Write vocabulary words in the air. (It looks silly, but it works!)

11. Make predictions.

12. Prioritize information.

13. Tell what you knew, learned, and questioned.

14. Sketch three ideas that you want to remember.

15. Use graphic organizers to compare and contrast, show cause and effect, and summarize.

16. To review vocabulary words, write the dictionary definition, write your own definition, draw a picture of the word, and create a sentence using the word.

17. Use a thinking skill cube to create good questions. Roll the cube and use the verb that lands faceup to create a question.

18. Use the 3-2-1 strategy: list three things about . . ., tell two things that are dependent upon . . ., and identify the one most important thing about . . . and tell why it is the most important.

19. Use the connect-remember-question strategy: This reminds me of . . . , I want to remember because . . . , I still don't understand . . .

20. Sort information into facts, opinions, and not sure.

21. Have a small-group discussion about a topic of your choice.

22. Research for more information or to clarify information.

23. Blog about the content.

24. Think about the content. Discuss it with a friend. Then find two other partners to share your thoughts with.

Pathways and Playlists

Pathway 1:		
Playlist 1	Grouping Arrangement	Formative and Summative Scores

Pathway 2:		
Playlist 2	Grouping Arrangement	Formative and Summative Scores

Pathway 3:		
Playlist 3	Grouping Arrangement	Formative and Summative Scores

Formative Assessment Questions

Student name: _____ Date: _____

Topic: _____

Formative Assessment

1. What is the purpose of _____? Give as much detail as possible.

2. Describe the link between _____ and _____.

3. Analyze the causes and the effects of __ _____ _____. Elaborate on your answer.

4. What if _____? Could you predict _____?

5. Summarize what you have learned so far about _____.

6. Why is it important to know about _____ _____?

7. Generate a list of your unanswered questions about _____.

Reflection

1. How do you feel about your responses to the questions above? Check one:
   ☐ good   ☐ bad   ☐ so-so

2. Do you feel ready to move on, or do you think you need more review? Check one:
   ☐ move on   ☐ not ready   ☐ not sure

3. If you want to review, what activity or activities will help you?

Manage

1. Record your progress on your management tracker and date it.

2. Begin your next subtopic exploration or let the teacher know if you are ready for your summative assessment.

Student Feedback Form

What I learned	☐ I had no choice about what I learned.	☐ I had some choice about what I learned.	☐ I had total choice about what I learned.	Comments:
Tasks or activities	☐ I had no choice of tasks or activities.	☐ I had some choice of tasks or activities.	☐ I had total choice of tasks or activities.	Comments:
Products	☐ I had no choice of products.	☐ I had some choice of products.	☐ I had total product choice.	Comments:
Interest	☐ I learned things but they didn't interest me.	☐ I learned some things that interested me.	☐ I was very interested in what I learned.	Comments:
Understanding	☐ I didn't really have enough time to understand my new learning.	☐ I mostly had time to understand my new learning.	☐ I had enough time to fully understand my new learning.	Comments:
Group work	☐ I did not work with others.	☐ I worked a little with others.	☐ I worked with others.	Comments:
Feedback	☐ I received feedback that won't really help me for next time.	☐ I received feedback that will maybe help me for next time.	☐ I received feedback that will definitely help me for next time.	Comments:
Sharing	☐ I didn't have time to share with others.	☐ I had some time to share with others.	☐ I had plenty of time to share with others.	Comments:
Peers	☐ I didn't feel listened to by my peers.	☐ My peers listened to me a little.	☐ My peers really listened to me.	Comments:
Teacher	☐ I didn't feel listened to by the teacher.	☐ My teacher listened to me sometimes.	☐ My teacher always listened to me.	Comments:
Challenge	☐ I didn't feel challenged.	☐ I felt slightly challenged.	☐ I was consistently challenged.	Comments:
Expectations	☐ The expectations were unclear.	☐ The expectations were somewhat clear.	☐ The expectations were very clear.	Comments:
Strategies	☐ I did not learn any strategies that will help me improve my learning.	☐ I learned one strategy that might help me improve my learning.	☐ I learned several strategies that will improve my learning.	Comments:

Student Personalized Learning Plan

Student name:

School year:

Academic strengths and interests:	Academic weaknesses:	Areas to be addressed:

Competency skills strengths:	Competency skills weaknesses:	Areas to be addressed:

Executive function strengths:	Executive function weaknesses:	Areas to be addressed:

Differentiation strategies:	Personalized learning strategies:	Habits of work strategies:

	Academic	Executive Function	Habits of Work
Goals			
Teacher Comments			
Student Comments			
Parent Comments			

Student-Led Conference Prep

Standard:

Skill or topic:

Check one:

☐ I had trouble learning about this topic. It was really hard.

☐ I really learned a lot about this topic, and I can share what I know with others.

☐ This topic was so easy. I learned what I needed to know before the others, and I actually had time to go beyond what I needed to know. I can teach my classmates about this topic.

What I'm most proud of:

What worked best for me:

What really didn't work for me:

What I need to do next time:

I don't want to forget to tell my teacher about:

CHAPTER 8

Empowerment, Personalization, and Social and Emotional Learning (SEL)

Student empowerment and personalized learning can occur only when the classroom climate is safe and supportive of students' academic and social and emotional needs. The importance of climate cannot be overstated. In a survey of ten high-poverty schools that included half high-performing schools and half low-performing schools, the teachers who fostered positive classroom and school climate were over four times more likely to be in a high-performing school (Jensen 2009). Classroom climate is critical to the success of a strong personalized learning program. Without a positive climate, all the great ideas you've been reading in this book will be ineffective.

The Classroom Climate

In a 2015 survey of twenty-two thousand high school students, the top three words students used to describe how they felt in school were *tired*, *stressed*, and *bored* (Yale Center for Emotional Intelligence 2015). In a similar survey of seven thousand educators in 2017, the top three feelings were *frustrated*, *overwhelmed*, and *stressed* (Brackett and Baron 2018). Research indicates that stress is related to and affects classroom climate (Collie, Shapka, and Perry 2012).

The Classroom Environment

The classroom should not be a stressful place; it should be a place that inspires innovative thinking and empowers students. When the classroom environment is welcoming, students and visitors feel it the moment they walk in the room. Students want to spend time in such a classroom. The trick is to create a sense of student comfort, belonging, and inspiration in the classroom regardless of the school building's age or condition. A

positive classroom environment can't eliminate stress for students and teachers, but it *can* minimize it.

In a traditional classroom, students stay in their chairs most of the time. The chairs may be arranged in rows or in small groupings. A personalized learning classroom is much more dynamic. Empowered students may design their own classroom layout. Their chairs and desks may be arranged in a pattern of their choosing. Students are free to move around and get whatever resources they need. They feel comfortable asking questions and sharing ideas in their self-designed space. There may be a lot of activity going on in this type of classroom, which sometimes looks chaotic from the outside, but students do not bother one another because they are comfortable and engaged. The amount of movement may be reduced if the classroom uses a substantial amount of technology for research, writing, and other work.

Regardless of the amount of technology usage, a classroom is a small space in which many people need to get along. It is empowering for students to create classroom rules that work for them. Ideally, these rules include nonnegotiable codes of conduct determined by the teacher or the school as well as rules students come up with on their own.

The amount and type of movement in the classroom is partly dependent upon whether the space is defined in learning areas (also known as stations or centers). Many classrooms consist of three areas: a quiet area for thinking or reading, a small-group area for discussion, and an area for hands-on or physically active learning. Sometimes, classrooms are divided into three areas designated as teacher-directed, practice, and independent work areas. When classrooms are arranged in these ways, students rotate through the areas in the course of one class period.

Just as the layout of the classroom must be welcoming and conducive to learning, so must the lighting. Fluorescent lighting, while common in schools, can be hard on the eyes and may even cause headaches. To address this problem, some teachers use table lamps or floor lamps to generate a cozy feeling in their classrooms. To create an environment conducive to computer work, a teacher might turn off the fluorescent lights in the computer room and use many-colored lamps and lights projected on the ceiling.

Some teachers and students take great care in creating a quiet area. They might build a loft for students to read in or set up a secluded nook for retreating from the high energy of a crowded classroom. The quiet nook might have low lighting, beanbag chairs, and the sounds of soft music, the ocean, or chirping birds. The area might be closed off with netting or fabric.

Student-Teacher Relationships

As important as the physical environment is to classroom climate, relationships matter most. Teachers can build relationships with their students by acknowledging them academically. Student effort matters, so a quick comment recognizing that effort matters too. Encourage your students rather than praising them. Make sure they know that you recognize their progress. You might write positive comments on sticky notes and place them on students' desks, encourage students aloud, or write comments on students' papers to acknowledge success or progress or to remind them of past successes. Students see teachers as role models, so it is important that your students see you as a learner as well as a teacher. For example, if you don't know the answer to a student's question, you can respond, "I don't know, but I'll find out" or "Let's find the answer together."

You can also build relationships with students by acknowledging them on a personal level. A simple gesture like smiling can set—or reset—a student's mood. Some students come from homes where yelling, arguing, and put-downs are common daily experiences. When these students come to school, where people smile and support one another, they can refill their emotional tanks with positivity. Another way to show appreciation for students is to acknowledge their birthdays, either privately or publicly.

In a personalized learning classroom, it's important for the teacher to create a community of belonging

and safety. Create an emotional tone that says, "All are welcome here." Model respect for all members of your classroom community and for everyone's unique characteristics. Be available to your students and show an interest in their interests. Show them that it is okay to tell it like it is, to be honest, and to trust one another. If necessary, remind students that frankness and honestly aren't excuses for rudeness or disrespect.

The Importance of Social and Emotional Skills

Your classroom climate depends not only on your physical space and your relationships with students, but also on the students' social and emotional competence. "Social and emotional competence is the ability to understand, manage, and express the social and emotional aspects of one's life in ways that enable the successful management of life tasks such as learning, forming relationships, solving everyday problems, and adapting to the complex demands of growth and development" (Elias et al. 1997, 2). Social and emotional learning (SEL) helps students develop social and emotional competence.

According to the Collaborative for Academic, Social, and Emotional Learning (CASEL), SEL involves applying "the knowledge, attitude, and skills necessary to understand and manage emotions, set and achieve positive goals, feel and show empathy for others, establish and maintain positive relationships, and make responsible decisions" (CASEL 2012). CASEL's SEL model includes five competencies:

1. self-management
2. self-awareness
3. responsible decision-making
4. relationship skills
5. social awareness

The Every Student Succeeds Act (ESSA) of 2015 expanded the definition of student success to include nonacademic skills. This act, along with the research that says social and emotional skills are better predictors of success in the workplace than academic scores are, focused public attention on SEL. SEL helps students understand themselves and others, communicate effectively and with respect, resolve conflicts, and develop healthy relationships.

Executive Function, Empowerment, and Personalized Learning

Executive function—*a set of processes related to managing oneself and one's resources to achieve a goal*—is crucial to social and emotional competence and to personalized learning. *Executive functions are brain-based skills involving mental control and self-regulation* (Cooper-Kahn and Dietzel 2019).

Executive function plays a role in students' social and emotional well-being and their academic success. It helps students manage time, pay attention, switch focus, plan and organize, remember details and instructions, avoid saying or doing the wrong thing, do things based on experience, and multitask (WebMD 2019; Center on the Developing Child 2019). Students control their behavior and impulsivity—think before they act—using their executive function. It also involves the ability to think flexibly about situations. Cognitive flexibility allows students to be strong creative problem solvers. Researchers point out that executive function is a better predictor of academic success than IQ and socioeconomic status are (May 2019). That's why it is important for teachers to know about and attend to students' executive function.

Executive function is closely tied to student empowerment and personalized learning in that students must use executive function when they direct their own learning. Students do not feel empowered when teachers act as the students' executive function. For example, when you direct students' attention to the board or tell students to slow down their reading so they do not miss details, you are using your executive function—the students aren't using theirs. Instead, you should encourage students to ask themselves while doing a task, "Is this what the teacher would tell me to do?" The goal is to transition students from you telling them what to do, to them thinking about what you would want them to do, to knowing what to do themselves. When students become aware of what they need to do and the tasks they need to do it, they feel empowered and capable of making their learning personal.

Executive function also involves the ability to initiate tasks. The student knows what to do and when to do it. Once the task is initiated, students use their working memory to hold the information necessary for completing it and use their executive function skills to plan and organize the task and materials. Students use self-monitoring to monitor their own performance and reflect on it.

How Stress Affects Executive Function

Stress can affect any or all of the three main areas of executive function: working memory, self-control, and cognitive flexibility. Stress causes the body to release chemicals that overwhelm the prefrontal cortex and interfere with its ability to think clearly and exercise self-control (Diamond and Ling 2016). Students should be empowered with knowledge about how they might minimize their stress. In the personalized classroom, students have opportunities to practice mindfulness, apply growth mindsets, be aware of their own challenges, and realize the work it will take to overcome these challenges.

The longer students are in a state of stress, the more that state becomes the default state. Students who experience chronic stress revert to stress because their brains think it is the normal state. These students may also experience anxiety, anger, feelings of being scattered, and despondency. Teachers should not expect to teach kids with stress disorders in the same way they would teach kids without stress (Jensen 2013).

When something activates stress in a student's brain, it takes thirty to ninety minutes for the brain to calm down. Learning does not take place while this calming down is happening. Students who are stressed need coping strategies so they can continue to learn. Some strategies you can use to reduce student stress are building relationships, providing more student control, teaching coping skills, teaching executive function skills, increasing engagement, teaching appropriate emotional responses, and teaching memory techniques.

Executive Function Problems

If your students are having behavior problems, consider whether they might have executive function problems. Students can take a test for this. A cognitive ability test asks students to make figural or verbal associations. For example, a cognitive test might say, "Cat is to dog as lion is to . . ." and offer the possible answers "snake," "fish," and "wolf." The correct answer is "wolf," because the association between cat and dog is that they are both mammals, as are a lion and a wolf. An executive function task, by contrast, would list many animals and ask which one goes with the lion. Students would have to figure out for themselves what the answer is, without the cat and dog stated as an example of association. The cognitive ability test assesses logical reasoning. The executive function test assesses the ability to organize information and use flexible thinking to make meaning.

Students who have executive function problems may experience one or more of the following:

- difficulty getting started
- inability to estimate time
- difficulty incorporating feedback
- inability to plan
- inability to change plans
- loss of train of thought when interrupted
- trouble switching gears
- lack of words to describe detail
- inability to multitask
- working too slowly or too quickly

Students with poor executive function have difficulty prioritizing which task is most important or deciding which of two or three tasks to do first. In the personalized learning classroom, where students themselves identify what projects they want to do and are expected to organize their learning in a logical, meaningful way, students with executive function problems find this to be a monumental task. Teachers will need to provide strategies such as the use of graphic organizers to help students structure and organize their thinking.

Self-Regulation and Personalized Learning

Self-regulation falls under the umbrella of executive function. It is the ability to act in one's own self-interest, control one's emotions, and self-manage work. Self-regulation is the ability to think before acting. In other words, self-regulation is the power to regulate your thoughts and behaviors through resilience, grit, perseverance, and mental fortitude. It enables students to complete a task. While students persist at a task, they need to maintain socially appropriate behaviors, such as moving without bothering others, helping others, sharing resources, and speaking quietly.

Expect your students to self-regulate their learning to an age-appropriate degree in the personalized learning classroom. Students feel empowered when they apply self-regulation skills successfully to their learning process. Without the ability to self-regulate their own learning, students become dependent upon the teacher to do it. When teachers keep managing students' work, students do not practice and learn how to do it for themselves.

Students use grit to persevere with their tasks in a personalized learning classroom. You can introduce the idea of grit by sharing stories of people who have overcome great odds by demonstrating persistence. These stories will likely inspire students, but students may also need a concrete experience of their own toughness to really understand grit. For example, an outdoor education experience gives students an opportunity to learn teamwork and practice fortitude as they overcome

EXECUTIVE FUNCTIONING AND GIFTED LEARNERS

Although we expect students to carry out many executive function skills, these skills do not fully develop in humans until they are about twenty-one years old. In 2006, researchers at the National Institute of Mental Health and McGill University published a study of MRIs investigating the brain development of children with IQs between 121 and 145, a range that is typically considered gifted. Their brain development differed significantly from that of children with above-average IQs of 109 to 120 and that of children with average IQs of 83 to 108. The cortex layer in the brains of the children with higher IQs was thinner at age seven than that of the other children, and it reached peak thickness later (Shaw et al. 2006).

This means that academically gifted students may not develop the executive function skills associated with cortex thickness until later than their age peers do. This may explain why gifted students sometimes have difficulty remembering their homework or appear disorganized. While their cognitive ability is accelerated, their executive function may take longer than average to develop. Therefore, teachers should not assume students have executive function abilities commensurate with their intellectual abilities.

physical and emotional challenges. They experience resilience, overcome fear, build confidence, and develop a can-do attitude. Meanwhile, their teachers learn not to overprotect them. When teachers are too protective, they send the message that they don't think students can do something. It is important for teachers to encourage calculated risk-taking; it is an excellent way to learn grit.

You can support students' self-regulation and overall executive function with the following tips:

- Explain the purpose of self-regulation strategies and discuss specific self-regulation strategies.

- Tell students they can trick their brains to become less impulsive through self-talk. Students can tell themselves to count to five before reacting, they can write down their impulsive reaction and decide later whether to share it with others, or they can tell themselves to refocus negative impulsive thoughts to identify possible positive thoughts first.

- Help students set goals, monitor progress, and get feedback. Direct students to a video game to demonstrate how gamers do these things.

- Learn about the Pomodoro Technique for time management at francescocirillo.com/pages /pomodoro-technique, then apply this technique in your classroom using a timer of your choice.

- Give your students examples of self-regulation and executive function strategies you use.

- Help students use tools to organize thinking by giving them graphic organizers that help them compare and contrast, draw conclusions, and prioritize.

- Give students a copy of the reproducible **Questions and Verbs Decoder** on page 177 and the reproducible **Test-Taking Tips** on page 178 to help them complete assignments, study for tests, and take tests.

- Use posters and sticky notes as visual reminders.

- When you give directions for a research or writing assignment, provide specific how-to information, such as how many citations, how many note cards, how many resources, or how many types of resources.

- Develop protocols with students for discussions and group work.

- Confer with students informally or have students confer with a peer informally, using a rubric to guide their conversation.

- Have students record their own progress and determine whether they are demonstrating grit.

- Students learn through play, so use games in your instruction and encourage students to pretend what they are doing is a game.

- Teach students relaxation techniques and other tools to quiet the mind.

- Encourage "I can" attitudes in your classroom.

- Limit the amount of time you lecture and use other more powerful strategies, such as imagery.

- Encourage students to wonder, wish, and dream. Curiosity and wonder drive students to learn because they want to, not because someone tells them to.

- Emphasize that students are responsible for their choices.

- Provide opportunities both formally and informally for students to experience and show empathy and kindness.

- Praise effort, not ability. The message should be "I can see how hard you worked on this," not "You got an A on this assignment—nice work!"

- Teach students to avoid negative thoughts and spend time with positive people.

- Teach students how to advocate for themselves.

Executive function and self-regulation skills are nonacademic skills students use to complete a task. They affect both SEL and cognitive achievement, particularly in a personalized learning classroom. When students drive their own learning, we do not want them to feel disempowered or discouraged if they lack these skills that are necessary for success. No matter where students fall on their journey to becoming independent and self-directed, teachers can empower students by sharing strategies and tools their students can use to help develop self-regulation.

Integrating SEL into the Curriculum

As you have seen, SEL is vital to student empowerment and personalized learning. Students need social and emotional skills to be productive in a personalized learning environment. If some of your students lack these skills, or if your district expects you to teach these skills, you may not know what to do. Perhaps you can't figure out how it would fit into your busy school day. Maybe you did not learn much about SEL during your teacher preparation coursework. Perhaps you view SEL as the guidance counselor's area. (Unfortunately, guidance counselors usually have time to work only with at-risk students.) Maybe your students are not comfortable talking about their feelings in front of others—and maybe you are not comfortable with this either. A solution that addresses all these issues is to use an SEL model that can be integrated into curriculum content. One such model is the Affective Perspectives model. The following section provides an overview of this model.

The Affective Perspectives Model

Affective Perspectives is a model that integrates what students need to know (content), how the students learn it (process), and how the students approach the learning process (affect) through producing a product (product). The model provides a safe way for students to talk about SEL by first connecting it to content and then transferring what they learn to themselves, which leads to student empowerment. The model is composed of five skill areas called strands:

1. understanding of self and others

2. leadership

3. risk-taking

4. insight

5. goal setting

In each strand, the Affective Perspectives model offers shared language you can use to create questions for your students or steps for them to follow. Using shared language with students helps them understand what you mean and in what ways you are asking them to think about the information and notice how they feel about it. See the **Affective Perspectives Shared Language** reproducible on page 179. The language can be simplified for younger children or made more complex for older students. You do not have to use all the shared language or use it in the suggested order. In a personalized learning classroom, once students know and understand how this language works, they can create their own questions using the same language. They can also create questions and trade questions with peers.

STRAND 1: UNDERSTANDING SELF AND OTHERS

The goal of this strand is for students to understand their own and others' feelings and to develop positive self-esteem and self-concept. We want students to better understand themselves and others so that they become clear and effective communicators, self-directed learners, responsible citizens, and collaborative workers. Students who have a healthy self-esteem believe they can do things, are in charge of their lives, and take on responsibility. They have strong values and a sense of purpose. They feel they belong.

Shared Language

1. List many varied observations about a circumstance or situation.

2. Give many varied feelings you feel when you are faced with a circumstance or situation.

3. Describe the many varied conditions you might need to feel comfortable in a circumstance or situation or with a person.

Following are some examples of the shared language for strand 1 in action.

In a space unit, students:

1. Identify what they know about space stations.

2. List feelings they might have about living in space.

3. List many varied conditions they need to feel comfortable about living on a space station.

In a math class, students:

1. Identify what they notice about themselves when they take a test.

2. Give many varied feelings they feel when taking a math test.

3. Describe many varied conditions they need to feel comfortable taking the math test.

In an ELA class, after reading *A Wrinkle in Time*, students:

1. List the many varied observations they notice about Meg's intelligence.

2. List the many varied ways Meg feels about herself and her intelligence. Have they ever felt the way Meg felt?

3. Describe the many varied conditions that they might need to feel comfortable faced with Meg's problems.

STRAND 2: LEADERSHIP

The goal of this strand is for students to understand and develop skills that allow them to lead. We want students to develop leadership skills because these skills empower students to direct their own learning. Good leaders value task completion. They are persistent in pursuing goals. Leaders demonstrate self-confidence and a sense of personal identity. They tolerate frustration, uncertainty, and stress. Leaders have strong communication skills and are good organizers and planners. They are able to sense what others need and help them achieve it. They demonstrate acceptance and empathy. In the personalized learning classroom, leaders often feel empowered.

Shared Language

1. Describe the many qualities of a leader.

2. List the variables that might affect a leader's judgment in a situation.

3. Make a network of ideas as to how a leader might peacefully resolve conflict.

Following are some examples of the shared language for strand 2 in action.

In a space unit, students:

1. List the many qualities that the leader of a space station should have.

2. List the variables that might affect the space station leader's judgment.

3. If conflict arises on a space station, how might the leader peacefully resolve such a conflict?

In a math class, students:

1. Describe the many qualities of a mathematician.

2. List the variables that might affect a math group leader's judgment in deciding whose answer to use for a group response.

3. Make a network of ideas about how the leader of a math group might peacefully resolve a conflict.

In ELA class, after reading *A Wrinkle in Time*, students:

1. Describe the leadership qualities Meg demonstrated at a specific point in the story.

2. List the variables that affected Meg's judgment as a leader.

3. Make a network of ideas about how Meg demonstrated a peaceful resolution to the conflict in the story.

A TEACHER'S TESTIMONY

One middle school teacher used this model with her social studies students. They were studying the Middle Ages, with a focus on the plague known as the Black Death. She asked her students to do the following:

1. List many varied observations they noticed about living during this time.

2. List many varied emotions the students might have had if they had been living at that time.

3. Think of many varied conditions that would be necessary for them to feel comfortable.

After the activity, the teacher asked the students if any of the things they listed as necessary to feel comfortable were available to the people living during the time of the plague. She said interesting personal biases came out of the discussion, as well as a better understanding of the facts. Notice how she integrated the model into content and then had the students apply their understandings to themselves.

STRAND 3: RISK-TAKING

The goal of this strand is for students to become comfortable taking calculated risks and to embrace a calculated risk-taking attitude. We want students to develop the ability to take calculated risks because it empowers them to grow. Students recall risks they have taken and learn from this behavior. They take small risks at first and stretch to larger ones. This strand does not promote impulsive risk. Rather, it is all about taking risks in which students weigh alternatives and anticipate outcomes.

Shared Language

1. Define the risk.

2. Establish the degree of excitement surrounding the risk.

3. Brainstorm positive and negative causes and effects of taking the risk.

4. Clarify the risk by researching information.

5. Create an action plan.

6. Just do it.

Figure 8-1 offers a detailed example of the shared language for strand 3 in action. A student filled out this questionnaire after reading the story of Cinderella. You'll find a blank reproducible version of this questionnaire on page 180.

STRAND 4: INSIGHT

The goal of this strand is for students to recognize and appreciate intuitive experiences and realize that input comes from a variety of sources. Insight is a deep intuitive understanding. We want students to develop insight because it enables them to access their thoughts and experiences quickly, formulate ideas without going through analytical and evaluative processes, and apply prior knowledge in a holistic manner. When students use insight, they see patterns, have hunches, and are often interested in the future. Students who use insight are accepting, open to experiences, willing to take risks, confident, secure, independent, focused on the long view, and tolerant of ambiguity. They are often creative and playful and enjoy

humor. Insight is a useful tool for creative thinking and making educated guesses. In the personalized learning classroom, learning about insight provides students with one more tool for their toolbelt. When students learn content through insight, new information resonates with them quickly, and they feel empowered.

Shared Language

1. Practice one of the many varied ways to quiet your thoughts.

2. Focus your thoughts on a mind picture.

3. Describe with or without words what you see, hear, smell, taste, and/or feel.

In the first step, to quiet their thoughts, students can do body stretches or body shakeouts, listen to quiet music, take deep breaths, or stare at a picture. In the

---

Figure 8-1 Sample Student Risk-Taking Questionnaire

1. Tell what the risk is. What's it all about? Cinderella took a risk going to the ball because the stepsisters might find out, the prince might find out who she really is, the prince might ignore her, or the prince might not like her.

2. How much excitement did Cinderella have about taking this risk? (Check one.)
   ☐ not much   ☐ some   ☒ quite a lot

3. Brainstorm possible causes and effects. What might cause Cinderella to take the risk? What might be the effects of Cinderella taking the risk?

Possible Causes	Possible Effects
She is curious.	She meets the prince.
She has magic on her side.	She gets caught and is punished.
She is not happy.	Prince might reject her.
She has nothing to lose.	Her dreams may come true or be dashed.
She wants to meet the prince.	

4. Clarify the risk by researching information.
   What have we learned about fairytales? They end happily ever after.
   What do we know about peasants attending royal balls? Royalty and peasants meet, and relationships begin, which may or may not end happily.

5. What activities are necessary to carry out taking the risk?

Who	Does What	When	Check When Completed
Cinderella	Finds advice about royalty fashion	Before the ball	
Cinderella	Speaks with her stepsister to find out what happens at a royal ball	Before the ball	
Cinderella	Borrows a watch	Just before the ball	

6. Just do it.

second step, students create an image in their heads. They might notice they've been doing this already without realizing it. They visualize scenes in a story or create images in their head as they read. In the third step, students might have a hard time verbally expressing what they imagined. The more senses they use, the stronger the description will be. Nonverbal forms of expression such as drawing and painting are great ways for students to share their insights.

Here are some examples of integrating insight into content by using the shared language for strand 4. First, the teacher asks students to quiet their thoughts, usually by taking a few deep breaths, closing their eyes, and focusing on a mind picture. Then teachers ask students to do the following.

In math, students:

* Describe with or without words what they see/hear/feel when attending the math meet.

* Visualize fractions and percents as animals. Draw pictures of them.

In reading, students:

* Imagine the taste, smell, and feelings Andrew had when he drank the freckle juice in *Freckle Juice* by Judy Blume.

* Describe the sights, sounds, and feelings of fear the three little pigs experienced as the wolf huffed and puffed at their house of straw.

In science, students:

* Imagine they are astronauts fixing the Hubble Space Telescope. Draw what they see and explain how they feel.

* Imagine they are plants. Describe the many changes they feel as they grow.

In social studies, students:

* Visualize being a patriot soldier in the Battle of Trenton on the day after Christmas in 1776. What do they see, smell, and feel?

* Imagine going to the New York World's Fair in 1964. What do they see, hear, smell, and feel?

* Visualize a ride on a magnetic levitation vehicle and present their impressions through metaphor.

STRAND 5: GOAL SETTING

The goal of this strand is not just to set achievable aims but also to feel good about achieving. Healthy achievement requires a healthy attitude. Goal setting is a strategy that can help students develop a healthy attitude and shift from nonproductivity to productivity. Teach your students how to set realistic goals, clarify consequences, and help them see progress. No matter how much work students do, they should notice how they feel when they complete their work.

When students underachieve, they are often suffering from lack of motivation, perfectionism, procrastination, or disorganization:

* **Lack of motivation:** To encourage intrinsic motivation, let students self-grade their work and allow them to choose their own projects, set up small-group projects, do experiments, and conduct interviews. In other words, personalize the learning as much as possible and empower the learners. When students feel empowered, they achieve.

* **Perfectionism:** Lack of motivation may be driven by the need to be perfect. When the drive for excellence becomes too intense, students are at risk for underachieving. Perfectionists feel there is never enough time to get everything done, so they do nothing. To help perfectionists, teach them how to become comfortable with uncertainty and leave room for spontaneous activities. Perfectionists need to learn that mistakes are okay. You can model this by pointing out your own mistakes. Perfectionists also need to set small, progressive goals. By stopping and noticing how they feel after completing each step of a goal, they learn to experience feelings of accomplishment in little steps along the way—not just in the end step.

* **Procrastination:** Perfectionism can lead to procrastination, but it is not the only reason students procrastinate. Some other reasons are boredom, stress, distraction, rebellion, lack of time-management skills, not finding the work meaningful, or simply preferring to do things at the last minute. Help procrastinators by showing them how to break goals into doable steps, remove distractions, do what is most difficult first (then the rest will seem easy), record progress, make a daily to-do list, or come up with their own assignment reminder strategy.

* **Disorganization:** Disorganization interferes with production and goes hand in hand with underachievement. Organization skills allow students to stay on track so they can achieve. These skills

include time management, scheduling, prioritizing, and communication.

Goal setting is the overall route to healthy achievement. In order to be an effective goal setter, behavioral researcher Shad Helmstetter claims, goals should be stated in the present tense, must be specific, must be practical and possible, must get the job done with minimal negative side effects, and must allow one to do their best (Helmstetter 2017). Many educators use SMART goals—goals that are **specific**, **measurable**, **attainable**, **relevant**, and **timely**.

Shared Language

1. State your goal.

2. List positive and negative ideas or concerns related to your goal.

3. Modify your goal to fit your feelings and needs and restate your goal.

4. Develop a plan that includes what, who, when, needs, a record of progress, and rewards for progress.

5. Visualize your completed goal.

Figure 8-2 offers a detailed example of the shared language for strand 5 in action. A student filled out this questionnaire after reading *The Gingerbread Man* by Karen Schmidt. (You'll find a blank reproducible version of this questionnaire on page 181.) In this example, the teacher is teaching goal setting, point of view, and story recall to primary students. She asks them to consider the fox's goal when answering the questions.

Here are some examples of integrating goal setting into content by using the shared language for strand 5.

In math, students:

- Set a goal to memorize the math facts. Develop a plan to accomplish this.

- Set a goal to create an illustrated poem that compares a geometric shape to an emotion and complete the goal-setting form.

In ELA, students:

- Identify Oberon's goal and analyze the goal in *A Midsummer Night's Dream*.

- Analyze Claudius's goal in *Hamlet* using the goal-setting process. What can they learn about goal setting from Claudius?

- Set a goal for Andrew from *Freckle Juice* regarding how he acts with Sharon. Use the goal-setting process to describe how his goal would be carried out.

In science, students:

- Use the goal-setting method to analyze what Marie Curie's work toward understanding radioactivity might have looked like.

Figure 8-2 Sample Student Goal-Setting Questionnaire

Answer these questions from the point of view of the fox in the story *The Gingerbread Man* by Karen Schmidt.

1. State your goal:
The fox's goal was to eat the Gingerbread Man.

2. List positive and negative ideas or concerns related to your goal.

Positive	Negative
The good thing about reaching his goal is that he gets something to eat.	There is nothing bad about reaching his goal.

3. Modify your goal to fit your feelings and needs and restate your goal.

He doesn't change his goal.

4. What do you think the fox's plan was?

What	Who	When	Needs	Date	Reward
He said he couldn't hear him.	Fox	Middle of the story			The gingerbread man came closer.
He kept saying it.	Fox	To the end of the story			He kept getting closer.

5. Visualize your completed goal. What do you think the fox visualized?

The fox visualized eating the Gingerbread Man.

- Define a specific goal for a change in wildlife management that will result in an increase in the herd. Go through the goal-setting process to analyze what this might look like.

In social studies, students:

- Imagine the South had won the American Civil War and analyze what its goal-setting process might have looked like.

- Define one of the goals of the Sons of Liberty before the American Revolution and how it was modified. Describe the action plan.

- Determine the most pivotal event in the US fight for civil rights, analyze the goal the people had at the time, and include the analysis in an informative or explanatory written piece.

Other SEL Frameworks

The Affective Perspective model appeals to teachers who want to integrate social and emotional skills into their required content. Some teachers don't want to approach SEL this way. They want to deal with social and emotional skills head-on. A variety of social and emotional curricula are available for purchase. Following are several examples of such frameworks that can effectively support student empowerment and personalized learning.

Open Circle is a social and emotional program for K–5 students. This model, like Affective Perspectives, uses common language to teach social and emotional skills. The goals of this program are to reduce negative behaviors, reduce bullying, and foster prosocial skills. Teachers have fifteen-minute Open Circle meetings with the class twice a week. This model includes the following curriculum topics: being together, managing ourselves, strengthening relationships, how to sort problems, and problem-solving. Find scope and sequence and curriculum materials at open-circle.org.

Michelle Garcia Winner, founder of Social Thinking, created—with Stephanie Madrigal—*Superflex*, a social thinking curriculum with a superhero angle. It includes many Superflex books and a Thinkables & Unthinkables card deck that students use to play games. Superflex teaches students how to be aware of their own thinking and social behavior. The materials also provide self-regulation strategies. Winner and Pamela Crooke wrote a book and app titled *You Are a Social Detective! Explaining Social Thinking to Kids*. This book

is a fun way to teach students what other students mean by assessing their actions and their words. Winner and Crooke's work addresses social self-awareness, perspective taking, self-regulation, executive functioning, social and emotional understanding, and more. At the website socialthinking.com, you can find out about social thinking at all grade levels.

The *Habits of Mind* framework developed by Arthur Costa and Bena Kallick identifies sixteen soft-skill areas: persisting, managing impulsivity, listening to others with understanding and empathy, thinking flexibly, thinking about our thinking, striving for accuracy and precision, questioning and posing problems, applying past knowledge to new situations, thinking and communicating with clarity and precision, gathering data through all senses, creating/imagining/innovating, responding with wonderment, taking responsible risks, finding humor, thinking independently, and learning continuously. The developers recommend students use these skills consciously to gain maximum benefit. The use of pedagogy built into the framework creates a mindfulness approach for students to be able to know and apply the set of positive behaviors.

Other districts use the *Restorative Practices* model. One of the goals of this model is to teach students how to self-regulate positive behavior. Another goal is for students to build and maintain healthy, positive relationships. As with Habits of Mind, this model helps develop a positive school culture. The restorative practice model is often used to teach students about how to deal with bullying. It encourages students to use their voice and be heard. Students are taught about the importance of emotions. This approach can also be used to help students self-regulate positive behavior. The restorative classroom is based on the restorative justice philosophy, which emphasizes accountability, responsibility, and repairing wrongdoing. Students are taught how to resolve conflict in respectful ways.

The *Responsive Classroom* is another model that addresses social and emotional needs. One of its guiding principles is that teaching social and emotional skills is just as important as teaching academic skills. This model identifies five social and emotional competencies. They include cooperation, assertiveness, responsibility, empathy, and self-control. Subcategories include establishing relationships, resolving conflicts, accepting differences, taking initiative, considering consequences, choosing positive solutions, appreciating differences, having

SEL BOOKS

A few popular books that many guidance counselors recommend are *Social Skills Activities for Special Children* by Darlene Mannix, *Counseling Toward Solutions A Practical Solution-Focused Program for Working with Students, Teachers, and Parents* by Linda Metcalf, and *Social Skills Activities for Secondary Students with Special Needs* by Darlene Mannix.

concern for others, understanding other perspectives, and regulating thoughts/emotions/behaviors.

Research evidence shows that SEL can improve students' attitude, behavior, and academic performance. In one study, SEL programs reduced aggression and improved student attitudes and performance (Durlak et al. 2011). Another meta-analysis found positive effects on several areas, including academic achievement (Sklad et al. 2012). Regardless of whether SEL improves academic performance, this type of learning is important for its own sake.

Chapter Summary

Classroom climate influences the effectiveness of differentiated instruction and personalized learning. Students do not fully engage or feel empowered in a classroom that does not feel safe. They need to learn in a place of comfort, joy, community, and belonging. Students thrive in an environment with a physical layout that creates a feeling of oneness. The chair arrangement, desk or table arrangement, lighting, and areas of coziness all contribute to a place where students want to be.

Researchers say that students' social and emotional skills are indicators of success. You can help students develop these skills by practicing mindfulness techniques, giving students breaks, providing choice, extending wait time, sharing humor, and demonstrating patience. Executive function and self-regulation affect engagement

and empowerment too. Students need to be able to initiate tasks and follow through. They need to demonstrate grit and monitor their progress. Students may need tools to control impulsivity and strategies to help them focus and concentrate.

Many districts use programs to promote SEL. These programs consist of specific social and emotional skill areas that are targeted in little *e* empowerment or big *E* empowerment experiences in personalized learning classrooms. Some of these models are Open Circle, Superflex, Habits of Mind, Restorative Practices, and Responsive Classroom. One model that integrates cognition and affect into curriculum is the Affective Perspectives model, which is designed to combine thinking and feeling with learning content. Its goal is to empower students with knowledge about themselves in five specific SEL skill areas and to provide ways for students to change their behavior. In the personalized learning classroom, students become not just consumers of knowledge but also healthy producers of knowledge. To achieve this, teachers need to address both academic and social and emotional learning.

Discussion Questions

1. If your school hasn't adopted an SEL program, do you think it should? Why or why not?

2. How much responsibility should classroom teachers take on for students' social and emotional learning compared to guidance counselors?

3. What should teachers know about executive function and self-regulation, and what are they expected to do with this information?

4. How might you apply the Affective Perspectives model in your content area?

5. In what ways does SEL help students become self-directed lifelong learners?

After you've thought about your answers to these questions, visit this website for a video chapter review with the author: freespirit.com/empower-videos.

Questions and Verbs Decoder

Decoding Questions

Word	Refers to . . .	Response looks like . . .
who	a person	a description: the person is . . .
what	details	an elaboration: for example . . .
when	time	a date, time, or relative time: first, next, finally . . .
where	a place	a location
why	reasons	one reason or the most important reason is . . . because . . .
how	ways	the first way is . . . the second way is . . . the third way is . . .

Decoding Verbs

Verb	Meaning
explain	describe in your own words; help the reader understand; give the reason for
compare or *contrast*	describe similarities or differences
infer	draw a conclusion
summarize	explain the main points briefly
categorize	classify or group things by shared traits

Test-Taking Tips

1. Can you use any of the following tools to prepare and present your ideas?

   - webs

   - bullet charts

   - outlines

   - information tables

   - graphs

   - Venn diagrams

   - flowcharts

   - outlincs

2. When you respond to *explain your thinking*:

   - Restate the question.

   - Use the word because.

   - Give examples.

   - Use text references.

   - State a conclusion.

3. There are four types of answers to test questions:

   - personal responses that deal with feelings and experiences

   - opinion responses that ask for interpretations and reactions

   - logical responses that give reasons and list facts

   - sequential responses that prioritize or organize information

4. Watch out for "and" questions:

   - Give two responses.

   - Respond in two separate paragraphs.

5. Watch out for "would" and "could" questions:

   - The word would requires either a judgment or a prediction.

   - The word *could* requires imagination.

Affective Perspectives Shared Language

Understanding Self and Others

1. List many varied observations about a circumstance or situation.

2. Give many varied feelings you feel when you are faced with a circumstance or situation.

3. Describe the many varied conditions you might need to feel comfortable in a circumstance or situation or with a person.

Leadership

1. Describe the many qualities of a leader.

2. List the variables that might affect a leader's judgment in a situation.

3. Make a network of ideas as to how a leader might peacefully resolve conflict.

Risk-Taking

1. Define the risk.

2. Establish the degree of excitement surrounding the risk.

3. Brainstorm positive and negative causes and effects of taking the risk.

4. Clarify the risk by researching information.

5. Create an action plan.

6. Just do it.

Insight

1. Practice one of the many varied ways to quiet your thoughts.

2. Focus your thoughts on a mind picture.

3. Describe with or without words what you see, hear, smell, taste, and/or feel.

Goal Setting

1. State your goal.

2. List positive and negative ideas or concerns related to your goal.

3. Modify your goal to fit your feelings and needs and restate your goal.

4. Develop a plan that includes what, who, when, needs, a record of progress, and rewards for progress.

5. Visualize your completed goal.

Student Risk-Taking Questionnaire

1. Tell what the risk is. What's it all about?

2. How much excitement is there about this risk?
   ☐ not much   ☐ some   ☐ quite a lot

3. Brainstorm possible causes and effects of taking the risk.

Possible Causes	Possible Effects

4. Clarify the risk by researching information.

5. What activities are necessary to carry out taking the risk?

Who	Does What	When	Check When Completed

6. Just do it.

Student Goal-Setting Questionnaire

1. State your goal.

2. List positive and negative ideas or concerns related to your goal.

Positive	Negative

3. Modify your goal to fit your feelings and needs and restate your goal.

4. Plan how you will achieve your goal.

What	Who	When	Needs	Date	Reward

5. Visualize your completed goal.

Final Thoughts on Empowerment and Personalized Learning

As engagement and autonomy increase in the classroom, students become more and more empowered. Empowering students and creating a culture that supports empowerment helps students succeed academically and sparks their investment in the learning process. You can empower students by giving them opportunities to become responsible and involved citizens. You can support an empowering classroom climate by sharing stories and images of people—especially of your students' age—who have made an impact on their world. You can demonstrate the use of empowering language. You can make sure that little *e* and big *E* empowerment happen regularly in your classroom.

Empowerment is a key element of personalized learning. Personalized learning empowers learners to drive their own learning. Personalized learning is a natural extension of differentiation. Differentiation is meeting more of the learners' needs more of the time. Personalized learning is students directing their own learning more of the time. But it is just one educational philosophy that embraces empowerment. There are many ways to empower students. Personalized learning does, however, provide a natural framework for empowering experiences.

You may want to shift your instruction from engagement to empowerment or from differentiation to personalized learning, but you may be apprehensive about doing so. Thinking through the following questions can help you decide whether to make changes to your educational approach:

- Why do you want to empower students?
- What do you know about personalized learning?
- Do you want to make changes to your instruction based on an existing model or design your own instruction?
- What research informs your decision to empower students?
- Will you visit other schools?
- What local data will you consider in your decision-making?
- How will you plan for the changes you want to make?
- How will you find the time to do research and make changes?
- What kind of administrative support do you have for making changes?
- What are the benefits and what are the limitations of making the changes you envision?
- How will these changes align with current district or state initiatives? Will existing initiatives compete with a new initiative for teachers' attention?
- How will you ensure high-quality curriculum for all students?
- How will you ensure that standards will be covered with personalized learning?
- What specific aspects of programming, instruction, assessment, and management will change?
- Will the shift play out differently in various content areas?
- What role will you play in building support for students?
- To what degree will technology play a role in the new instructional approach?
- Have you used empowerment or personalized learning to some degree already? If so, have you seen any changes in your students' achievement or attitudes?

Your responses to these questions will differ from those of other educators. Educators may have differing beliefs and values. Schools and districts may have different demographics and missions. What works well in one classroom, school, or district does not necessarily work well in another. Even after reviewing the research and observing empowerment and personalized learning in action, you, your school, or your district must decide independently what works best for you.

If a school- or district-wide change isn't possible, you can still empower your students and personalize their learning in individual classrooms. If you make a conscious effort to do little *e* activities twice a week and a big *E* activity once a year, the effort will have a positive impact. So will using empowering language. Remember, the feeling of empowerment is as important as acts of empowerment are.

When it comes to personalized learning, not all students are ready to drive their own learning—nor do they want to. You must respect your students by differentiating their personalized learning experiences. When your students direct their own learning, you may fear that they will not be challenged. You needn't worry about this if you give students tools to teach them how to drive their own learning, such as the ones described in this book.

Teachers, schools, and districts can be found at many points along a continuum from a little to a lot of engagement, empowerment, differentiation, and personalized learning. None of them is at rest; all are constantly trying to improve. Most probably aspire to a blend of engagement, empowerment, differentiation, and personalized learning rather than a redesign of their entire educational system to create classrooms where students direct their own learning 100 percent of the time.

The shift from engagement to empowerment and from differentiation to personalized learning is not a race, and there is no finish line. Rather, it is a journey. There is no golden ticket that leads you down the "right" path. There are lots of golden tickets and many paths. You can choose the ones that work best for you. I hope you have collected enough golden tickets from this book to move your student empowerment and personalized learning practices forward with confidence.

After you've thought about what you've learned from this book, visit this website for a few parting words from the author: freespirit.com/empower-videos.

References and Resources

Abramovich, Samuel, Christian Schunn, and Ross Mitsuo Higashi. 2013. "Are Badges Useful in Education?: It Depends on the Type of Badge and Expertise of Learner." *Educational Technology Research and Development* 61 (2): 217–232. lrdc.pitt.edu/schunn /research/papers/Abramovich-Schunn-Higashi.pdf.

Achiron, Marilyn. 2014. "Why Policy Makers Should Care About Motivating Students." OECD Education and Skills Today. oecdedutoday.com/why-policy-makers-should-care-about -motivating-students.

AFS-USA. 2017. "5 Things All Top Global Learning Schools Have in Common." AFS-USA Blog. afsusa.org/educators/blog /article/?article_id=9039.

Amabile, Teresa, and Stephen Kramer. 2011. *The Progress Principle: Using Small Wins to Ignite Joy, Engagement, and Creativity at Work*. Boston: Harvard Business Review Press.

Amaral, Olga Maia, Leslie Garrison, and Michael Klentschy. 2002. "Helping English Learners Increase Achievement Through Inquiry-Based Science Instruction." *Bilingual Research Journal* 26 (2): 213–239.

Anand, Anika, and Ann Schimke. 2015. "Grade Levels Could Be a Thing of the Past in Schools Focused on Competency." PBS NewsHour. pbs.org/newshour/education/say-goodbye-fifth -grade-k-12-schools-test-competency-based-learning.

Anderson, Lorin W., David R. Krathwohl, Peter W. Airasian, Kathleen A. Cruikshank, Richard E. Mayer, Paul R. Pintrich, James Raths, and Merlin C. Wittrock. 2000. *A Taxonomy for Learning, Teaching, and Assessing: A Revision of Bloom's Taxonomy of Educational Objectives*. New York: Pearson.

Applebee, Arthur N., Judith A. Langer, Martin Nystrand, and Adam Gamoran. 2003. "Discussion-Based Approaches to Developing Understanding: Classroom Instruction and Student Performance in Middle and High School English." *American Educational Research Journal* 40 (3): 685–730.

Archambault, Isabelle, Michel Janosz, Julien Morizot, and Linda S. Pagani. 2009. "Adolescent Behavioral, Affective, and Cognitive Engagement in School: Relationship to Dropout." *Journal of School Health* 79 (9): 408–415.

Asia Society. 2019. "Leadership is a Global Competence." Center for Global Education. asiasociety.org/education /leadership-global-competence.

Aydin, Kubilay, Kader Karli Oguz, Ozlem Ozmen Okur, Ayaz Agayev, Zeynep Unal, Sabri Yilmaz, and Cengizhan Ozturk. 2007. *American Journal of Neuroradiology* 28 (10):1859–1864. ajnr.org /content/28/10/1859.long.

Barnum, Matt. 2018. "Maine Went All In on 'Proficiency-Based Learning'—Then Rolled It Back. What Does That Mean for the Rest of the Country?" chalkbeat.org/posts/us/2018/10/18/maine -went-all-in-on-proficiency-based-learning-then-rolled-it-back -what-does-that-mean-for-the-rest-of-the-country.

Barwick, Melanie. 2010. "Underachieving Kids: No Quick Fix." CBC News. cbc.ca/news/technology/underachieving-kids-no -quick-fix-1.928130.

Bates Prins, Samantha C. 2009. "Student-Centered Instruction in a Theoretical Statistics Course." *Journal of Statistics Education* 17 (3). jse.amstat.org/v17n3/batesprins.html.

Beecher, Margaret, and Sheelah M. Sweeny. 2008. "Closing the Achievement Gap with Curriculum Enrichment and Differentiation: One School's Story." *Journal of Advanced Academics* 19 (3): 502–530. doi.org/10.4219/jaa-2008-815.

Bill & Melinda Gates Foundation. 2010. "Next Generation Learning." docs.gatesfoundation.org/Documents /nextgenlearning.pdf.

Bloom, Benjamin S. 1968. "Learning for Mastery." *Evaluation Comment* 1 (2): 1–11. files.eric.ed.gov/fulltext/ED053419.pdf.

Brackett, Marc A., and Wendy Baron. 2018. "Research Insights: Improving Teacher Well-Being." National Association of Independent Schools. nais.org/magazine/independent-school /spring-2018/feelings-matter.

Bray, Barbara, and Kathleen McClaskey. 2017. *How to Personalize Learning: A Practical Guide for Getting Started and Going Deeper*. Thousand Oaks, CA: Corwin.

Brighton, Catherine M., Holly L. Hertberg, Tonya R. Moon, Carol A. Tomlinson, and Carolyn M. Callahan. 2005. *The Feasibility of High-End Learning in a Diverse Middle School* (RM05210). Storrs: University of Connecticut, National Research Center on the Gifted and Talented.

British Council. 2017. "The Value of Enterprise and Entrepreneurship Education." britishcouncil.org/education /skills-employability/what-we-do/vocational-education-exchange -online-magazineoctober-2017value-enterprise-entrepreneurship -education.

Brockway, David. 2015. "Equality Workshops Teach Boys to Be Empowered, Not Ashamed." *The Telegraph*. telegraph.co.uk/men /thinking-man/11755745/Equality-workshops-teach-boys-to-be -empowered-not-ashamed.html.

Brown, Peter C., Henry L. Roediger III, and Mark A. McDaniel. 2014. *Make It Stick: The Science of Successful Learning*. Cambridge, MA: Belknap Press.

Brulles, Dina, and Susan Winebrenner. 2019. *The Cluster Grouping Handbook. Revised and Updated Edition*. Minneapolis: Free Spirit Publishing.

Bulger, Monica. 2016. "Personalized Learning: The Conversations We're Not Having." Data and Society Research Institute. datasociety.net/pubs/ecl/PersonalizedLearning_primer_2016.pdf.

Calaprice, Alice, ed. 2000. *The Expanded Quotable Einstein*. Princeton, NJ: Princeton University Press. assets.press.princeton .edu/chapters/s6908.pdf.

Calderon, Valerie J., and Daniela Yu. 2017. "Student Enthusiasm Falls as High School Graduation Nears." Gallup News. news. gallup.com/opinion/gallup/211631/student-enthusiasm-falls-high -school-graduation-nears.aspx.

Callahan, Rebecca M. 2013. *The English Learner Dropout Dilemma: Multiple Risks and Multiple Resources*. Santa Barbara, CA: California Dropout Research Project. cdrpsb.org/researchreport19.pdf.

Campbell, Frances A., Elizabeth P. Pungello, Shari Miller-Johnson, Margaret Burchinal, and Craig T. Ramey. 2001. "The Development of Cognitive and Academic Abilities: Growth Curves from an Early Childhood Educational Experiment." *Developmental Psychology* 37 (2): 231–242.

CASEL. 2012. "2013 CASEL Guide: "Effective Social and Emotional Learning Programs: Preschool and Elementary School Edition." casel.org/wp-content/uploads/2016/01/2013 -casel-guide-1.pdf.

Center on the Developing Child. 2019. "Executive Function and Self-Regulation." developingchild.harvard.edu/science/key -concepts/executive-function.

Collie, Rebecca J., Jennifer D. Shapka, and Nancy E. Perry. 2012. "School Climate and Social-Emotional Learning: Predicting Teacher Stress, Job Satisfaction, and Teaching Efficacy." *Journal of Educational Psychology* 104 (4): 1189–1204. reset-mindbody.com /wp-content/uploads/2017/02/school-climate-and-sel-predicting -teacher-stress.pdf.

Common Core State Standards Initiative. 2019. "English Language Arts Standards." corestandards.org/ELA-Literacy.

Cook-Sather, Alison. 2006. "Sound, Presence, and Power: Exploring 'Student Voice' in Educational Research and Reform." *Curriculum Inquiry* 36 (4): 359–390.

Cooper-Kahn, Joyce, and Laurie Dietzel. 2019. "What Is Executive Functioning?" LD OnLine. ldonline.org/article/29122.

Costa, Arthur L., and Bena Kallick, eds. 2008. *Learning and Leading with Habits of Mind: 16 Essential Characteristics for Success.* Alexandria, VA: ASCD.

Couros, George. 2015. *The Innovator's Mindset: Empower Learning, Unleash Talent, and Lead a Culture of Creativity.* San Diego, CA: Dave Burgess Consulting, Inc.

———. 2017. "Seven Things That Happen When Kids Embrace a Maker Mindset." The Principal of Change. georgecouros.ca/blog/archives/tag/seven-things-that-happen -when-kids-embrace-a-maker-mindset.

Csikszentmihalyi, Mihalyi. 2013. *Creativity: Flow and the Psychology of Discovery and Inventions.* New York: Harper Perennial.

Diamond, Adele, and Daphne S. Ling. 2016. "Conclusions About Interventions, Programs, and Approaches for Improving Executive Functions That Appear Justified and Those That, Despite Much Hype, Do Not." *Developmental Cognitive Neuroscience* 18: 34–48. sciencedirect.com/science/article/pii/S1878929315300517.

Drapeau, Patti. 2004. *Differentiated Instruction: Making It Work.* New York: Scholastic.

———. 2009. *Differentiating with Graphic Organizers: Tools to Foster Critical and Creative Thinking.* Thousand Oaks, CA: Corwin.

Duckworth, Angela. 2016. *Grit: The Power of Passion and Perseverance.* New York: Scribner.

Duckworth, Angela L., and Martin E. P. Seligman. 2005. "Self-Discipline Outdoes IQ in Predicting Academic Performance of Adolescents." *Psychological Science* 16 (12): 939–944.

Durlak, Joseph, Roger P. Weissberg, Allison Dymnicki, Rebecca Taylor, and Kriston Schellinger. 2011. "The Impact of Enhancing Students' Social and Emotional Learning: A Meta-Analysis of School-Based Universal Interventions." *Child Development* 82 (1): 405–432.

Dweck, Carol S. 2016. *Mindset: The New Psychology of Success.* Updated ed. New York: Random House.

Elias, Maurice J., Joseph E. Zins, Roger P. Weissberg, Karin S. Frey, Mark T. Greenberg, Norris M. Haynes, Rachael Kessler, Mary E. Schwab-Stone, and Timothy P. Shriver. 1997. *Promoting Social and Emotional Learning: Guidelines for Educators.* Alexandria, VA: ASCD.

Elliott, Julian G., Susan E. Gathercole, Tracy P. Alloway, Joni Holmes, and Hannah Kirkwood. 2010. "An Evaluation of a Classroom-Based Intervention to Help Overcome Working Memory Difficulties and Improve Long-Term Academic Achievement." *Journal of Cognitive Education and Psychology* 9 (3): 227–250.

Erickson, Lynn H. 2008. *Stirring the Head, Heart, and Soul: Redefining Curriculum, Instruction, and Concept-Based Learning.* 3rd ed. Thousand Oaks, CA: Corwin Press.

Evans, Gary W., and Michelle A. Schamberg. 2009. "Childhood Poverty, Chronic Stress, and Adult Working Memory." *PNAS* 106 (16): 6545–6549. ncbi.nlm.nih.gov/pmc/articles/PMC2662958.

Finlay, Krystina A. 2008. "Quantifying School Engagement: Research Report." National Center for School Engagement. schoolengagement.org/wp-content/uploads/2013/12 /QuantifyingSchoolEngagementResearchReport-2.pdf.

Fisher, Douglas, and Nancy Frey. 2013. *Better Learning Through Structured Teaching: A Framework for the Gradual Release of Responsibility.* 2nd edition. Alexandria, VA: ASCD.

Fleming, Laura, and Billy Krakower. 2016. "Makerspaces and Equal Access to Learning." Edutopia. edutopia.org/blog /makerspaces-equal-access-to-learning-laura-fleming-billy-krakower.

Fletcher, Adam. 2014. *The Guide to Meaningful Student Involvement.* Olympia, WA: SoundOut. soundout.org/wp -content/uploads/2015/05/The-Guide-to-Meaningful-Student -Involvement.pdf.

———. 2018. "Student Empowerment and Meaningful Student Involvement." SoundOut. soundout.org/student-empowerment.

Flowerday, Terri, and Gregory Schraw. 2000. "Teacher Beliefs About Instructional Choice: A Phenomenological Study." *Journal of Educational Psychology* 92 (4): 634–645.

Fredricks, Jennifer A., Phyllis C. Blumenfeld, and Alison H. Paris. 2004. "School Engagement: Potential of the Concept, State of the Evidence." *Review of Educational Research* 74 (1): 59–109.

Frymier, Ann Bainbridge, Gary M. Shulman, and Marian Houser. 1996. "The Development of a Learner Empowerment Measure." *Communication Education* 45 (3): 181–199.

Games and Learning. 2014. "Teachers Surveyed on Using Digital Games in Class: A Games and Learning Research Report." gamesandlearning.org/2014/06/09/teachers-on-using-games -in-class.

Gentry, Marcia. 2014. *Total School Cluster Grouping and Differentiation: A Comprehensive, Research-Based Plan for Raising Student Achievement and Improving Teacher Practices. 2nd ed.* Waco, TX: Prufrock Press.

Gerloff, Pamela. 2011. "You're Not Laughing Enough, and That's No Joke." *Psychology Today* blog. psychologytoday.com/us/blog /the-possibility-paradigm/201106/youre-not-laughing-enough -and-thats-no-joke.

Gewertz, Catherine. 2016. "Vermont High School Takes Student Voice to Heart." Education Week. edweek.org/ew/articles/2016/06/02/vt-high-school-takes-student-voice-to.html.

Girl Talk. 2018. "Our Impact." mygirltalk.org.

The Global Future Education Foundation and Institute. 2017. global-future-education.org.

GLSEN. 2018. "Model School District Policy on Transgender and Gender Nonconforming Students." glsen.org/sites/default/files/Model-School-District-Policy-on-Transgender-and-Gender-Nonconforming-Students-GLSEN_0.pdf.

Goodwin, Bryan. 2014. "Curiosity Is Fleeting, but Teachable." *Educational Leadership* 72 (1): 73–74.

Great Schools Partnership. 2019. "Habits of Work Grading and Reporting." greatschoolspartnership.org/proficiency-based-learning/grading-reporting/habits-work-grading-reporting.

Gregory, Gayle H. and Kaufeldt, Martha. 2015. *The Motivated Brain: Improving Student Attention, Engagement, and Perseverance.* Alexandria, VA: ASCD.

Gross, Betheny, and Michael DeArmond. 2018. "Personalized Learning at a Crossroads: Early Lessons from the Next Generation Systems Initiative and the Regional Funds for Breakthrough Schools Initiative." Seattle, WA: Center on Reinventing Public Education (CRPE). crpe.org/sites/default/files/crpe-personalized-learning-crossroads.pdf.

Guskey, Thomas R. 1997. *Implementing Mastery Learning.* Belmont, CA: Wadsworth Cengage.

———. 2001. "Mastery Learning." In *International Encyclopedia of Social and Behavioral Sciences*, edited by Neil J. Smelser and Paul B. Baltes, 9372–9377. Oxford, UK: Elsevier Science.

———. 2009. "Mastery Learning." Education.com.

Guthrie, John T., ed. 2008. *Engaging Adolescents in Reading.* Thousand Oaks, CA: Corwin.

Guthrie, John T., and Marcia H. Davis. 2003. "Motivating Struggling Readers in Middle School Through an Engagement Model of Classroom Practice." *Reading and Writing Quarterly* 19 (1): 59–85.

Hall, Tracey, Nicole Strangman, and Anne Meyer. 2003. "Differentiated Instruction and Implications for UDL Implementation." CAST. cast.org/udlcourse/DifferInstruct.doc.

Halverson, Erica Rosenfeld, and Kimberly Sheridan. 2014. "The Maker Movement in Education." *Harvard Educational Review* 84 (4): 495–504.

Hanover Research. 2012. "Best Practices in Personalized Learning Environments." hanoverresearch.com/media/Best-Practices-in-Personalized-Learning-Environments.pdf.

Hattie, John. 2009. *Visible Learning: A Synthesis of Over 800 Meta-Analyses Relating to Achievement.* New York: Routledge.

———. 2012. *Visible Learning for Teachers: Maximizing Impact on Learning.* New York: Routledge.

Helmstetter, Shad. 2017. *What to Say When You Talk to Yourself.* New York: Gallery Books.

Hughes, Jan N., Wen Luo, Oi-Man Kwok, and Linda K. Loyd. 2008. "Teacher-Student Support, Effortful Engagement, and Achievement: A 3-year Longitudinal Study." *Journal of Educational Psychology* 100 (1): 1–14. doi:10.1037/0022-0663.100.1.1.

Hunt, Abigail. 2013. "Education and Empowerment: You're Nobody Until Somebody Trains You." The Guardian. theguardian.com/global-development-professionals-network/2013/aug/02/education-empowerment-adolescent-girls.

Indiana University. 2010. "Latest HSSSE Results Show Familiar Theme: Bored, Disconnected Students Want More from Schools." newsinfo.iu.edu/news-archive/14593.html.

Jensen, Eric. 2009. *Teaching with Poverty in Mind: What Being Poor Does to Kids' Brains and What Schools Can Do About It.* Alexandria, VA: ASCD.

———. 2013. *Engaging Students with Poverty in Mind: Practical Strategies for Raising Achievement.* Alexandria, VA: ASCD.

Jensen, Eric, and Carole Snider. 2013. *Turnaround Tools for the Teenage Brain: Helping Underperforming Students Become Lifelong Learners.* San Francisco: Jossey-Bass.

Johnson, Amy, and Erika Stump. 2018. "Proficiency-Based High School Diploma Systems in Maine: Educator Perceptions of Implementation." usm.maine.edu/sites/default/files/cepare/Proficiency_based_High_School_Diploma_Systems_in_Maine_Educator_Perceptions_of_Implementation.pdf.

Jones, Stephanie, Rebecca Bailey, Katharine Brush, and Jennifer Kahn. 2018. Harvard Graduate School of Education. wallacefoundation.org/knowledge-center/Documents/Preparing-for-Effective-SEL-Implementation.pdf.

Jordan, Anna E. 2018. "School Around Us: A Learning Community Built on Trust." *Maine Women Magazine.* July 30, 2018. mainewomenmagazine.com/school-around-us.

Kajtaniak, Tara Nuth. 2016. "Five Ways Global Education Is Transforming My School." Education Week's Global Learning Blog. blogs.edweek.org/edweek/global_learning/2016/02/teacher_global_education_is_transforming_my_school.html.

Kalick, Bena, and Costa, Arthur L. 2008. *Learning and Leading with Habits of Mind: 16 Essential Characteristics of Success.* Alexandria, VA: ASCD.

Kamenetz, Anya. 2018. "The Future of Learning? Well, It's Personal." npr.org/2018/11/16/657895964/the-future-of-learning-well-it-s-personal.

Kanevsky, Lannie, and Tacey Keighley. 2003. "To Produce or Not to Produce? Understanding Boredom and the Honor in Underachievement." *Roeper Review* 26 (1): 20–28. doi.org/10.1080/02783190309554235.

Kena, Grace, Susan Aud, Frank Johnson, Xiaolei Wang, Jijun Zhang, Amy Rathbun, Sidney Wilkinson-Flicker, and Paul Kristapovich. 2014. *The Condition of Education 2014 (NCES 2014-083).* Washington, DC: US Department of Education, National Center for Education Statistics. nces.ed.gov/pubs2014/2014083.pdf.

Klem, Adena M., and James P. Connell. 2009. "Relationships Matter: Linking Teacher Support to Student Engagement and Achievement." *Journal of School Health* 74 (7): 262–273. doi: 10.1111/j.1746-1561.2004.tb08283.x.

Kohn, Alfie. 1993. "Choices for Children: Why and How to Let Students Decide." *Phi Delta Kappan* 75 (1): 8–16, 18–21. alfiekohn.org/article/choices-children/?print=pdf.

Larmer, John. 2014. "Project-Based Learning vs. Problem-Based Learning vs. X-BL." Edutopia. edutopia.org/blog/pbl-vs-pbl-vs-xbl-john-larmer.

Leahy, Siobhán, and Dylan Wiliam. 2012. "From Teachers to Schools: Scaling Up Professional Development for Formative Assessment." In *Assessment and Learning*, 2nd ed., edited by John Gardner, 49–71. Thousand Oaks, CA: Sage Publications.

Little Kids Rock. 2019. littlekidsrock.org.

Luethi, Mathias, Beat Meier, and Carmen Sandi. 2008. "Stress Effects on Working Memory, Explicit Memory, and Implicit Memory for Neutral and Emotional Stimuli in Healthy Men." *Frontiers in Behavioral Neuroscience* 2 (5). ncbi.nlm.nih.gov/pmc/articles/PMC2628592.

Lynch, Matthew. 2018. "Five Ways to Use Digital Badges in the Classroom." The Tech Edvocate. thetechedvocate.org/5-ways-to-use-digital-badges-in-the-classroom.

Maker Education Initiative. 2013. "Makerspace Playbook." makered.org/wp-content/uploads/2014/09/Makerspace-Playbook-Feb-2013.pdf.

Mansilla, Veronica Boix, and Anthony Jackson. 2011. "Educating for Global Competence: Preparing Our Youth to Engage the World." Council of Chief State School Officers' EdSteps Initiative and the Asia Society Partnership for Global Learning. New York: Asia Society.

Marks, Helen M. 2000. "Student Engagement in Instructional Activity: Patterns in the Elementary, Middle, and High School Years." *American Education Research Journal* 37 (1): 153–184.

Martinez, Sylvia Libow, and Gary Stager. 2013. *Invent to Learn: Making, Tinkering, and Engineering in the Classroom*. Torrance, CA: Constructing Modern Knowledge Press.

Marzano, Robert J., and Debra J. Pickering. 2011. *The Highly Engaged Classroom*. Bloomington, IN: Marzano Research Laboratory.

Maslyk, Jacie, and Scott Miller. 2014. "Making in the Classroom: Changing Places and Practices." *Pennsylvania Administrator* 18 (3): 11–13.

Matteson, Addie. 2016. "It's Genius Hour!" *School Library Journal* 62 (10): 36. slj.com/?detailStory=its-genius-hour.

May, Catherine. 2019. "Stronger Than IQ: Executive Function." intentionalfutures.com/work/executive-function.

McCloskey, George. 2017. "Executive Functions and Classroom Learnings and Production." Presentation at Learning and the Brain Workshop, Dedham, Massachusetts.

McQuarrie, Lynn, Philip McRae, and Holly Stack-Cutler. 2008. *Differentiated Instruction Provincial Research Review*. Edmonton: Alberta Initiative for School Improvement. assembly.ab.ca/lao/library/egovdocs/2008/aled/168784.pdf.

Mentored Pathways. 2019. mentoredpathways.org

Mitra, Dana L., and Steven Jay Gross. 2009. "Increasing Student Voice in High School Reform: Building Partnerships, Improving Outcomes." *Educational Management Administration and Leadership* 37 (4): 522–543.

Morrow, Beth. 2014. "The Myth of Student Engagement." ASCD Inservice. inservice.ascd.org/the-myth-of-student-engagement.

Motamedi, Vahid. 2011. "Mastery Learning: An Effective Teaching Strategy." *Journal of Online Education*. nyu.edu/classes/keefer/waoe/motamediv.htm.

Mullgardt, Brian. 2008. "Introducing and Using the Discussion (AKA Harkness) Table." National Association of Independent Schools. nais.org/magazine/independent-teacher/fall-2008/introducing-and-using-the-discussion-(aka-harkness/.

Murphy, Marilyn, Sam Redding, and Janet S. Twyman, eds. 2016. *Handbook on Personalized Learning for States, Districts, and Schools*. Philadelphia: Center on Innovation in Learning. files.eric.ed.gov/fulltext/ED568173.pdf.

Murphy, P. Karen, and Patricia A. Alexander. 2000. "A Motivated Exploration of Motivation Terminology." *Contemporary Educational Psychology* 25 (1): 3–53.

Namahoe, Kanoe. 2017. "Cultivating Student Voice." SmartBriefsmartbrief.com/original/2017/03/cultivating-student-voice.

National Center for Transgender Equality. 2019a. "Issues: Youth Students." transequality.org/issues/youth-students.

National Center for Transgender Equality. 2019b. "Know Your Rights: Schools." transequality.org/know-your-rights/schools.

National Mentoring Partnership. 2019. mentoring.org.

NC State University. 2019. "College of Engineering: Educators." engr.ncsu.edu/theengineeringplace/educators.

Noble, Kimberly G., M. Frank Norman, and Martha J. Farah. 2005. "Neurocognitive Correlates of Socioeconomic Status in Kindergarten Children." Developmental Science 8 (1):74–87.

O'Byrne, W. Ian. 2018. "What Is 'Empowerment' in Education?" wiobyrne.com/empowerment.

Pane, John F., Elizabeth D. Steiner, Matthew D. Baird, and Laura S. Hamilton. 2015. "Continued Progress: Promising Evidence on Personalized Learning." RAND Corporation. rand.org/pubs/research_reports/RR1365.html.

Panskepp, Jaak. 1998. *Affective Neuroscience: The Foundations of Human and Animal Emotions*. New York: Oxford University Press.

Panskepp, Jaak, and Lucy Biven. 2012. *The Archaeology of Mind: Neuroevolutionary Origins of Human Emotions*. New York. W. W. Norton.

Panskepp, Jaak, Steve Siviy, and Larry Normansell. 1984. "The Psychobiology of Play: Theoretical and Methodological Perspectives." *Neuroscience and Biobehavioral Reviews* 8 (4): 465–492.

Perdue, Neil H., David P. Manzeske, and David B. Estell. 2009. "Early Predictors of School Engagement: Exploring the Role of Peer Relationships." *Psychology in the Schools* 46 (10): 1084–1097.

Perrin, Andrew. 2018. "5 Facts About Americans and Video Games." pewresearch.org/fact-tank/2018/09/17/5-facts-about-americans-and-video-games.

Pettig, Kim L. 2000. "On the Road to Differentiated Practice." *Educational Leadership* 58 (1): 14–18.

Pierce, Dennis. 2016. "Can You Teach Students to Think More Like Entrepreneurs?" eSchool News. eschoolnews.com/2016/06/20/can-you-teach-students-to-think-more-like-entrepreneurs.

Pink, Dan. 2009. "The Puzzle of Motivation." TEDGlobal 2009. ted.com/talks/dan_pink_on_motivation/transcript.

Project Tomorrow. 2016. "Nearly Half of All Teachers Now Use Games as Part of Instruction, Marking a Big Jump Since 2010." Project Tomorrow Speak Up Survey Results. tomorrow.org /speakup/pdfs/Speak%20Up%20May%202015_PR1.pdf.

RAND Corporation. 2014. "Early Progress: Interim Research Report on Personalized Learning." k12education.gatesfoundation.org/resource /early-progress-interim-research-on-personalized-learning.

———. 2019. "Personalized Learning." rand.org/topics /personalized-learning.html.

Regeluth, Charles M. 2013. *Instructional-Design Theories and Models: A New Paradigm of Instructional Theory.* London: Routledge.

Renzulli, Joseph S., and Linda H. Smith. 1979. *A Guidebook for Developing Individualized Educational Programs (IEP) for Gifted and Talented Students.* Mansfield Center, CT: Creative Learning Press.

Responsive Classroom. 2019. "Responsive Classroom Is an Evidence-Based Approach as Defined in the ESSA." responsiveclassroom.org/about/research.

Ritchhart, Ron. 2015. *Creating Cultures of Thinking: The 8 Forces We Must Master to Truly Transform Our Schools.* San Francisco: Jossey-Bass.

Robinson, Ken. 2009. *The Element: How Finding Your Passion Changes Everything.* New York: Penguin.

Robinson, Melia. 2015. "Why the Classes at Phillips Exeter Are Different Than at Any Other Private School." *Business Insider.* businessinsider.com/phillips-exeter-harkness-table-2014-11.

Rock, Marcia L., Madeleine Gregg, Edwin Ellis, and Robert A. Gable. 2008. "REACH: A Framework for Differentiating Classroom Instruction." *Preventing School Failure* 52 (2): 31–47.

Rogers, Karen B. 2007. "Lessons Learned About Educating the Gifted and Talented: A Synthesis of the Research on Educational Practice." *Gifted Child Quarterly* 51 (4): 382–396.

Roker-Jones, Marie. 2015. "The Pressure to Raise Great Men." goodmenproject.com/featured-content/the-pressure-to-raise -great-men-kerj.

Ronan, Amanda. 2015. "Seven Ways to Hack your Classroom to Include Student Choice." edudemic.com/7-ways-to-hack -your-classroom.

Rush, Elizabeth Barrera. 2015. "Genius Hour in the Library." *Teacher Librarian* 43 (2): 26–30. teacherlibrarian.com/wp-content /uploads/2017/07/6B-rush.pdf.

Ryan, Richard M., and Edward L. Deci. 2000. "Self-Determination Theory and the Facilitation of Intrinsic Motivation, Social Development, and Well-Being." *American Psychologist* 55 (1): 68–78. selfdeterminationtheory.org/SDT /documents/2000_RyanDeci_SDT.pdf.

Savery, John R. 2006. "Overview of Problem-Based Learning: Definitions and Distinctions." *Interdisciplinary Journal of Problem-Based Learning* 1 (1): 9–20. citeseerx.ist.psu.edu/viewdoc /download?doi=10.1.1.557.6406&rep=rep1&type=pdf.

Shakman, Karen, Brandon Foster, Noman Khanani, Jill Marcus, and Josh Cox. 2018. "Understanding Implementation of Proficiency-Based Education in Maine." edc.org/sites/default /files/uploads/Understanding%20implementation%20of%20 PBE%20in%20Maine_EDC%2020180917.pdf.

Shapiro, Jordan, Katie Salen Tekinba, Katrina Schwartz, and Paul Darvasi. 2014. "MindShift Guide to Digital Games and Learning." a.s.kqed.net/pdf/news/MindShift -GuidetoDigitalGamesandLearning.pdf.

Shaw, Philip, David E. Greenstein, Jason P. Lerch, Liv S. Clasen, Rhoshel K. Lenroot, Nitin Gogtay, Alan C. Evans, Judith L. Rapoport, and Jay N. Giedd. 2006. "Intellectual Ability and Cortical Development in Children and Adolescents." *Nature* 440: 676–679.

Singh, Maanvi. 2014. "What's Going on Inside the Brain of a Curious Child?" KQED News: Mind/Shift. kqed.org/mindshift /38260/whats-going-on-inside-the-brain-of-a-curious-child.

Skinner, Ellen A., J. G. Wellborn, and J. P. Connell. 1990. "What It Takes to Do Well in School and Whether I've Got It: A Process Model of Perceived Control and Children's Engagement and Achievement in School." *Journal of Educational Psychology* 82 (1): 22–32.

Sklad, Marcin, Rene Diekstra, Monique DeRitter, Jehonathan Ben, and Carolien Gravesteijn. 2012. "Effectiveness of School-Based Universal Social, Emotional, and Behavior Programs: Do They Enhance Students' Development in the Area of Skill, Behavior, and Adjustment?" *Psychology in the Schools* 49 (9): 892–909.

Smith, Andrew F. 2007. *The Oxford Companion to American Food and Drink.* New York: Oxford University Press.

Smith, Meshelle. 2017. "Genius Hour in Elementary School." Edutopia. edutopia.org/article/genius-hour-elementary-school.

Sousa, David A., and Carol Ann Tomlinson. 2018. *Differentiation and the Brain: How Neuroscience Supports the Learner-Friendly Classroom.* Bloomington, IN: Solution Tree.

Spencer, John. 2016. "10 Ways to Incorporate Student Choice in Your Classroom." The Synapse (blog). medium.com/synapse /10-ways-to-incorporate-student-choice-in-your-classroom -e07baa449e55.

Spencer, John, and A. J. Juliani. 2017. *Empower: What Happens When Students Own Their Learning.* San Diego, CA: Impress Books.

Spencer, Kyle. 2017. "A New Kind of Classroom: No Grades, No Failing, No Hurry." *New York Times* August 11, 2017. nytimes.com/2017/08/11/nyregion/mastery-based-learning-no -grades.html.

Strauss, Valerie. 2017. "It's 2017, and Girls Still Don't Think They Are as Smart as Boys, Research Shows." Washington Post. washingtonpost.com/news/answer-sheet/wp/2017/02/14 /its-2017-and-girls-still-dont-think-they-are-as-smart-as-boys -research-shows.

Suárez-Orozco, Carola, Allison Pimentel, and Margary Martin. 2009. "The Significance of Relationships: Academic Engagement and Achievement Among Newcomer Immigrant Youth." *Teachers College Record* 111 (3): 712–749.

Taylor, Ronald D., and Azeb Gebre. 2016. "Teacher-Student Relationships and Personalized Learning: Implications of Person and Contextual Variables." in *Handbook on Personalized Learning for States, Districts, and Schools*, edited by Marilyn Murphy, Sam Redding, and Janet S. Twyman, 205–220. Philadelphia: Center on Innovations in Learning.

Tichnor-Wagner, Ariel. 2018. "Why Global Education Matters." ASCD InService. inservice.ascd.org/why-global-education-matters.

Tieso, Carol. 2005. "The Effects of Grouping Practices and Curricular Adjustments on Achievement." *Journal for the Education of the Gifted* 29 (1): 60–89.

Tomlinson, Carol, Kay Brimijoin, and Lane Narvaez. 2008. *The Differentiated School: Making Revolutionary Changes in Teaching and Learning*. Alexandria, VA: ASCD.

Toshalis, Eric, and Michael J. Nakkula. 2012. Motivation, Engagement, and Student Voice." studentsatthecenterhub.org/wp-content/uploads/2012/04/Motivation-Engagement-Student-Voice-Students-at-the-Center-1.pdf.

Tough, Paul. 2013. *How Children Succeed: Grit, Curiosity, and the Hidden Power of Character*. New York: Mariner Books.

Tucker, Carolyn M., Rose A. Zayco, Keith C. Herman, Wendy M. Reinke, Mark Trujillo, Kirsten Carraway, Cory Wallack, and Phyllis D. Ivery. 2002. "Teacher and Child Variables as Predictors of Academic Engagement Among Low-Income African American Children." *Psychology in the Schools* 39 (4): 477–488.

Tucker, Marc. "Globally Ready—or Not?" 2016–2017. *Educational Leadership* 74 (4): 30–35.

Turner, Duane. 2010. "Student-Centered Teaching: A Look at Student Choice in the Classroom." Paper for the Center for Teaching Excellence, United States Military Academy, West Point, NY.

University College London. 2017. "One in Four Girls Is Depressed at Age 14, New Study Reveals." UCL Institute of Education. ucl.ac.uk/ioe/news/2017/sep/one-four-girls-depressed-age-14-new-study-reveals.

US Department of Education. 2012. "Succeeding Globally Through International Education Engagement: US Department of Education International Strategy 2012–2016." ed.gov/about/inits/ed/internationaled/international-strategy-2012-16.pdf.

———. 2015. "Fundamental Change: Innovation in America's Schools Under Race to the Top." ed.gov/programs/racetothetop/rttfinalrptfull.pdf.

von Stumm, Sophie, Benedikt Hell, and Tomas Chamorro-Premuzic. 2011. "The Hungry Mind: Intellectual Curiosity Is the Third Pillar of Academic Performance." *Perspectives on Psychological Science* 6 (6): 574–588.

WebMD. 2019. "Executive Function and Executive Function Disorder." webmd.com/add-adhd/guide/executive-function#1.

Wiggins, Grant, and Jay McTighe. 2005. *Understanding by Design*. 2nd ed. Alexandria, VA: ASCD.

Wiliam, Dylan, and Siobhán Leahy. 2015. *Embedding Formative Assessment: Practical Techniques for K–12 Classrooms*. West Palm Beach, FL: Learning Sciences International.

Willis, Judy. 2011a. "A Neurologist Makes the Case for the Video Game Model as a Learning Tool." Edutopia. edutopia.org/blog/neurologist-makes-case-video-game-model-learning-tool.

———. 2011b. "How to Plan Instruction Using the Video Game Model." Edutopia. edutopia.org/blog/how-to-plan-instruction-video-game-model-judy-willis-md.

Wolf, Mary Ann. 2010. "Innovate to Educate: System [Re]Design for Personalized Learning—A Report from the 2010 Symposium." library.educause.edu/-/media/files/library/2010/1/csd6181-pdf.pdf.

Wolpert-Gawron, Heather. 2015. "Kids Speak Out on Student Engagement." Edutopia. edutopia.org/blog/student-engagement-stories-heather-wolpert-gawron.

Wrabel, Stephani L., Laura S. Hamilton, Anamarie A. Whitaker, and Sean Grant. 2018. "Investing in Evidence-Based Social and Emotional Learning: Companion Guide to *Social and Emotional Learning Interventions Under the Every Student Succeeds Act: Evidence Review*." RAND Corporation. wallacefoundation.org/knowledge-center/Documents/Investing-in-Evidence-Based-Social-and-Emotional-Learning.pdf.

Yale Center for Emotional Intelligence. 2015. "Emotion Revolution—Student." ei.yale.edu/what-we-do/emotion-revolution-student.

Yazzie-Mintz, Ethan. 2007. "Voices of Students on Engagement: A Report on the 2006 High School Survey of Student Engagement." Bloomington, IN: Center for Evaluation and Education Policy.

———. 2009. "Engaging the Voices of Students: A Report on the 2007 and 2008 High School Survey of Student Engagement." Bloomington, IN: Center for Evaluation and Education Policy.

———. 2010. "Charting the Path from Engagement to Achievement: A Report on the 2009 High School Survey of Student Engagement." Bloomington, IN: Center for Evaluation and Education Policy.

Yeager, David S., and Gregory M. Walton. 2011. "Social-Psychological Interventions in Education: They're Not Magic." *Review of Educational Research* 81 (2): 267–301.

Zeldin, Shepherd. 2004. "Youth as Agents of Adult and Community Development: Mapping the Processes and Outcomes of Youth Engaged in Organizational Governance." *Applied Developmental Science* 8 (2): 75–90.

Index

About the Author

Patti Drapeau (pattidrapeau.com) is an internationally active educational consultant, author, and presenter, with more than twenty-five years of classroom experience. Patti conducts keynote sessions as well as short- and long-term workshops in the United States and abroad. She commonly presents on the following topics: differentiation, creativity, engagement, gifted education, student empowerment, and personalized learning.

Patti is the founder of Patti Drapeau Educational Consulting Services and has received the New England Region Gifted and Talented award for outstanding contributions in gifted education and the Maine Educators of the Gifted and Talented award for exemplary service. Patti coached programs such as Odyssey of the Mind, Future Problem Solving, Explorer Vision, and math teams. She also developed a curriculum model for the regular classroom called "Affective Perspectives: Combining Critical Thinking, Creative Thinking, and Affect," and authored a variety of articles for *Maine Exchange*, *Teaching Matters*, and *Understanding Our Gifted*. Her other books include *Sparking Student Creativity: Practical Ways to Promote Innovative Thinking and Problem Solving*, *Differentiating with Graphic Organizers: Tools to Foster Critical and Creative Thinking*, *Differentiated Instruction: Making It Work*, and *Great Teaching with Graphic Organizers*.

Patti currently works as a consultant, and she is a part-time faculty member at the University of Southern Maine. She lives in Freeport, Maine. Follow her on Twitter @ptdrapeau.

Other Great Resources from Free Spirit

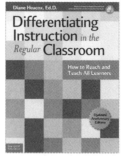
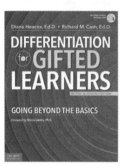